Lecture Notes in Computer Sci

Edited by G. Goos, J. Hartmanis, and J. vai

T0250717

Springer

Berlin
Heidelberg
New York
Barcelona
Hong Kong
London
Milan
Paris
Tokyo

Alejandro Buchmann   Fabio Casati
Ludger Fiege   Mei-Chun Hsu
Ming-Chien Shan (Eds.)

Technologies for E-Services

Third International Workshop, TES 2002
Hong Kong, China, August 23-24, 2002
Proceedings

Springer

Volume Editors

Alejandro Buchmann
Ludger Fiege
TU Darmstadt
Wilhelminenstr. 7, 64283 Darmstadt, Germany
E-mail: buchmann@informatik.tu-darmstadt.de, fiege@gkec.tu-darmstadt.de

Fabio Casati
Hewlett Packard
1501 Page Mill road, MS 1142
Palo Alto, CA, 94304, USA
E-mail: fabio_casati@hp.com

Mei-Chun Hsu
Commerce One
19191 Vallco Parkway, Cupertino, CA 95014, USA
E-mail: meichun.hsu@commerceone.com

Ming-Chien Shan
Hewlett Packard
13264 Glasgow court, Saratoga, CA 95070, USA
E-mail: shan@hpl.hp.com

Cataloging-in-Publication Data applied for

Die Deutsche Bibliothek - CIP-Einheitsaufnahme

Technologies for E-services : third international workshop ; proceedings /
TES 2002, Hong Kong, China, August 23 - 24, 2002. Alejandro Buchmann ...
(ed.). - Berlin ; Heidelberg ; New York ; Barcelona ; Hong Kong ; London ;
Milan ; Paris ; Tokyo : Springer, 2002
   (Lecture notes in computer science ; Vol. 2444)
   ISBN 3-540-44110-7

CR Subject Classification (1998): H.2, H.4, C.2, H.3, J.1, K.4.4, I.2.11

ISSN 0302-9743
ISBN 3-540-44110-7 Springer-Verlag Berlin Heidelberg New York

This work is subject to copyright. All rights are reserved, whether the whole or part of the material is
concerned, specifically the rights of translation, reprinting, re-use of illustrations, recitation, broadcasting,
reproduction on microfilms or in any other way, and storage in data banks. Duplication of this publication
or parts thereof is permitted only under the provisions of the German Copyright Law of September 9, 1965,
in its current version, and permission for use must always be obtained from Springer-Verlag. Violations are
liable for prosecution under the German Copyright Law.

Springer-Verlag Berlin Heidelberg New York,
a member of BertelsmannSpringer Science+Business Media GmbH

http://www.springer.de

© Springer-Verlag Berlin Heidelberg 2002
Printed in Germany

Typesetting: Camera-ready by author, data conversion by PTP-Berlin, Stefan Sossna e.K.
Printed on acid-free paper   SPIN: 10871039   06/3142   5 4 3 2 1 0

Preface

The 2002 VLDB workshop on Technologies for E-Services (VLDB-TES 02) is the third workshop in a series of annual workshops endorsed by the VLDB Conference. It serves as a forum for the exchange of ideas, results and experience in the area of e-commerce and e-business.

VLDB-TES 02 took place in Hong Kong, China. It featured the presentation of 14 regular papers, focused on major aspects of e-business solutions. In addition, the workshop invited five industrial speakers to share their vision, insight, and experience with the audience.

The workshop would not have been a success without help from many people. Special thanks go to Fabio Casati, who recruited the world-class speakers from various e-business fields, Ludger Fiege who served as the publicity and publication chair, and Eleana Kafeza, who organized and planned the local arrangements. We also thank the authors for submitting their papers and the members of the program committee and external reviewers for their thorough work, which greatly contributed to the quality of the final program.

We hope that the participants found the workshop interesting and stimulating, and we thank them for attending and for contributing to the discussions.

Juli 2002

Ming-Chien Shan
Mei-Chun Hsu
Alejandro Buchmann

Organization

Workshop Officers

General Chair
Ming-Chien Shan, Hewlett-Packard
shan@hpl.hp.com

Program Chairs
Mei-Chun Hsu, Commerce One
Meichun.Hsu@commerceone.com

Alejandro Buchmann, Darmstadt University of Technology
buchmann@informatik.tu-darmstadt.de

Industrial Track Chair
Fabio Casati, Hewlett-Packard
casati@hpl.hp.com

Local Arrangements Chair
Eleana Kafeza, Hong Kong University of Science and Technology
kafeza@cs.ust.hk

Publicity Chair
Ludger Fiege, Darmstadt University of Technology
fiege@gkec.tu-darmstadt.de

Program Committee

Gustavo Alonso, ETH Zürich, Switzerland
Jean Bacon, Cambridge University, UK
Martin Bichler, IBM, USA
Christof Bornhoevd, IBM, USA
Paul Brebner, CSIRO, Australia
Christoph Bussler, Oracle Corp., USA
Arvola Chan, TIBCO, USA
Jen-Yao Chung, IBM, USA
Umesh Dayal, Hewlett-Packard, USA
Oscar Diaz, U. del Pais Vasco, Spain
Asuman Dogac, Middle East Technical University, Turkey
Peter Fankhauser, Fraunhofer IPSI, Germany
Dan Fishman, Avaya Labs., USA
Matthew Fuchs, Stele Corp., USA
Dimitrios Georgakopoulos, Telcordia, USA
Bob Glushko, Commerce One, USA
Eleana Kafeza, Hong Kong University of Science and Technology, China
Roger Kilian-Kehr, T-Systems Nova, Germany
Johannes Klein, Microsoft, USA
Winfried Lamersdorf, Hamburg University, Germany
Frank Leymann, IBM, Germany
Christoph Liebig, SAP, Germany
Oded Shmueli, Technion, Israel
Joe Sventek, Agilent, UK
Stefan Tai, IBM, USA
Aphroditi Tsalgatidou, U. of Athens, Greece
Dick Tsur, Real-Time Enterprise Group, USA
Steve Vinoski, IONA, USA
Hartmut Vogler, SAP Research Lab, USA
Claus von Rieger, SAP, Germany
Gerhard Weikum, U. of the Saarland, Germany

Additional Referees

George Athanassopoulos
Yildiray Kabak
Nuri Gokhan Kurt
Gokce Banu Laleci
Thomi Pilioura
Uwe Wilhelm

Table of Contents

Dynamic E-business: Trends in Web Services 1
   C. Mohan

Telecom Databases for the E-services Industry 6
   Mikael Ronström, Vinay P. Joosery

Improving the Functionality of UDDI Registries through Web
Service Semantics 9
   Asuman Dogac, Ibrahim Cingil, Gokce Laleci, Yildiray Kabak

Public Process Inheritance for Business-to-Business Integration 19
   Christoph Bussler

A Model-Transformers Architecture for Web Applications 29
   Alexey Valikov, Alexei Akhounov, Andreas Schmidt

Modeling E-service Orchestration through Petri Nets 38
   Massimo Mecella, Francesco Parisi Presicce, Barbara Pernici

Composite Applications: Process Based Application Development 48
   Anil K. Nori, Rajiv Jain

Design Methodology for Web Services and Business Processes 54
   Mike P. Papazoglou, Jian Yang

E-service Based Information Fusion: A User-Level Information
Integration Framework 65
   Abdelsalam Helal, Jingting Lu

A Request Language for Web-Services Based on Planning and
Constraint Satisfaction 76
   M. Aiello, Mike P. Papazoglou, Jian Yang, M. Carman, M. Pistore,
   L. Serafini, P. Traverso

Communication Flow Expressions in a Notification and Response System . 86
   Joann J. Ordille, Thomas Petsche

A Coverage-Determination Mechanism for Checking Business
Contracts against Organizational Policies 97
   Alan S. Abrahams, David M. Eyers, Jean M. Bacon

Managing Business Relationships in E-services Using Business
Commitments 107
   Haifei Li, Jun-Jang Jeng, Henry Chang

Ad-Hoc Transactions for Mobile Services 118
    Andrei Popovici, Gustavo Alonso

Advanced Web Session Provider for Suspensible E-services 131
    Jing Li, Xin Zhang, Zhong Tian

PLM_{flow}–Dynamic Business Process Composition and Execution
by Rule Inference 141
    Liangzhao Zeng, David Flaxer, Henry Chang, Jun-Jang Jeng

Trust-Based Security Model and Enforcement Mechanism for Web
Service Technology 151
    Seokwon Yang, Herman Lam, Stanley Y.W. Su

Fair Exchange under Limited Trust 161
    Chihiro Ito, Mizuho Iwaihara, Yahiko Kambayashi

Author Index 171

Dynamic E-business: Trends in Web Services

C. Mohan

IBM Almaden Research Center
650 Harry Road, K01/B1
San Jose, CA 95120, USA
http://www.almaden.ibm.com/u/mohan
mohan@almaden.ibm.com

Abstract. In the last couple of years, the concept of a web service (WS) has emerged as an important paradigm for general application integration in the internet environment. More particularly, WS is viewed as an important vehicle for the creation of dynamic e-business applications and as a means for the J2EE and .NET worlds to come together. Several companies, including Microsoft, have been collaborating in proposing new WS standards. The World Wide Web Consortium has been the forum for many WS-related standardization activities. Many traditional concepts like business process management, security, directory services, routing and transactions are being extended for WS. This extended abstract traces some of the trends in the WS arena. After the TES2002 workshop is over, more information could be found in the presentation material at http://www.almaden.ibm.com/u/mohan/WebServices_TES2002_Slides.pdf

1 Introduction

With the popularity of the world wide web has come the need for businesses to exploit the web not only for disseminating information but also for improving their *interactions* with their customers, distributors, suppliers and partners. This way of integrating applications and conducting business using the internet has come to be called *dynamic e-business* [7]. The web service (WS) paradigm has emerged as an important mechanism for interoperation amongst separately developed distributed applications in such a dynamic e-business environment. One definition of WS is: *Web services are a new breed of web application. They are self-contained, self-describing, modular applications that can be published, located, and invoked across the web. Web services perform functions, which can be anything from simple requests to complicated business processes. Once a web service is deployed, other applications (and other web services) can discover and invoke the deployed service.* XML messaging is used to interact with a WS.

WS is also viewed as an important interoperability mechanism for the J2EE [15] and Microsoft's .NET [26] worlds to come together. WS has become so popular that, in addition to conferences and workshops, even magazines devoted to WS are currently in existence (see, e.g., [17]). In this extended abstract, I trace some of the trends

A. Buchmann et al. (Eds.): TES 2002, LNCS 2444, pp. 1-5, 2002.
© Springer-Verlag Berlin Heidelberg 2002

in the WS arena and provide pointers to numerous papers, specifications and web sites for much more detailed information. Links to a number of tutorials on WS topics can be found in [25].

The World Wide Web Consortium (W3C) has been the sponsoring organization for many WS-related standardization activities [18]. In May 2000, IBM, Microsoft and others released the specification for SOAP 1.1 (Simple Object Access Protocol) [2]. SOAP is an XML-based protocol for information exchange in a decentralized, distributed environment like the internet. It is essentially a flexible form of the traditional remote procedure call (RPC) mechanism for use in the web context. While SOAP was originally designed to work using HTTP and be able to tunnel through firewalls, more recently, other transport protocol bindings have been proposed for SOAP. In March 2001, IBM, Microsoft and Ariba submitted to W3C the Web Services Description Language (WSDL) specification [3] as a starting point for standardization activities. WSDL is a language intended to be used to describe interfaces of web services and to describe how to interact with them. UDDI is intended to be the means for publishing and discovering services on the web [16].

2   Business Process Management

Business process or workflow management is one area where pre-existing work [13] is being extended to take into account WS requirements [30]. Just recently, BEA, Sun, Intalio and SAP have released the specification for what has been called Web Service Choreography Interface (WSCI) [1]. WSCI is an interface description language based on WSDL for describing the flow of messages exchanged by a WS participating in choreographed interactions with other WSs. It is an attempt to standardize an XML-based syntax for service choreography. IBM and Microsoft are also currently working together on a similar proposal that would merge IBM's WSFL [22] and Microsoft's XLANG [19]. The relationship between WSCI and related technologies like WSFL, XLANG, ebXML's BPSS, BTP, BPMI.org's Business Process Modeling Language (BPML), HP's Web Service Conversation Language (WSCL), XML Pipeline Definition Language and OMG's Enterprise Distributed Object Computing (EDOC) has been discussed in [24].

3   Implementations

Many software vendors are actively working on supporting WS in their products. This is especially true of the application server vendors [15]. In July 2000, IBM released on its alphaWorks site a WS toolkit which has been steadily enhanced with additional functionality ever since [5, 9]. This kit includes a run-time environment, a demo and examples to help users in designing and executing applications that are built by combining web services. IBM has also released what is called the WebSphere SDK (WSDK) for Web Services [10]. IBM has also developed the Web Services Invocation

Framework (WSIF) for supporting the invocation of web services without worrying about transport protocols or the locations of the services [6]. WSIF frees a software developer from the constraints of having to develop services for particular transport protocols or service environments. To enable quicker adoption and standardization IBM has donated the WSIF source code to the Apache XML project under the auspices of the Axis work.

IBM's DB2 has been extended to include support for WS [12]. Consequently, now it is possible to very easily make existing DB2 stored procedures available across the web as services. In July 2001, IBM released the Beta version of Web Services Object Runtime Framework (WORF) [4]. WORF allows the DB2 XML Extender to support WS.

In June 2002, BEA released WebLogic Workshop which allows even developers with no knowledge of J2EE to develop WSs using visual controls [32]. Recently, Google has made available a SOAP-based web service to access its search engine from applications [8]. On the IBM developerWorks web site, demo applications of some public web services can be found [11].

4 Work in Progress

Microsoft has released the specification for an asynchronous routing protocol, called WS-Routing, for SOAP messages over a variety of protocols like HTTP, TCP and UDP [28]. The entire route for a SOAP message (as well as a return route) can be described directly within the SOAP envelope. WS-Routing supports one-way messaging, two-way messaging (e.g., request/response and peer-to-peer conversations) and long-running dialogs. It does not define any reliability or retransmission policies. Other groups are extending transaction management concepts like JTS to make web service invocations become transactional. In this context, IBM has defined a reliable version of HTTP called HTTPR [23]. A draft of a specification for WS for J2EE has just been released [20]. It relies on JAX-RPC as the base technology. Research work is currently in progress in IBM Almaden and IBM Tokyo to extend existing support for caching [14] to deal with results of invocations of WS.

WS is becoming more popular in the intranet environment compared to the internet environment [27]. Private UDDI directories are being used to enable this. They are also being used within a company to catalog information regarding the partner companies whose services the former makes use of. They are also useful for keeping track of services developed within the company itself by various groups of people for intra-company usage. A rating system for trustworthiness and quality of service is needed for companies whose services are made available via a public UDDI directory. Another crucial feature is security. Work is currently in progress to add security to WS [21, 31]. In April 2002, IBM, Microsoft and VeriSign defined the specification for WS-Security [29]. It defines a set of SOAP headers that could be used to specify security measures like encryption and digital signatures for WS. It also defines a general mechanism for passing around a set of arbitrary security tokens.

Once the 3rd VLDB Workshop on Technologies for E-Services (TES2002) is over, the slides of the talk for which this extended abstract has been written will be available at http://www.almaden.ibm.com/u/mohan/WebServices_TES2002_Slides.pdf

References

1. Arkin, A., Askary, S., Fordin, S., Jekeli, W., Kawaguchi, K., Orchard, D., Pogliani, S., Riemer, K., Struble, S., Takacsi-Nagy, P., Trickovic, I., Zimek, S. *Web Service Choreography Interface 1.0 Specification*, BEA, Intalio, SAP and Sun, June 2002. http://ftpna2.bea.com/pub/downloads/wsci-spec-10.pdf
2. Box, D., Ehnebuske, D., Kakivaya, G., Layman, A., Mendelsohn, N., Nielsen, H., Thatte, S., Winer, D. *Simple Object Access Protocol (SOAP) 1.1*, W3C Note, May 2000. http://www.w3.org/TR/SOAP/
3. Christensen, E., Curbera, F., Meredith, G., Weerawarana, S. (Eds.) *Web Services Description Language (WSDL) 1.1*, W3C Note, March 2001. http://www.w3.org/TR/2001/NOTE-wsdl-20010315
4. *DB2 XML Extender Web Services Object Runtime Framework (WORF)*, July 2001. http://www.ibm.com/software/data/db2/extenders/xmlext/docs/v72wrk/WORF.html
5. Feller, J. *IBM Web Services Toolkit – A Showcase for Emerging Web Services Technologies*, IBM, http://www.ibm.com/software/solutions/webservices/wstk-info.html
6. Fremantle, P. *Applying the Web Services Invocation Framework – Calling Services Independent of Protocols*, IBM DeveloperWorks, June 2002. http://www.ibm.com/developerworks/webservices/library/ws-appwsif.html
7. Gisolfi, D. *Web Services Architect Part 1: An Introduction to Dynamic e-Business*, IBM, April 2001. ftp://www.software.ibm.com/software/developer/library/ws-arc1.pdf
8. Google Web APIs, Google, http://www.google.com/apis/
9. *Web Services Toolkit*, IBM alphaWorks, July 2000. http://www.alphaworks.ibm.com/tech/webservicestoolkit/
10. *WebSphere SDK for Web Services (WSDK)*, IBM DeveloperWorks, http://www.ibm.com/developerworks/webservices/wsdk/
11. *Web Services Demos: Learn by Example – GUI, Code and Documentation*, IBM DeveloperWorks, http://www.ibm.com/developerworks/offers/wsdemos.html
12. *Dynamic e-Business with DB2 and Web Services*, IBM, 2001. http://www.ibm.com/software/data/pubs/papers/ db2webservices/db2webservices.pdf
13. Mohan, C. *Tutorial: Workflow Management in the Internet Age*, EDBT Foundation's Sumer School, La Baule-les-Pins, France, May 1999. http://www.almaden.ibm.com/u/mohan/workflow.pdf
14. Mohan, C. *Tutorial: Caching Technologies for Web Applications*, 27th International Conference on Very Large Data Bases, Rome, September 2001. http://www.almaden.ibm.com/u/mohan/Caching_VLDB2001.pdf
15. Mohan, C. *Tutorial: Application Servers and Associated Technologies*, 28th International Conference on Very Large Data Bases, Hong Kong, August 2002. http://www.almaden.ibm.com/u/mohan/AppServersTutorial_VLDB2002_Slides.pdf
16. *Universal Description, Discovery and Integration (UDDI) Version 2.0 Specification*, June 2001, http://uddi.org/specification.html
17. Web Services Journal, http://www.sys-con.com/webservices/

18. *Web Services Activity*, W3C, http://www.w3.org/2002/ws/
19. Thatte, S. *XLANG Web Services for Business Process Design*, Microsoft, 2001. http://www.gotdotnet.com/team/xml_wsspecs/xlang-c/default.htm
20. *Web Services for J2EE*, Version 1.0, Public Draft v0.3, JSR 109, April 2002. http://www.ibm.com/software/solutions/webservices/pdf/websvcs-0_3-pd.pdf
21. Snell, J. *Securing Web Services*, IBM, May 2002. http://www.ibm.com/software/solutions/webservices/pdf/wp_securingws.pdf
22. Leymann, F. *Web Services Flow Language (WSFL 1.0)*, IBM, May 2001. http://www.ibm.com/software/solutions/webservices/pdf/WSFL.pdf
23. Todd, S., Parr, F., Conner, M. *A Primer for HTTPR – An Overview of the Reliable HTTP Protocol*, IBM, April 2002. http://www.ibm.com/developerworks/library/ws-phtt/
24. *Web Service Choreography Interface (WSCI) FAQ*, BEA, Intalio, SAP and Sun, June 2002. http://ftpna2.bea.com/pub/downloads/wsci-faq-060302.html
25. *Web Services Tutorials*, xml.com. http://www.xml.com/pub/rg/Web_Services_Tutorials
26. *Microsoft .Net Framework SDK QuickStart Tutorials*, Microsoft, http://samples.gotdotnet.com/quickstart/
27. Wong, W. *Web 'Yellow Pages' Still a Dream*, ZDNet News, July 2002. http://zdnet.com.com/2100-1106-941184.html
28. *WS-Routing Specification Index Page*, Microsoft, October 2001. http://msdn.microsoft.com/library/en-us/dnglobspec/html/wsroutspecindex.asp
29. Atkinson, B., Della-Libera, G., Hada, S., Hondo, M., Hallam-Baker, P., Kaler, C., Klein, J., LaMacchia, B., Leach, P., Manferdelli, J., Maruyama, H., Nadalin, A., Nagaratnam, N., Prafullchandra, H., Shewchuk, J., Simon, D. *Web Services Security (WS-Security) Version 1.0*, IM, Microsoft and VeriSign, April 2002. ftp://www.software.ibm.com/software/developer/library/ws-secure.pdf
30. Leymann, F., Roller, D., Schmidt, M.-T. *Web Services and Business Process Management*, IBM Systems Journal, Vol. 41, No. 2, 2002. http://www.research.ibm.com/journal/sj/412/leymann.pdf
31. Hondo, M., Nagaratnam, N., Nadalin, A. *Securing Web Services*, IBM Systems Journal, Vol. 41, No. 2, 2002. http://www.research.ibm.com/journal/sj/412/hondo.pdf
32. WebLogic Workshop, BEA, 2002. http://edocs.bea.com/workshop/docs70/index.html

Telecom Databases for the E-services Industry

Mikael Ronström and Vinay P. Joosery

Ericsson Business Innovation AB / Alzato Venture
LM Ericssons väg 8 (Telefonplan)
S-126 25 Stockholm, Sweden
{ mikael.ronstrom , vinay.joosery }@inn.ericsson.se
http://www.alzato.com

Extended Abstract

The Internet has revolutionized the business landscape over the last decade. E-services is about externalizing business processing to customers and partners. As more customers and partners use the e-services infrastructure, managing availability and performance becomes a crucial business goal. This level of interdependence has uncovered a class of problems that telecommunications vendors have typically solved in the past. Next generation e-services platforms will need to address similar data management problems as those handled in the telecom systems today.

Providing non-stop, always-available service to large numbers of concurrent users is a major challenge today for e-services providers. Database technology is needed for storing session-oriented data that reflects the state of ongoing connections and communication services. Preserving session data during partial system failures is crucial in achieving high availability. But this is considered hard and expensive to achieve. Low cost shared-nothing clusters are beginning to be used to distribute processing over several processors and automatically mask out partial system failures.

Major application server vendors have started to introduce support for running their platforms in clustered environments. This has been necessary in order to satisfy the scalability requirements of large e-business sites, e.g. online banking portals. There is still an availability challenge that is to distribute and replicate in-memory sessions within the cluster in order to avoid disruption of service. Solutions based on conventional disk-based RDBMS have not been suitable, the main problems being high response times, high switchover times and asynchronous replication.

In the case of mobile portals, there are other types of data that need to be handled almost in real-time. Examples are logging, personalization, security, micro payments etc. Records are fairly simple, usually a few hundred bytes, but volumes are growing constantly as more and more users start using these services.

Let us take a look at a popular online bookstore. A session is the timeframe in which a visitor navigates the web site. Typically, several web servers and application servers handle the requests. A session object would be created on one of the application servers for each visitor. As a visitor browses the site and adds books to her shopping basket, the session object is kept updated. What happens if one of the application servers fails? The session objects on that server would disappear, thus

A. Buchmann et al. (Eds.): TES 2002, LNCS 2444, pp. 6-8, 2002.
© Springer-Verlag Berlin Heidelberg 2002

affecting users processed by that server. Shopping baskets would be emptied and users would have to start again.

A relational database would be too slow to handle the session objects. One could build a proprietary database that replicates data in the memory areas of the different servers, but this will not cater for other needs that may arise. For instance, the bookshop may want to gather and analyze information about the visitors of the web site in order to understand the patterns of visitors and provide customized services to them. It could be useful to understand for example what kind of books a visitor likes, and suggest books that the visitor may be interested in. Every click translates into information being created and logged. Tens of thousands of visitors would imply thousands of short records being created. The proprietary database would have to be built out to contain a model of the data being stored and to manipulate that data in different ways.

These requirements are quite familiar to the telecom world. At the heart of telecom systems are data management systems for processing subscriber and network information. The database systems typically have to:

– Answer massive amounts of rather simple queries (almost always through primary key or unique secondary key)
– Manage simple data with frequent updates
– Be highly available, with downtime of less than half a minute per year
– Have very short response times measured in a few milliseconds

As an example, Authentication, Authorization and Accounting (AAA) servers in wireless networks control access to network services, enforce policies, audit usage and provide information to bill for services. A subscriber base of several millions for a network operator is not too uncommon. Servers are being developed to handle a subscriber base in the range of 10 millions including visiting subscribers belonging to other operators. In the near future, the same server infrastructure will be shared by several operators, and thus will need to support even more users. In a more distant future, subscribers may even be mobile devices built into machines, e.g. cars. The number of connected users to the system will then increase by several orders of magnitude. There are today more than a billion mobile phone users in the world and this number is constantly increasing.

Network users demand and expect continuous availability of services. This implies always-on services and connections that are maintained without disruption. The communications infrastructure is usually built on large distributed clusters of shared nothing or multi-processor nodes with redundant high speed interconnects.

Telecom databases have been used to handle these types of requirements. These are parallel, main-memory database systems with synchronous replication of data placed on different nodes. They scale well on shared-nothing clusters that is not the case for most traditional RDBMSs. At failures the database system automatically reconfigures and masks out the faulty processor. Fail-over at a fraction of a second is required to guarantee uninterrupted services. Synchronous replication and dynamic reconfiguration are also used for providing support for online (rolling) upgrades, which is required for high availability.

As an example of such a telecom database, the NDB Cluster was developed by Ericsson in order to cater for the data management needs of the company's telecom products. It was recently launched as a generally available product.

E-services platforms are today using alternative solutions including main-memory databases, relational databases or proprietary databases but this strategy is not sustainable in the long run. Commercial main-memory databases are focused on performance, and it is not possible to distribute them on several processors. Replication is usually asynchronous. Some of the commercial relational databases have started to provide support for clustering and synchronous replication, but they are still too slow to handle thousands of transactions per second and response times under 10 milliseconds. The most common alternative has been to develop proprietary databases to suit the need of the platform. But this is very expensive to develop, as it requires a lot of specialized knowledge. The database is but one component among many other components in a platform. Since a proprietary database is tailor-made for specific needs, it needs to evolve over time to keep up with the changing needs of the platform, taking unnecessary time and resources.

A commercial telecom database is indeed a necessity for the e-services industry. At a time where time to market is determining for success, e-services platform vendors need a new generation of commercially available database systems to address their new challenges in data management.

Improving the Functionality of UDDI Registries through Web Service Semantics

Asuman Dogac, Ibrahim Cingil, Gokce Laleci, and Yildiray Kabak

Software Research and Development Center
Middle East Technical University (METU)
06531 Ankara Turkiye
asuman@srdc.metu.edu.tr

Abstract. In this paper we describe a framework for exploiting the semantics of Web services through UDDI registries. As a part of this framework, we extend the DAML-S upper ontology to describe the functionality we find essential for e-businesses. This functionality includes relating the services with electronic catalogs, describing the complementary services and finding services according to the properties of products or services. Once the semantics is defined, there is a need for a mechanism in the service registry to relate it with the service advertised. The ontology model developed is general enough to be used with any service registry. However when it comes to relating the semantics with services advertised, the capabilities provided by the registry effects how this is achieved. We demonstrate how to integrate the described service semantics to UDDI registries.

1   Introduction

Web services are modular and self-describing applications that can be mixed and matched with other Web services to create business processes and value chains. Recently, there have been a number of initiatives related with service discovery and composition lead by IT companies and consortiums like e-Speak [11] from HP, UDDI [19] from IBM and Microsoft, and ebXML [10] from United Nations/CEFACT and OASIS. Furthermore, HP has developed a platform, called eFlow [3,4], for specifying, enacting, and monitoring composite Web services.

However the lack of standard business semantics creates inefficiencies in exploiting the Web service registries. Describing the semantics of Web services provides the ability for automatic Web service discovery, invocation, composition and interoperation, and Web service execution monitoring [7]. Recently there is an important iniative in this respect, namely, DAML-S [7]. DAML-S is a comprehensive effort based on DAML+OIL [5,6] defining an upper ontology for Web services.

In this paper, we describe a framework for Web service semantics where we exploit the upper ontology defined by DAML-S to extend it with the functionality we find essential for the e-businesses and integrate it with UDDI registries.

A. Buchmann et al. (Eds.): TES 2002, LNCS 2444, pp. 9–18, 2002.
© Springer-Verlag Berlin Heidelberg 2002

Universal Description, Discovery and Integration (UDDI) is jointly proposed by IBM, Microsoft and Ariba. It is a service registry architecture that presents a standard way for businesses to build a registry, discover each other, and describe how to interact over the Internet. Conceptually, the information provided in UDDI registries consist of three components: "white pages" of company contact information; "yellow pages" that categorize businesses by standard taxonomies; and "green pages" that document the technical information about services.

Currently there are no mechanisms to describe the metadata of services in UDDI. For example, locating parties that can provide a specific product or service at a given price, which we believe is an essential functionality of the e-businesses, is currently not available in UDDI. We give the following example to motivate the reader for the work presented in this paper:

Assume that a business user in Ankara wishes to buy second hand IBM desktop computers for the cheapest price that she can get, for over a period of time (that is, she wishes to establish a long term business relationship). The user also wishes to find services for possible products that may add value to the desktop, for example, a scanner. There is a need for the purchases to be delivered, and therefore complementary services like "delivery" are also necessary.

This business user can find a standard products and services code (like UN-SPSC [20]) for desktops and the geography code for Ankara, and search for businesses in a UDDI registry. However there are a number of problems in this process:

- First, the user has to go through all the businesses found to check their services. These services could be anything related with desktops, not only the services that sell desktops. Therefore the user has to go through all the services found to distinguish the ones that "sell" desktops. With the projected near-term population of several hundred thousand to million distinct entities in a UDDI registry, it is unlikely that even this result set will be manageable.
- Second, it is not possible in UDDI to enforce a relationship between the service names and their functionality. Note that Web service description languages like WSDL only provide the signature of the operations of the service, that is, the name, parameters and the types of parameters of the service. Trying to discover services by name may not be always very meaningful since a service name could be anything and in any language. So it is not easy to figure out which of the services in the UDDI registry indeed realize the "sell" functionality.
- Third, among the services discovered that sell desktops there is no hint on which of these services actually sell "IBM" desktops and also their prices, since UDDI does not provide a mechanism to discover services on the basis of product instances. In other words, although it is possible to find the services according to the category of the products, it is not possible to find services by giving specific product information like their brand names or prices.
- Notice that the user is looking for a service that has a property: the service should deal with "second hand" products. There is no way to find such services since it is not possible to define properties for the services in UDDI.

- Products may have attributes that cannot be defined in product taxonomies like UNSPSC. For example given an anchor product, say a desktop, there could be a number of products that add value to this product, say a scanner or a printer, and the user may wish to find the services related with these products as in the case of our example.
- Since there is no mechanism to define relationships among service types, it is hard to identify complementary services. Continuing with our example, the user cannot locate a complementary "delivery" service for the reason stated.

These limitations are not inherent in the UDDI specification, but rather stem basically from the lack of semantic descriptions of the Web services. Currently, describing the semantic of Web in general [1], and semantic of Web services in particular are very active research areas. There are a number of efforts for describing the semantics of Web services such as [13,14,9]. Among these DAML-S is a comprehensive effort defining an upper ontology.

In defining an ontology for e-businesses, there are certain functionality that we believe should be present. The first one is describing a standard way of relating the Web services with electronic catalogs. Also, we believe it is necessary to discover services with complementary functionality. For example a "delivery" service may be complementary to a "sell" service, and it should be possible to discover the related complementary "delivery" service instances given a "sell" service instance.

There is another issue to be handled once the semantics is defined: There should be a mechanism in the service registry to relate the semantics defined with service advertised. We also address this issue.

The paper is organized as follows: In Section 2, we very briefly summarize the ontology language used in this paper, namely, DAML-S. Section 3 describes the service ontology we propose. In this section, we also show how to integrate the proposed framework to UDDI. Section 4 concludes the paper.

2   DAML-S: Semantic Markup for Web Services

DAML-S [7], which is based on DAML+OIL [6], defines an upper ontology for describing service semantics and the top level class is the *Service* class. *Service* class has three properties:

- *presents.* The class Service *presents* a *ServiceProfile* to specify what the service provides for its users as well as what the service requires from its users; that is, it gives the type of information needed by a service-seeking agent to determine whether the service meets its needs. *ServiceProfile* class has properties to describe the necessary inputs and outputs used or generated by a service; preconditions and postconditions, and binding patterns. Other properties of the *ServiceProfile* include *serviceParameter* to define parameters of services like maximum response time; *serviceType* to refer to a high level classification of services, such as B2B or B2C; and *serviceCategory* to refer to an ontology of services.

- *describedBy.* The class Service is *describedBy* a *ServiceModel* to specify how it works.
- *supports.* The class Service *supports* a *ServiceGrounding* to specify how it is used. A service grounding specifies the details of how an agent can access a service. It should be noted that DAML-S ServiceGrounding specification overlaps with WSDL [8].

3   The Proposed Semantic Framework

In order to better expolit the service registries, service semantics need to be defined. In developing ontologies for e-business applications, there are some important functionality that must be provided by Web services in a standard way, such as:

- *Discovering services with complementary functionality:* For example, a "Sell" service can complement a "Delivery" service. A standard property, say, "addOn" can be used to describe such complementary services to help with their discovery.
- *Finding services according to the properties of services or products:* Given an anchor product, a customer may be intersted in products that add value to this product. As an example, a customer willing to buy a computer, may also be willing to buy a "scanner" or a "ups", and may therefore be interested in finding services providing these products.

  Also services themseves may have properties; for example a "sell" service may be dealing with only "second hand" products; or a "payment" service may have properties such as "Credit Card Payment".

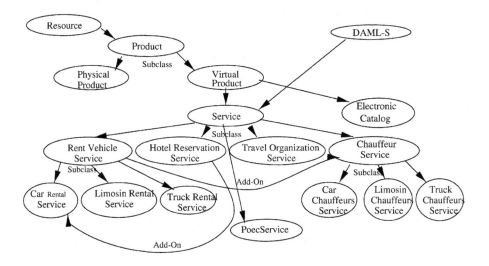

Fig. 1. An example service taxonomy

– *Relating the services with electronic catalogs:* For example a user may not only wish to rent a car but a specific model like "Chevrolet Model 1956". Unless the instances of a "Car_Rental_Service" provide a standard way to access electronic catalogs, providing the user what he wants in an automated way, may become impossible.

We extend DAML-S upper ontology to provide this functionality. We further note that most of the services are related with products, let it be physical products or virtual products, i.e., information. Specifying services and products in the same taxonomy has the following advantages: the properties applicable to both physical and virtual products, such as "addOn" property is defined only once at the top level product class and inherited by the subclasses. Secondly, in this way it becomes possible to relate services and products in the same ontology, in a compact way. We use DAML+OIL as the ontology language both because of its richer semantic modelling primitives and to be able to be compatible with DAML-S.

In the proposed framework, both the services and the products are classified in a single top level taxonomy as shown in Figure 1. That is, under the top level class defined to be "resource" by RDF, we define a "Product" class that has "Physical Products" and "Virtual Products" as subclasses. The service class we define, namely "PoecService", is a subclass of "Virtual Products". In the following subsections we describe how the required functionality is achieved through the proposed semantic framework.

3.1   Discovering the Services According to Their Functionality

We will first describe how a service ontology is used to find the services with desired functionality. A "generic" type service in an ontology defines service functionality; that is, an ontology associates generic classes with well-defined meanings. In order to discover the services according to their functionality, the generic service class of the desired functionality should be known. In other words, the generic service class name is the input for discovering services according to their functionality. Once the generic class is known, it is necessary to query the ontology to obtain all the subclasses of the given generic class as well as the "implementation" instances. The implementation instances thus found satisfy the required functionality.

To differentiate between the "generic" type services in the ontology from the service instances, we use DAML-S "serviceType". "PoecService" inherits both from the "Service" specification of DAML-S and from the "Virtual_Product" specification. "PoecService" class restricts the DAML-S "serviceType", and defines the type of the service to be a "generic" type or an "implementation" instance as shown in the following:

```
<daml:Class ID="PoecService">
  <rdfs:subClassOf rdf:resource="#Virtual_Product"/>
  <rdfs:subClassOf rdf:resource="http://www.daml.org/services/daml-s/2001/05/Service.daml"/>
  <rdfs:subClassOf>
    <daml:Restriction>
      <daml:onProperty rdf:resource="&profile;#serviceType"/>
```

```
      <daml:toClass rdf:resource="#ServiceTypes"/>
    </daml:Restriction> </rdfs:subClassOf> </daml:Class>
<daml:Class ID="ServiceTypes">
  <daml:oneOf rdf:parseType="daml:collection">
    <ServiceTypes rdf:ID="Generic"/>
    <ServiceTypes rdf:ID="Implementation"/>
  </daml:oneOf> </daml:Class>
```

An "implementation" instance gives the description of a particular service implementation. Consider the example service taxonomy provided in Figure 1. The services presented in this schema are generic services such as "Car_Rental_Service". Any implementation of this service, such as "My_Car_Rental_Service" declares itself to be an instance of the "Car_Rental_Service" class. Then, in order to find the implementations of "Rent_Vehicle_Service", it is necessary to query the ontology to find all subclasses of this class and all of their implementations. Since the queries involved have well defined goals like finding all subclasses of a given class, they can easily be standardized. It should be noted that DAML+OIL documents can be queried through DAML APIs or through any XML query language since the serialization syntax of DAML+OIL documents are XML. However, to the best of our knowledge, there are no DAML+OIL query languages yet.

3.2   Relating Services with Complementary Functionality

Consider the ontology given in Figure 1. Assume that a customer needs a driver after renting a car. Given the generic name of the car rental service in the ontology, "Car_Rental_Service", to find out what kind of add on services are available for this service, we need to find out the add on services of this class and the add on services of all of its super classes. Such a search (through a query mechanism) will give us the "Chauffeur" service as the complementary (add on generic service) to the "Rent_Vehicle_Service" service. Now in order to find drivers for the car we plan to rent, we need to search the UDDI registry for services that contain the tModel for "Chauffeur" in their catagory bags. This issue is further elaborated in Section 3.5.

The "Added_Value" and "AddOn_To" properties defined in the following are used to express complementary services:

```
<rdf:Property ID="AddOn_To">
    <rdfs:domain resource="#Product"/>
    <rdfs:range   resource="#Product"/> </rdf:Property>
<rdf:Property ID="Added_Value">
    <rdfs:domain resource="#Product"/>
    <rdfs:range   resource="#Product"/> </rdf:Property>
```

Notice that since "PoecService" is a subclass of "Product", the "Added_Value" and "AddOn_To" properties are applicable to both services and products. Further note that, add on products of a super class are also add on products for all of its subclasses due to the inheritance in class hierarchies.

As noted previously, the process of finding the properties of services can be automated through a set of standardized queries to traverse DAML+OIL descriptions for the super classes of a given class and retrieving the necessary properties.

3.3 Discovering the Services According to the Attributes of Product Types

The attributes of the products can be used to discover the services in a similar way as described in Section 3.2. For example, a user, after locating a service for an anchor product, may want to discover the services providing add on products. The "Add-On" property defined in Figure 1 is used to express complementary products. Notice that these properties are applicable to both services and products.

Given an anchor product, in order to find the services for add on products, it is necessary to find the super classes of this anchor product, since add on products of its super classes are also add on products of this class. For example, the super class of "desktop" is "computer" which declares "scanner" as its add on product. This process can be automated through standardized queries as mentioned previously. Once the add on products are discovered, the services for these products can be obtained from the UDDI registries by using their UNSPSC codes.

3.4 Relating Services with Product Instances

Discovering services related with a specific product is of strategic importance for Web services. For example, a user may wish not only to rent a car but a specific model like "Chevrolet Model 1956". In such a case it is necessary to find car rental services that rent this specific model. However in order to discover services according to product instance information, it is necessary to form a relationship between the two.

To be able to associate service implementations with their related product instances, we first define a class called "ElectronicCatalog" to be a subclass of "Virtual_Product". Electronic catalog has the following properties, defined as a subproperty of "input" property of DAML-S ServiceProfile class:

- Catalog Schema Type
- Catalog Schema
- Catalog URI

These are, we believe, the minimum set of properties for an electronic catalog to be queried automatically. The range of these properties are the most generic class DAML Thing, which can be restricted in the individual schemas.

We then define a "QueryCatalog" standard service as a subclass of "PoecService". The services that provide a "QueryCatalog" service declare this through "has_Query_Catalog" service which is a sub property of "serviceParameters" property of DAML-S ServiceProfile class. The "QueryCatalog" class has the following properties: "inputCatalog", "inputQuery" (defined as subproperties of DAML-S "ServiceProfile input" property) and "QueryResult" (subproperty of DAML-S "ServiceProfile output") as shown in the following:

```
<daml:Class ID="ElectronicCatalog">
    <rdfs:subClassOf resource="#Virtual_Product"/> </daml:Class>
<rdf:Property rdf:ID="CatalogURI">
```

```
    <rdfs:subPropertyOf rdf:resource="&profile;#input"/>
    <rdfs:domain rdf:resource="#ElectronicCatalog"/>
    <rdfs:range rdf:resource="&daml;#Thing"/> </rdf:Property>
<rdf:Property rdf:ID="CatalogSchema">
    <rdfs:subPropertyOf rdf:resource="&profile;#input"/>
    <rdfs:domain rdf:resource="#ElectronicCatalog"/>
    <rdfs:range rdf:resource="&daml;#Thing"/> </rdf:Property>
<rdf:Property rdf:ID="CatalogSchemaType">
    <rdfs:subPropertyOf rdf:resource="&profile;#input"/>
    <rdfs:domain rdf:resource="#ElectronicCatalog"/>
    <rdfs:range rdf:resource="&daml;#Thing"/> </rdf:Property>
<daml:Class ID="QueryCatalog">
    <rdfs:subClassOf rdf:resource="#PoecService"/>
    <rdfs:subClassOf>
        <daml:Restriction>
          <daml:onProperty rdf:resource="&profile;#inputCatalog"/>
          <daml:toClass rdf:resource="#ElectronicCatalog"/>
        </daml:Restriction> </rdfs:subClassOf> </daml:Class>
<rdf:Property ID="has_Query_Catalog">
    <rdfs:subPropertyOf rdf:resource="serviceParameters"/>
    <rdfs:domain rdf:resource="&service;#ServiceProfile"/>
    <rdfs:range rdf:resource="&poec;QueryCatalog"/> </rdf:Property>
<rdf:Property rdf:ID="inputCatalog">
    <rdfs:subPropertyOf rdf:resource="&profile;#input"/>
    <rdfs:domain rdf:resource="#QueryCatalog"/> </rdf:Property>
<rdf:Property rdf:ID="inputQuery">
    <rdfs:subPropertyOf rdf:resource="&profile;#input"/>
    <rdfs:domain rdf:resource="#QueryCatalog"/>
    <rdfs:range rdf:resource="&daml;#Thing"/> </rdf:Property>
<rdf:Property rdf:ID="QueryResult">
    <rdfs:subPropertyOf rdf:resource="&profile;#output"/>
    <rdfs:domain rdf:resource="#QueryCatalog"/>
    <rdfs:range rdf:resource="&daml;#Thing"/> </rdf:Property>
```

To provide interoperability, the queries and the electronic catalogs must conform to standards. Possible standards for electronic catalogs include the Common Business Library (CBL) [2] catalog definition or RosettaNet Technical Dictionary [17]. Possible query standards to be used depends on the catalog structure. For Common Business Library and RosettaNet Technical Dictionaries, since they are defined in XML [22], XQuery [23] is a possible candidate. Note that for catalogs with a well-known schema like RosettaNet Technical Dictionary, there is no need to specify the Catalog Schema. However if the catalog is on a database, it is necessary to provide the database schema.

When it comes to service invocation, DAML-S specifies service grounding to describe how the service is used. In this respect, DAML-S specification is overlaping with Web Services Description Language (WSDL). WSDL is a well established standard for describing the interface and binding information of Web services. DAML-S service grounding specification has the same functionality as WSDL except for preconditions and post conditions for executing Web services. Yet this information is also available from DAML-S service profile definitions.

3.5   Relating Service Ontology with Service Instances

It is also necessary to provide the DAML+OIL descriptions of the service instances. The server where the service is defined can host the DAML+OIL description of service implementation instance. Storing a DAML+OIL description individually in this way isolates the description of each implementation instance and facilitates their maintenance by the service providers. However there are times, when it is necessary to query all the individual service descriptions, and this implies accessing all of them one by one, which may be inefficient. Therefore a combined schema per industry domain containing all the descriptions of the services pertaining to this domain may be necessary to facilitate querying. Note that the combined schema needs to be updated to contain the newly registered services.

There is one more issue to be handled to exploit the semantics defined for the Web services: there should be a mechanism in the service registry to relate the semantics defined with the service advertised. The semantic framework proposed can be integrated with UDDI as follows: Similar to WSDL, DAML+OIL Schema should also be classified as "damlSpec" with "uddi-org:types" taxonomy. A seperate tModel of type "damlSpec" can be created for the combined schema of each industry domain, and OverviewDoc element of the corresponding tModel can be made to point at the combined schema. The services in an industry domain contain the key of this tModel in their category bags and the OverviewDoc elements associated with these tModel keys point at the DAML+OIL description of service instances.

Furthermore, a tModel should be assigned to each generic service as well as service implementations. We therefore define the following in the common schema:

```
<daml:UniqueProperty rdf:ID="tModelKey">
  <rdfs:domain rdf:resource="#PoecSercive"/>
  <rdfs:range rdf:resource="&xsd;#decimal"/>
</daml:UniqueProperty>
```

4 Conclusions

When looking towards the future of web-services, it is predicted that the breakthrough will come when the software agents start using web-services rather than the users who need to browse, discover and compose the services. Among the challenges this breakthrough involves is the semantics of Web services.

Although some progress has been made in the area of web service description and discovery, and there are some important standards like SOAP, WSDL, and UDDI, and efforts for defining semantics like DAML-S; there is still more work needed in this area.

In this paper, we extend the DAML-S upper ontology to describe some functionality that we find essential for e-businesses like discovering services with complementary functionality, discovering services according to the properties of products or services and relating services with electronic catalogs. We then describe how to use the defined semantics through UDDI registries.

Our future work includes extending this work to ebXML [10] registries. ebXML registries allow to store classification hierarchies and relate registry items with classification nodes through classification objects. This feature of ebXML facilitates associating semantics with the services. However classification structure provided by ebXML is not adequate to store DAML+OIL ontologies and need to be extended to be used for this purpose. Also ebXML registry interface needs to be extended to query DAML+OIL ontologies.

References

1. Berners-Lee, T., Hendler, J., Lassila, O., "The Semantic Web", Scientific American, May 2001.
2. Common Business Library (CBL) URL. http://www.xCBL.org/
3. F. Casati and M-C. Shan "Definition, Execution, Analysis and Optimization of Composite E-Services" IEEE Data Engineering Bulletin, Vol. 24, No.1, pp. 29-34.
4. F. Casati and M-C. Shan "Dynamic and Adaptive Composition of E-Services" Information Systems, to appear.
5. DARPA Agent Markup Language, http://www.xml.com/pub/a/2002/01/30/daml1.html
6. DAML+OIL, http://www.w3.org/2001/10/daml+oil
7. DAML Services Coalition (A. Ankolekar, M. Burstein, J. Hobbs, O. Lassila, D. Martin, S. McIlraith, S. Narayanan, M. Paolucci, T. Payne, K. Sycara, H. Zeng), DAML-S: Semantic Markup for Web Services, in Proceedings of the International Semantic Web Working Symposium (SWWS), July 2001.
8. The DAML Services Coalition, "DAML-S: Web Service Description for the Semantic Web", to appear in The First International Semantic Web Conference (ISWC), Sardinia, Italia, June 9-12th, 2002.
9. Denker, G., Hobbs, J. R., Narayan, S., Waldinger, R., "Accessing Information and Services on DAML-Enabled Web, Semantic Web Workshop, Hong Kong, China, 2001.
10. ebXML http://www.ebxml.org/
11. e-Speak http://www.e-speak.hp.com/
12. IBM UDDI registry http://www-3.ibm.com/services/uddi/find
13. McIlraith, S. A., Son, T. C., Zeng, H., "Semantic Web Services", IEEE Intelligent Systems, March/April 2001, pp. 46-53.
14. McIlraith, S. A., Son, T. C., Zeng, H., "Mobilizing the Semantic Web with DAML-Enaled Web Services", Semantic Web Workshop 2001, Hongkong, China.
15. Resource Description Framework (RDF) Schema Specification 1.0 W3C Candidate Recommendation, http://www.w3.org/TR/CR-rdf-schema, 2000.
16. Resource Description Framework (RDF) Model and Syntax Specification, W3C Recommendation, http://www.w3.org/TR/REC-rdf-syntax, 1999.
17. RosettaNet http://www. rosettanet.org.
18. Simple Object Access Protocol (SOAP) http://www.w3.org/TR/SOAP/
19. Universal Description, Discovery and Integration (UDDI) www.uddi.org
20. Universal Standard Products and Services Classification (UNSPSC) http://eccma.org/unspsc
21. Web Service Description Language (WSDL) http://www.w3.org/TR/wsdl
22. XML, "Extensible Markup Language (XML) 1.0", W3C Recommendation, http:// www.w3.org/ TR/REC-xml-19980210, 1998.
23. XQuery, "An XML Query Language 1.0", W3C Working Draft, http://www.w3.org/TR/2002/WD-xquery-20020430.

Public Process Inheritance for Business-to-Business Integration

Christoph Bussler

Oracle Corporation, Redwood Shores, CA 94065, U. S. A.
Chris.Bussler@Oracle.com

Abstract. Trading partners exchanging Business-to-Business (B2B) messages like purchase orders in context of B2B integration over networks like the Internet or value added networks (VANs) follow the concept of public processes for the definition and execution of B2B message exchange sequences. Experience shows that in most cases trading partners specialize them slightly to accommodate their specific needs. Currently, there is no language support for the structured modification or specialization of public processes. This paper applies the concept of public process inheritance that allows a trading partner to specialize public processes without loosing the modification path starting from the public process as defined by a standard.

1 Introduction

In order to make inter-enterprise processes work, each enterprise has to implement not only its internal processes ("private processes"), but also its external behavior ("public processes") [2] [7] [11] [16]. A public process is the definition of a formal message exchange with other enterprises (trading partners) with a pre-defined sequence and with pre-defined message formats over networks like the Internet.

The public processes of two enterprises have to match in order to allow inter-enterprise processes to work together seamlessly. E. g., if one enterprise sends a purchase order (PO) then the other enterprise must be able to receive the PO in the format sent over the same network. The formal definition of matching public processes is called business-to-business (B2B) protocols. Several efforts are ongoing [6] that define B2B protocols so that enterprises do not have to mutually agree on their own proprietary B2B protocols but instead can follow a given defined standard.

In contrast, private processes are internal to an enterprise. The definition of a private process is solely determined by an enterprise and it is not subject to agreement with its trading partners. Private processes are invisible to trading partners. The technology of choice to implement private processes is workflow management systems (WFMSs) [1] [19] [20]. Private processes are not relevant for the discussion in this paper and are therefore not discussed further. [6], [7] and [8] discuss private processes and their relationship to public processes in more detail.

In reality it is wishful thinking that the public processes as defined by a standards organization like RosettaNet [23] are agreed upon and accepted by all enterprises of a whole industry without requiring any modification to accommodate specific cases. In order for this to happen the definition of public processes would have to cover all the

A. Buchmann et al. (Eds.): TES 2002, LNCS 2444, pp. 19–28, 2002.
© Springer-Verlag Berlin Heidelberg 2002

specific needs of all enterprises that use the public processes to exchange B2B messages.

Needless to say that this is very unlikely. Either the message formats of existing messages have to be changed (e. g. adding fields for additional data in a purchase order) or the protocol itself is changed (e. g. including additional error messages). This requires the specialization of the public processes in order to accommodate the specific requirements. In this case, the enterprises that exchange messages have to agree on the modified public processes instead of the ones as defined by the standard. However, an enterprise does not modify a public process without keeping the original since it is possible that different trading partners need different modifications. All modifications have a common root and might be descendants of each other as well. The appropriate mechanism to support all required variations through specialization is process inheritance [9].

Process inheritance is based on the notion of overwriting existing elements or adding elements to a process definition. If a process (subprocess class) inherits from another process (superprocess class), the complete process definition is inherited. If no change is applied to the subprocess class it behaves exactly like its superprocess class. For example, if a process step is overwritten in the subprocess class then the execution of the subprocess class is the same than the superprocess class except that the overwritten process step would be executed instead of the one defined in the superprocess class.

The contribution of this paper is to apply the notion of process inheritance to public processes in order to accommodate enterprise specific changes in public processes. The notion of inheritance allows to manage public process variation on a large scale. Section 2 will discuss public processes. Section 3 will introduce inheritance of public processes with examples. Section 4 discusses related work.

2 Public Processes

B2B protocols like RosettaNet [23] are specifically designed for inter-enterprise message exchange. B2B protocols are outward focused in the sense that they are concerned about the message exchange between enterprises and not about private processes. In general, the concepts of B2B protocols are [6]:

- **Message format**. The message format defines the business content of messages. E. g., each business document like a purchase order described as a DTD [32].
- **Business messages and administration messages**. One type of message contains business content whereas other types of messages contain acknowledgments or error notifications. For example, a message can acknowledge that a message with business content was received.
- **Activities for sending and receiving of messages**. Messages have to be sent to enterprises as well as received from enterprises (steps labeled "S" and "R" in Figure 1). Distinct steps in B2B protocols define when a message is to be received and when a message must be sent. This allows to check if two public processes from two different enterprises match.
- **Time-out and retry logic**. B2B protocols must achieve reliable messaging over unreliable networks. Time-outs defined on messages as well as retry logic allow to handle failures (steps labeled "T" in Figure 4). E. g., a time-out can specify that an

acknowledgment message has to be received within two hours of sending a business message. If no acknowledgment message is received within two hours it is assumed that the business message was lost and it will be re-sent.
- **Duplicate check and avoidance**. B2B protocols must implement an exactly once message transfer. This ensures that messages are received as well as are received exactly once. Due to the time-out and retry requirement it might be the case that the same message is sent twice (e. g. when the message was not really lost but the acknowledgment was late). In this case the duplicate must be eliminated.

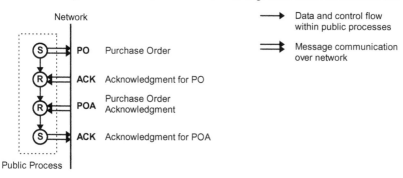

Fig. 1. Sample public process for sending purchase orders and receiving purchase order acknowledgments with individual message acknowledgments

Figure 1 shows a graphical representation of a public process that implements the behavior of a buyer. It refers to the messages being exchanged as well as the sequence of steps involved in the exchange. This public process sends a purchase order (PO) and expects a message acknowledgement afterwards (ACK). Then it expects a purchase order acknowledgement message (POA) and sends an ACK. This example will later on serve as a basis for specialization according to specific requirements.

The following specification shows the specification of the public process in the language as discussed in [9].

```
WORKFLOW_CLASS S /* SEND */ (IN message: send_message)
   /* internal implementation of send, not further detailed here */
END_WORKFLOW_CLASS

WORKFLOW_CLASS R /* RECEIVE */ (OUT message: received_message)
   /* internal implementation of receive, not further detailed here */
END_WORKFLOW_CLASS

WORKFLOW_CLASS PO_POA
   SUBWORKFLOWS
     S: send_PO_step, send_POA_ACK_step;
     R: receive_PO_ACK_step, receive_POA_step;
   END_SUBWORKFLOWS
   CONTROL_FLOW
     cf_1: sequence(send_PO_step, receive_PO_ACK_step);
     cf_2: sequence(receive_PO_ACK_step, receive_POA_step);
     cf_3: sequence(receive_POA_step, send_POA_ACK_step);
```

```
   END_CONTROL_FLOW
   WORKFLOW_DATA
     PO: PO_message;
     ACK: PO_ACK, POA_ACK;
     POA: POA_message;
   END_WORKFLOW_DATA
   DATA_FLOW
     df_1: PO_message -> send_PO_step.send_message;
     df_2: receive_PO_ACK_step.received_message -> PO_ACK;
     df_3: receive_POA_step.received_message -> POA_message;
     df_4: POA_ACK -> send_POA_ACK_step.send_message;
   END_DATA_FLOW
END_WORKFLOW_CLASS
```

3   Public Process Modification through Process Inheritance

A public process might be appropriate to govern the B2B message exchange between an enterprise and one of its trading partners but not for another trading partner. In this case it needs to be specialized for that particular trading partner to accommodate the specific change. The two types of changes can be:

- **Message format.** In this case the public process defines the desired exchange sequence of the B2B messages correctly, but their definition is not appropriate.
- **Message exchange protocol.** In this case the message formats are fine but the exchange protocol needs to be modified.

Both types of changes can of course be required at the same time, too. In the following three examples are discussed, one for each type of change and one that combines the two types of changes at the same time. Figure 2 shows the process inheritance hierarchy that will be defined throughout the discussion. The process inheritance concept followed is described in [9].

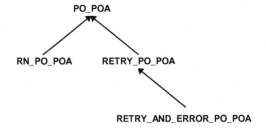

Fig. 2. Process inheritance hierarchy of the examples

3.1   Modification of Message Format Definition in Public Processes

The first example changes only the message format and does not modify the exchange protocol at all. Figure 3 shows the public process after the change. Only the message format has been changed from "PO" to "RN_PO" (for RosettaNet PO), from "POA" to "RN_POA (for RosettaNet POA) and from "ACK" to "RN_ACK" (for RosettaNet ACK).

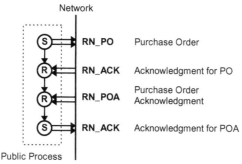

Fig. 3. Modification of message format

The following specification shows the process graphically depicted in Figure 3 using process inheritance. Only the messages formats are overwritten. The rest of the public process remains the same.

```
WORKFLOW_CLASS RN_PO_POA SUBCLASS_OF PO_POA
    WORKFLOW_DATA
    RN_PO: PO_message;
    RN_ACK; PO_ACK, POA_ACK;
    RN_POA: POA_message;
    END_WORKFLOW_DATA
END_WORKFLOW_CLASS
```

3.2 Modification of Exchange Protocol in Public Processes

The second example modifies the exchange protocol but leaves the message formats unchanged. In this example time-outs and retries are added as follows. Once a PO is sent out, a time-out step is started. If the time-out occurs, the PO is resent provided that the upper retry limit is not exhausted yet. If an ACK comes within the time-out limit the time-out step is canceled and the execution of the public process is continued. Otherwise the public process is aborted with failure (step "A" in Figure 4).

It is possible that the ACK is received right after the time-out happened. This means that the PO is sent again and it seems that this is unnecessary (since the ACK for the first PO arrived). However, according to the message exchange definition the PO has to be sent if the time out happens. Consequently, the late ACK has to be ignored. This is correct behavior because the first PO was not acknowledged in the time limit of the time-out. The public process continued processing (resending the PO). The trading partner has to acknowledge the second PO, too, even thought the trading partner received the first PO. In total, the trading partner received two POs and has to detect the duplicate PO due to the resend.

The incoming ACK triggers another time-out step. This time-out is required because the POA is expected to be received within a specific time limit. If this is not the case, the PO is sent again (that in turn triggers the first time-out loop again). After a predetermined number of retries in order to receive a POA the public process aborts (second abort). Otherwise, if one POA is received within the time limit, the ACK for the POA is sent out.

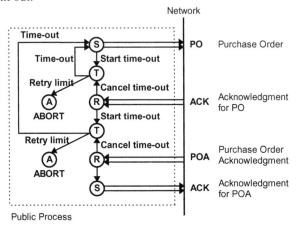

Fig. 4. Modification of exchange protocol

The following specifications defines the process in Figure 4. The time-out step "T" returns either that a time-out happened or that the retry-limit is reached. Both values are used in the control flow in order to branch the flow in the public process later on.

```
WORKFLOW_CLASS T /* Time-out step */ (OUT result: TIMEOUT | RETRY_LIMIT)
    /* internal implementation of time-out, not further detailed here */
END_WORKFLOW_CLASS
```

The new step type "A" (for abort) does not take any parameter. It just executes the unconditional abort of the public process.

```
WORKFLOW_CLASS A /* Abort */ ()
    /* internal implementation of abort, not further detailed here */
END_WORKFLOW_CLASS
```

The new public process is defined as follows through process inheritance. The data flow of "PO_POA" remains unchanged. However, the control flow changes by incorporating the new steps as well as conditional branching. As can be seen through the reference to already existing control flow names overwrites of control flow take place. Also, the additional four new steps have to be introduced. In this case no overwrite takes place but only extensions.

```
WORKFLOW_CLASS RETRY_PO_POA SUBCLASS_OF PO_POA
    SUBWORKFLOWS
        T: first_time_out_step, second_time_out_step;
        A: first_abort_step, second_abort_step;
    END_SUBWORKFLOWS
    CONTROL_FLOW
        cf_1: sequence(send_PO_step, first_time_out_step);
        cf_4: conditional(first_time_out_step.result == TIMEOUT,
            send_PO_step, first_abort_step)
```

```
   cf_2: parallel(receive_PO_ACK_step,
      first_time_out_step, second_time_out_step);
   cf_5: conditional(second_time_out_step.result == TIMEOUT,
      send_PO_step, second_abort_step);
   cf_3: parallel(receive_POA_step,
      second_time_out_step, send_POA_ACK_step);
   END_CONTROL_FLOW
END_WORKFLOW_CLASS
```

"cf_1" overwrites the one of the superclass to thread the time-out step. "cf_4" defines the conditional branch after the first time-out step. "cf_2" is overwritten defining that after receiving the "ACK" for the "PO" control flow goes to both, "first_time_out" as well as "second_time_out". "cf_5" defines the conditional branching after the second time-out step. "cf_3" is overwritten defining that after receiving the "POA" the second time-out step is cancelled as well as the "ACK" for the "POA" is sent.

3.3 Modification of Message Format and Exchange Protocol

The third example shows both, a modification of the message format as well as a modification of the exchange protocol. In contrast to the second example, an error message is sent to the trading partner each time before an abort happens. This informs the trading partner about the retry failure through an error message. The document formats introduced in the first example are used again in the third example. Furthermore, one new message format for error messages ("RN_ERR") is introduced in order to define the error message (see Figure 5).

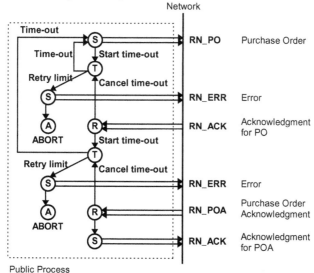

Fig. 5. Modification of exchange protocol as well as message format

First, two additional step are introduced for sending the error messages. Two different error messages are added to the local variables. Additional data flow is added to "flow" the local variables to the two additional steps. Finally, two control flow definitions are overwritten to add the additional steps to the control flow.

```
WORKFLOW_CLASS RETRY_AND_ERROR_PO_POA SUBCLASS_OF RETRY_PO_POA
    SUBWORKFLOWS
    S: send_first_error_step, send_second_error_step;
    END_SUBWORKFLOWS
    WORKFLOW_DATA
      RN_PO: PO_message;
      RN_ACK; PO_ACK, POA_ACK;
      RN_POA: POA_message;
      RN_ERROR: first_ERROR_message, second_ERROR_Message;
    END_WORKFLOW_DATA
    DATA_FLOW
      df_5: first_ERROR_message -> send_first_error_step.send_message;
      df_6: second_ERROR_message -> send_second_error_step.send_message;
    END_DATA_FLOW
    CONTROL_FLOW
      cf_4: conditional(first_time_out_step.result == TIMEOUT,
        send_PO_step,
        sequence(send_first_error_step, first_abort_step));
      cf_5: conditional(second_time_out_step.result == TIMEOUT,
        send_PO_step,
        sequence(send_second_error_step, second_abort_step));
    END_CONTROL_FLOW
END_WORKFLOW_CLASS
```

Through all three examples it becomes clear that changes cannot be made unilaterally, but both involved trading partners have to agree on the changes. The reason is that both trading partners have to agree on the message formats since otherwise it is impossible to interpret the contents. In addition, they have to agree on the behavior of the message exchange since otherwise message are expected and not sent or messages are sent by one trading partner whereby the other trading partner is not waiting for one.

4 Related Work

Two examples of standards addressing public processes are RosettaNet [23] and ebXML [13]. RosettaNet pre-defines specific public processes called Partner Interface Processes (PIPs) whereby ebXML allows to define arbitrary public processes through Collaborations. EbXML as a standard does not define specific public processes like RosettaNet but only provides a language for defining those. This means that in case of RosettaNet two enterprises can inter-operate by virtue of being RosettaNet compliant. In the case of ebXML two enterprises have to agree on a definition of their public processes first. This is facilitated by Collaboration Partner Agreements (CPAs) [14]. Standards like EDI [15] are neither defining public processes nor providing a mechanism to define public processes. In this case enterprises need to borrow the mechanism from e. g. ebXML to define public processes. None of the standards addresses public process inheritance in order to allow public process modification.

Web services [28] are currently being defined. From [28] can be derived that the concept of web services is not well-defined yet. However, efforts in registries like UDDI [25] and description languages like WSDL [29] show that the current thinking in this space is more along the lines of remote function calls than public process descriptions. With WSDL an elaborate scheme is given to define signatures of remote functions as well as their binding to physical locations. However, public process descriptions are impossible to define due to missing activity, control flow and data flow concepts.

WSFL [30] is concerned about a flow language describing web services composition (very similar to the workflow definition language of [17]). It is not concerned about providing a mechanism in order to specialize public processes as described in this paper. Alternative proposals like [4] [13] [31] do not provide public process inheritance either.

In [2] workflow inheritance is used to bind a public process to a private process. This binding is achieved by inheriting the exchange sequence from the public process into the private process and extend the public process with enterprise internal behavior. A discussion of the benefits and downsides of this approach of binding can be found in [5]. However, this approach does not mention at all the need for specializing public processes and hence does not discuss this functionality.

In [10] the authors discuss how to use workflow management to orchestrate web services and describe web service invocation order through workflow management. However, public process inheritance is not discussed. Other works of the same authors do not deal with the aspect of process specialization through process inheritance either.

Products of vendors like [3] [12] [18] [21] [22] [24] [26] [27] support inter-enterprise message exchange following specific selected standards. However, it is impossible to derive from the data made available by the vendors how the internal implementation would support the approach of public process inheritance as proposed in this paper.

References

1. Aalst,, W. M. P. van der; Hee, Kees van: *Workflow Management. Models, Methods, and Systems*. The MIT Press, 2002
2. Aalst, W. M. P. van der; Weske, M.: The P2P Approach to Interorganizational Workflows. In: *Proceedings of the 13th International Conference on Advanced Information Systems Engineering* (CAiSE'01), Vol. 2068 of Lecture Notes in Computer Science, Springer-Verlag, Berlin, 2001.
3. BEA Collaborate. www.bea.com/products/weblogic/collaborate/index.shtml
4. BPML. www.bpmi.org
5. Bussler, C.: Workflow Class Inheritance and Dynamic Workflow Class Binding. In: *Proceedings of the Workshop Software Architectures for Business Process Management* at the 11th Conference on Advanced Information Systems Engineering CAiSE*99, Heidelberg, Germany, June 1999
6. Bussler, C.: B2B Protocol Standards and their Role in Semantic B2B Integration Engines. In: *Bulletin of the Technical Committee on Data Engineering*. IEEE Computer Society, Vol. 24, No.1 (2001)
7. Bussler, C.: The Role of B2B Protocols in Inter-enterprise Process Execution. In: *Proceedings of Workshop on Technologies for E-Services* (TES 2001) (in cooperation with VLDB2001). Rome, Italy, September 2001

8. Bussler, C.: The Application of Workflow Technology in Semantic B2B Integration. *Distributed and Parallel Databases*, to appear.
9. Bussler, C.: Workflow Inheritance. In: *Proceedings of the 14th Conference on Advanced Information Systems Engineering CAiSE*02*, Toronto, Canada, June 2002
10. Casati, F.; Shan, M.-C.: Models and Languages for Describing and Discovering E-Services. *2001 SIGMOD International Conference on Management of Data*. Santa Barbara, CA, USA, May 2001
11. Chen, Q.; Hsu, M.: *Inter-Enterprise Collaborative Business Process Management*. Technical Report HPL-2000-107, HP Laboratories Palo Alto, August 2000
12. Cyclone Commerce. www.cyclonecommerce.com/
13. ebXML Business Process Specification Schema. Version 1.01. May 2001. www.ebxml.org
14. ebXML Collaboration-Protocol Profile and Agreement Specification. Version 1.0. May 2001. www.ebxml.org
15. EDI. www.x12.org
16. Georgakopoulos, D.; Cichocki, A.; Schuster, H.; Baker, D.: Process-based E-Service Integration. In: *Proceedings of the Workshop on Technologies for E-Services* (TES 2000), Cairo, Egypt, September 2000
17. IBM MQ Series Workflow. www-4.ibm.com/software/ts/mqseries/
18. IONA Netfish XDI. www.iona.com/products/
19. Jablonski, S.; Bussler, C.: *Workflow Management. Concepts, Architecture and Implementation*. International Thomson Publisher, 1995
20. Leymann, F.; Roller, D.: *Production Workflow. Concepts and Techniques*. Prentice Hall PTR, 2000
21. Microsoft Biztalk Server. www.microsoft.com/biztalkserver
22. Peregrine B2B Integration Platform. www.peregrine.com
23. RosettaNet. www.rosettanet.org
24. Tibco Active Exchange. www.tibco.com/products/activeexchange
25. UDDI: Universal Description, Discovery and Integration. www.uddi.org
26. Vitria Business Ware. www.vitria.com/products/businessware/overview.html
27. Webmethods B2Bi. www.webmethods.com/content/1,1107,B2BiSolutions,FF.html
28. W3C Web Services Workshop. www.w3c.org/2001/03/wsws-program
29. WSDL. *Web Services Description Language*. Version 1.1. Ariba, IBM, Microsoft. January 2001. msdn.microsoft.com/xml/general/wsdl.asp
30. WSFL. Web Services Flow Language. Version 1.0. IBM Software Group, May 2001. www-4.ibm.com/software/solutions/webservices/pdf/WSFL.pdf
31. XLANG. www.gotdotnet.com/team/xml_wsspecs/
32. XML. www.w3c.org/xml

A Model-Transformers Architecture for Web Applications

Alexey Valikov, Alexei Akhounov, and Andreas Schmidt

Forschungszentrum Informatik
Haid-und-Neu Str. 10-14
76131 Karlsruhe, Germany
{valikov, akhounov, aschmidt}@fzi.de

Abstract. This paper proposes a web application-oriented modification of Model-View-Controller architecture, which allows generic implementations of the controller and the view. Proposed architecture is based on the conjunction of two techniques: remote procedure calls for HTML/HTTP based web applications in the controller part and automatic presentation of the model state information with several XSLT transformations on the view part.

1 Introduction

Accessibility through the web has become an important feature of modern information systems. This surely has a lot of advantages. For instance, global system accessibility and low-cost software support due to the absence of local installations are made possible.

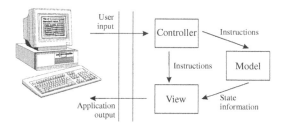

Fig. 1. General architecture of MVC paradigm

Nonetheless, there are certain serious complexities in development of web interfaces. User interface development is a very complex issue even in traditional systems, especially when taking into account that modifications to the UI are quite frequent because of changing user wishes. For more complex applications, this leads to problems of maintenance. In traditional "fat-client" environments, the idea of the model-view-controller architecture [4] has separated different tasks: the state of the application (model), the presentation thereof (view) and the response to user actions (controller) that may result in modifications of the state and the presentation (figure 1).

In web applications, the main difference to traditional UI development is the thin-client approach with a constrained interaction channel between the presentation and

A. Buchmann et al. (Eds.): TES 2002, LNCS 2444, pp. 29-37, 2002.
© Springer-Verlag Berlin Heidelberg 2002

user actions on the one side and the application logic and response to user actions on the server side. The controller mainly receives HTTP requests with sets of name-value pairs while the view has to generate "an interpretable description" of the UI in form of HTML forms.

Obviously, procedures of handling parameters and forming an HTML page based on model state information depend on the application. It means that both development of a new application and changes to an existing application will require customization or complete rewrite of the controller and the view.

In this paper we propose an approach, which allows making controller and view objects generic and reusable for different web applications without any adaptation. This approach is based on the conjunction of two techniques: remote procedure calls for web applications and automatic model transformation.

2   Related Work

MVC with its origins in Smalltalk-80 [4] is a well-known approach and was used in numerous technologies. Nowadays, MVC is also employed in web application area, where separation of presentation and application logic is often crucial [1]. This is somehow done in the J2EE platform with Enterprise JavaBeans (EJB). The approach suggested in this paper follows more or less the same design principles. But as long as we are solving a much more specific problem, we may take an advantage of the pre-conditions we have in web applications and automate certain parts of processing (namely, method calls and presentations).

The approach proposed in this paper is partially based on possibility to invoke methods of model from the client. Despite there are well-developed technologies (RMI, CORBA) and protocols (SOAP) for remote invocation and interaction, they do not solve the problem because of the limitations of HTML/HTTP-based client-server communication. Extension of software or usage of scripting languages is required on the client side; this requirement often simply cannot be met. Model-Transformers architecture does not require usage of advanced features on the client side.

There also are several approaches for MVC-based web applications coming from the open-source community (Apache Turbine, Velocity and Struts). The novelty of Model-Transformers in comparison to these technologies is automatic mapping of the request onto the model's method calls and automatic model presentation.

3   The Controller: RPC for Web Applications

In a web application scenario, user input is mainly a set of parameters submitted via an HTTP request. Controller-model and controller-view communication is usually implemented in conventional systems via simple method calls: in order to change view or model, controller invokes the method of the appropriate object. Consequently, controller fulfils the task of mapping submitted parameters onto method calls (figure 2).

Fig. 2. Controller in web MVC applications

In first approximation, a controller in MVC-based web application actually behaves like a dispatcher for remote method invocations. Of course, it may handle many other useful tasks, but the "dispatcher" functionality is, clearly, the primary task, on which we will be focusing.

By changing control values, the user invokes methods of the model through the controller. The carrier between the user and the controller in this case is a parameter-value set submitted with the request.

This limitation makes it almost impossible to apply current RMI approaches. For instance, SOAP does require SOAP-aware browsers or JavaScript solutions on the client side, which especially poses a problem for very thin devices like handhelds etc. Client-side CORBA or RMI also require more than pure-HTML/HTTP interaction.

Our previous work on this topic [6] proposed a light-weight solution for this problem. The idea is to follow standard naming conventions for parameters, submitted with the request. Standard naming of the parameters allows mapping them correctly onto model method calls. In the simplest case, one parameter invokes one method; for instance parameter value-pair *setDate=12.01.1992* invokes method *setDate("12.01.1992")*. In more complex cases, several parameters may be used to invoke a single method. For example, parameters *setDate(birth).0=1998*, *setDate(birth).1=01* and *setDate(birth).2=12* are mapped altogether onto one call of the method *setDate("1998", "01", "12", "birth")*.

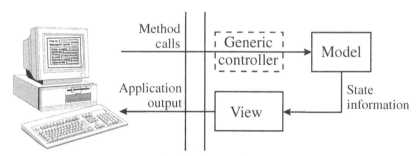

Fig. 3. MVC for web with a generic controller

The controller, which is built according to this specification, provides model-independent functionality of mapping parameters received from the client in an HTTP request onto the model's method calls. In other words, the development of the controller "vanishes" from the web application development. A modified architecture scheme is shown on figure 3.

4 The View: Automatic Model Transformation

The model in the MVC paradigm represents structured information about the state of the real world. This state information is processed by the view and the output is sent to the user. In the context of web applications, the output is an HTML document. In other words, the view is actually a processor, which converts structured model state information into an HTML document (figure 4).

Fig. 4. View in web MVC applications

Similar functionality is implemented in a declarative programming language called XSLT [7], (eXtensible Stylesheet Language for Transformations). Main purpose of XSLT is to transform structure of documents in general and XML documents in particular. If state information of the model could be viewed as a document, then XSLT may be employed to transform it into the required output format, like, for instance, an HTML page. The only question is how to present a model as a transformable document.

The basic idea is that the model exposes its state via readable properties. One of the readable properties is distinguished as a document property. Like in component architectures (e.g. JavaBeans), these properties are represented by methods which (a) are externally accessible, (b) have no input arguments and (c) return booleans, numbers, strings or sets of nodes (types, which can be manipulated in an XSLT transformation). These properties are the input for the transformation process: the document property is the input document for the transformation, and the other properties are mapped onto optional parameters. Via naming conventions, this mapping step can be completely automated.

The remaining problem is how to serialize the type system of the programming language to the data model of XSLT. For primitive types, this is straightforward. For more complex types, we can make use of techniques developed for XML serialization, e.g. SOAP bindings.

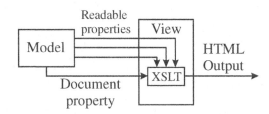

Fig. 5. Automatic model transformation

The task of mapping model's readable properties onto transformation's parameters and input document can be easily automated. Values of readable properties are assigned to parameters with appropriate names; then, transformation is applied to the document returned by document readable property (figure 5).

Obviously, the model-view interaction described above allows the view to be generic. This generic view does not depend on the model: it simply copies assigned readable property values to transformation parameters. For a specific application, only a transformation expressed in XSLT is required for adaptation

The approach may be slightly modified to allow multiple model presentations. This may be achieved with the view consisting of several transformations and the model having several document properties, one document property and one transformation for each presentation. A special *view property* of the model specifies active presentation.

To give an example of automatic view implementation, we will consider the Java programming language. Let the model be implemented as a single class. Then, properties are associated with public methods of the model with names starting with "*get*" and no input arguments. Names of document properties end with "*Document*". View property is associated with the *getView* method.

Mapping of properties onto transformation parameters is straightforward. For instance, *DocumentURL*, associated with *getDocumentURL* model method, defines the value of the *DocumentURL* parameter. View property defines active presentation. For example, "*Edit*" value of the view property means that user will receive the result of *getEditDocument* method previously processed by the *Edit.xsl* transformation.

Figure 6 provides a summary of the process of generating views for a given model.

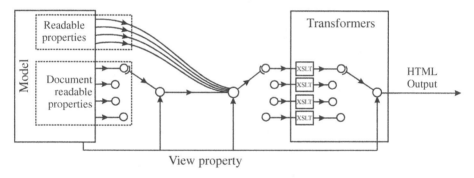

Fig. 6. Automatic model transformation with several transformers

5   Model-Transformers Instead of Model-View-Controller

With the automatic model presentation described above, the view implementation phase also disappears from the development of the web application; it is replaced with the design of one or more XSLT transformations (figure 7).

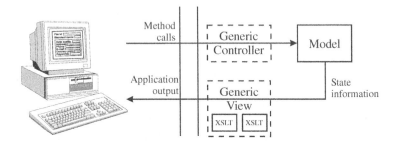

Fig. 7. MVC for web with generic controller and generic view

The solutions presented in the previous sections lead to a simplified design pattern, which consists of a **model** that represents real world and a set of **transformers**, which present the model to the user. We name this pattern *Model-Transformers* architecture; its overall scheme is presented on figure 8.

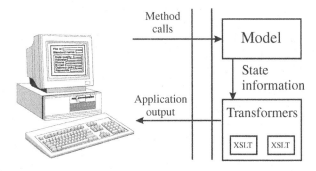

Fig. 8. The Model-Transformers architecture

The Model-Transformers architecture allows a clear separation of two typical application evolution tasks: adding/changing functionality and adding/changing presentations.

The functionality of the application is, basically, what a user may do with the application. In our case, functionality is clearly represented by accessible methods of the model. Hence, to extend functionality of the application, the developer extends the model with one or more methods, which become immediately available to the client. As functional modifications do not change declarations of readable property methods, they do not affect existing views.

New presentations are added by creating new model transformations. If needs of new presentation are not covered by existing model properties, more property methods have to be implemented; otherwise, no model extensions are required. In any case, modification of model presentation does not influence the application logic. Model's readable properties define the interface for accessing model state information. Thus, if application logic is changed but readable properties are not, transformations are not affected.

6 Evaluation

The proposed pattern was developed and implemented as an architectural part of XML-based metadata repository designed in FZI for the NOKIS project [3]. NOKIS is a distributed environmental metadata information system for the coasts of the North and the Baltic Sea. Based on previous experiences in CoastBase [2], we have developed a web-based metadata editing and management tool.

One of the key problems was the size of the metadata schema (based on ISO 19115) and the requirement of easy extension and adaptation for institution-specific metadata. We followed a schema-driven user interface generation approach.

Center component in NOKIS project is a web interface for managing metadata in form of XML documents. System requirements such as user-friendly interface for editing complex documents, type-dependent input fields, document validation, possibility to integrate additional applications and context-sensitive help system lead to complex HTML pages overloaded with input controls. Having this multiplied by the size of NOKIS XML Schema and taking into account its possible evolution, results a web application, which is difficult to implement and even more difficult to support.

Design and application of Model-Transformers architecture helped to solve two big issues: request parameters processing and presentation. Automatic handling of parameters and output transformations saved a lot of effort; it even allowed automatic generation of model transformations (including parts of user interface) based on document XML Schema. Support and extensions were drastically eased as well.

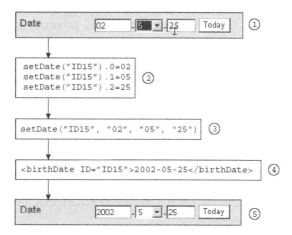

Fig. 9. Example of assigning date value to the element

One simple example, which may illustrate practical usage of Model-Transformers architecture, is assigning element values in document editor. NOKIS model was provided with several methods like *setString(...)*, *setDateTime(...)*, *setFloat(...)* etc., to validate user input and assign values to appropriate elements. Names of input controls displayed in the user interface encode method names. Typical process of assigning an element value is presented on figure 9.

User input (1) is submitted as a set of parameter-value pairs (2), which are automatically mapped onto method calls (3) to validate user input and assign values to the elements of the document (4), which are then presented in the user interface through an XSLT (5). In this example, *setDate(year, month, day)* method implements construction and validation of the date based on three parameters submitted by the client. The method checks and corrects the parameters, if required; for instance, two-digit year parameter was change by this method to four digits.

In addition, we have also found out that with Model-Transformers no custom mechanism is required to integrate external web applications. The generic controller makes no difference between a request from a user and an external application, if they both follow standard parameter naming conventions

Actual implementation of the proposed technique is done in Java programming language. The developed generic controller and view use Java Reflection API [5] to dynamically invoke methods of the model object. Proper caching of reflected method objects makes use of reflection quite efficient: our empirical measurements revealed insignificant invocation deceleration. Alternatively, runtime reflection usage may be avoided by static generation of code method calls.

7   Conclusions and Outlook

With the Model-Transformer architecture, we have provided a framework for easy development of complex web applications. There is no need to develop application-specific controller and view objects. The developer simply writes model methods and provides transformations. Moreover, as a method implemented in the model is already defined and (hopefully) documented, tasks of model extension and transformations design may be separated.

However, the Model-Transformer architecture has certain prerequisites. One big issue is the correspondence between parameters submitted by the user and the methods, which have to be invoked in response. A generic controller requires this correspondence to be generic as well. More precisely, it must be possible to encode method name and arguments in parameter name and value. Practice shows this to be true for most of the cases, but this is surely not a panacea.

Another problem is runtime method invocation. Modern programming languages like Java or C# provide runtime reflection capabilities while for older languages there has to be additional effort (for instance, pre-processing or source code).

Model-centricity of the MT approach also increases the model size. For instance, for automated presentation, complexly structured model state information must be transformed into document fragments.

Finally, a solution provided in MT architecture for HTML/HTTP based web applications is simple due to two prerequisites: primitiveness of the user input format and possibility to present the model as a document. These prerequisites are unlikely to be met in subject areas other than web applications. Moreover, development of the Web Services platform (driven by W3C Web Services Activity) may help to overcome complexities connected to the simplicity of HTML/HTTP based client-server communication in web applications. Technologies like WDSL, SOAP, XMLP may allow much more complex interactions over the web. However, general usage of these technologies will require general availability and wide distribution of client software that supports them. Until this is true, solutions like MT for more primitive web environments will continue to be useful.

General conclusion is that Model-Transformers architecture, when applied to the development of web applications gives considerable advantages of easy development, support and integration, while limitations in this context are insignificant. MT-based web applications are also open for integration with other systems from the very start. The model is manipulated through parameter-value sets, which follow defined naming conventions. Hence, it is easier to expose the application as a Web Service.

Although MT in the presented state is a complete solution pattern, several potential architecture extensions may be mentioned. One of the points that require special attention is XML serialization of complex model properties. Another possible improvement is the possibility of decomposing the model into several independent classes.

References

1. Althammer, E. and Pree, W. Design and Implementation of a MVC-Based Architecture for E-Commerce Applications. See http://citeseer.nj.nec.com/443079.html.
2. Kazakos, W., Kramer, R. and Schmidt, A. Coastbase - The Virtual European Coastal and Marine Data Warehouse. Computer Science for Environmental Protection '00. Environmental Information for Planning, Politics and the Public, volume II, pages 646-654.
3. Kazakos, W., Valikov, A., Schmidt, A. and Lehfeldt, R. Automation of Metadata Repository Development with XML Schema. Accepted for the EnviroInfo Vienna 2002 conference.
4. Krasner, G. E. and Pope, S. T. A Cookbook for Using the Model-View-Controller User Interface Paradigm in Smalltalk-80. In Journal of Object-Oriented Programming, Volume 1 Number 3, Aug/Sep 1988.
5. McCluskey, G. Using Java Reflection, 1998. See: http://developer.java.sun.com/developer/technicalArticles/ALT/Reflection/.
6. Valikov, A., Akhounov, A. and Kazakos, W. Remote method invocation for web applications. Submitted to CSIT 2002 conference.
7. World Wide Web Consortium. XSL Transformations (XSLT). W3C Recommendation, Nov. 16, 1999. See http://www.w3.org/TR/xslt.

Modeling *E*-service Orchestration through Petri Nets

Massimo Mecella[1], Francesco Parisi Presicce[2], and Barbara Pernici[3]

[1] Università di Roma "La Sapienza", Dipartimento di Informatica e Sistemistica
`mecella@dis.uniroma1.it`
[2] Università di Roma "La Sapienza", Dipartimento di Informatica
`parisi@dsi.uniroma1.it`
[3] Politecnico di Milano, Dipartimento di Elettronica e Informazione
`barbara.pernici@polimi.it`

Abstract. B2B interaction requires new forms of coordination between participating organizations. Indeed, the main requirement is that the autonomy of each participating partner is preserved during the interaction, guaranteeing at the same time that the overall goals of the common process are reached. Mechanisms for regulating distributed workflow evolution when the workflow is composed of the invocation of *E*-services of different organizations are needed. The *E*-service orchestration model proposed in this paper provides a mechanism for supporting control of process evolution in terms both of control and data flows, and for distributing and assigning process responsibilities.

1 Introduction

Current network technologies allow the development of new interaction business paradigms, such as virtual enterprises: different companies pool together their services to offer more complex, added-value products and services; network technologies and Internet make services readily accessible and thus they allow to compose virtual enterprises in very flexible ways. Although such a new business paradigm has initially emerged in the business context, indeed it has been spreading in many other contexts, e.g., for the definition of what is referred to as *E*-government [1].

Systems supporting such models are commonly referred to as Cooperative Information Systems (CIS's) [2]; various approaches are proposed for the design and development of CIS's: schema and data integration techniques, agent-based methodologies and systems, business process coordination and service-based systems (e.g., [3]). In the latter case, cooperation among different organizations is obtained by sharing and integrating services across networks; such services, commonly referred to as *E*-services and Web-Services, are exported by different organizations as semantically well defined functionalities that allow users and applications to access and perform tasks offered by back-end business applications. By using a service-based approach, the cooperative system consists of different

A. Buchmann et al. (Eds.): TES 2002, LNCS 2444, pp. 38–47, 2002.
© Springer-Verlag Berlin Heidelberg 2002

distributed applications which integrate the *E*-services offered by different organizations. Such an integration raises some interesting points regarding service composability, correctness, synchronization and coordination, as pointed out in [4].

In [5,6], an *E*-service framework, named PARIDE (Process-based frAmework for oRchestratIon of Dynamic E-services) has been presented, specifically addressing the issues of defining a common conceptual component model (and the related description language) for *E*-services, and defining the notions of compatibility and dynamic substitution of *E*-services, based on the concept of cooperative process. The composition of *E*-services requires the definition of rules for assembling *E*-services as needed and for the *orchestration* (also referred to as coordination or choreography) of different *E*-services. The orchestration of *E*-services should be specified through an *orchestration schema*, to be expressed in an appropriate orchestration language, which specifies interactions among them. Such an orchestration schema should act as a "script" (to be interpreted by appropriate orchestration engines) that coordinates the interactions among *E*-services. Orchestration is quite different from classical workflow management, as pointed out also in [4]: *E*-services need to be linked to the current enactment on the basis of dynamic assignments, and the task of the overall control can not be statically assigned to a single organization/system, but needs to be dynamically distributed among organizations. Indeed the aim of this paper is to introduce a model, based on Petri Nets, for describing the orchestration of *E*-services, and the related design of distributed orchestration engines, in the context of the PARIDE framework.

The remainder of this paper is as follows. In Section 2, the proposed framework for *E*-services is described, with specific focus on the distributed orchestration engines; Section 3 describes the proposed model for *E*-service orchestration based on Petri Nets. Section 4 presents an explanatory example in an *E*-government scenario. Section 5 presents related relevant research work and Section 6 concludes the paper by remarking which elements need to be further investigated.

2   The PARIDE Framework

In Figure 1 the framework for *E*-services is depicted; organizations willing to cooperate deploy software components on their *cooperative gateways* (possibly wrapping their internal legacy systems); such components realize E-*service schemas*, that are the abstract specifications of the offered services according to a conceptual component model. The coordination of different *E*-services is carried out by the *orchestration engines*, deployed on the cooperative gateways, which interpret *orchestration schemas*, possibly substituting compatible *E*-services at run-time. *E*-service schemas, orchestration schemas and component instance data are stored in a *repository*, which is accessed both by the orchestration engines and by the cooperative gateways.

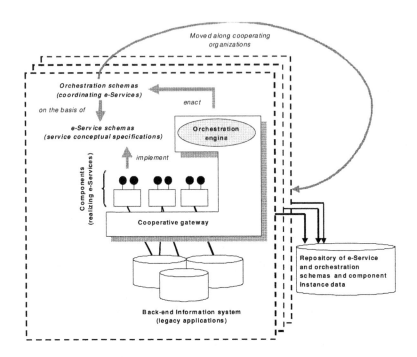

Fig. 1. The PARIDE framework

Cooperative gateways represent "where" and "how" different components are deployed. Each cooperating organization, through its cooperative gateway, offers to the others a specific element, i.e., the orchestration engine, which is able to interpret orchestration schemas and to effectively coordinate E-services.

Orchestration schemas are "scripts" which specifies how to create E-services and their correct synchronization. An orchestration schema $\mathbb{OS}$ refers to a set $(\mathbb{S}_1, \ldots, \mathbb{S}_n)$, $i = 1 \ldots n$, $n \geq 1$ of E-service schemas. An orchestration instance is a specific enactment of an orchestration schema; an orchestration instance $\mathcal{OI}$ of an orchestration schema $\mathbb{OS}$ uses a set of E-services $(\mathcal{S}_{11}, \ldots, \mathcal{S}_{m_1 1}, \ldots, \mathcal{S}_{1n}, \ldots, \mathcal{S}_{m_n n})$, where $\mathcal{S}_{ji}$, $j = 1 \ldots m_j$, $m_j \geq 1$, and $i = 1 \ldots n$, $n \geq 1$, is the j-th instance of the i-th E-service $\mathbb{S}_i$ which is referred to in $\mathbb{OS}$.

In our proposal, orchestration schemas are enacted by the orchestration engines, deployed by the different cooperating organizations on their cooperative gateways; a given orchestration schema, during its enactment, needs to be controlled and monitored by an organization, but such a task can not be assigned to a single organization, conversely it should be moved all along the enactment. Therefore an orchestration schema is moved from an orchestration engine to another one as the task of the overall coordination is assigned to some other organization; in a given time instant, only one and exactly one orchestration engine is enacting the schema, i.e., is coordinating the different *E*-services involved in the given enactment.

An *E*-service is an event-driven component: an *E*-service reacts to messages, does some internal actions (which are not visible outside) and sends some messages. The sending and receiving of messages are the events driving the *E*-service evolution. Messages are not only simple primitive signals, but they carry parameters (i.e., structured data). In such a way, the description of an *E*-service comprises only the external interfaces (input/output data and offered services) and the conversations (i.e., sequences of operations to be invoked) for interacting with it [6].

3   *E*-service and Orchestration Nets

In order to precisely design the orchestration of different *E*-services, models and techniques need to be provided, specifically addressing the definition of both the control and data flows. In this paper we propose the adoption of a Petri Net-based model, thus providing to designers of the overall cooperative applications appropriate tools for correctly assembling different *E*-services; as an example, deadlock freeness of the overall process and reachability of the final configuration of the involved *E*-services can be verified by analyzing the configuration graph of the net. The proposed model allows both to specify the external behaviour of the different *E*-services (in terms of possible sequences of messages they can be involved in) and the overall orchestration, as routing of such messages and the passing of the overall controlling and monitoring task among different organizations/engines.

Hereafter, we assume that the reader knows the basics both of Petri Nets and of Coloured Petri Nets; otherwise, the reader may refer to [7,8].

An *E*-service is specified both in its static interfaces and in its behaviour. Specifically, an *E*-service communicates through messages, including both the ones the *E*-service receives and the messages it produces. Upon receiving the message α, the *E*-service does some work (and it takes some time) and then it sends the message β as output; at this point, the *E*-service is ready to accept new input messages. This basic scenario can be represented as in Figure 2(a), in which a portion of an E-*service Net* is shown: when a token is available on the upper "circle" place and another one is available on the upper "square" place, the transition can fire, thus moving a token on the lower "circle" place and another one on the lower "square" place. A "circle" place is the graphical notation for a *control place*, representing a state of the *E*-service with respect to possible message exchanges it can be involved in; conversely a "square" place is the graphical notation for a *message place*, representing an input message (square with a thin border) and an output message (square with a thick border). A token available on a message place represents the reception/production of a message.

An E-*service Net (*E-S *Net) is a net where:*

❐ *places are of three different types, specifically control places, referred to as CP, input message places, referred to as IMP, and output message*

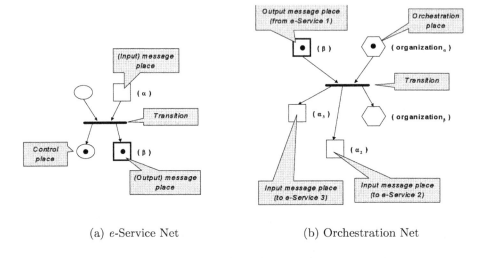

(a) *e*-Service Net   (b) Orchestration Net

Fig. 2. Basic elements of the Petri Net-based model

places, referred to as OMP; let us define $MP = IMP \cup OMP$ and $P = CP \cup MP$;

☐ tokens placed on control (input/output message) places are referred to as control (input/output message, respectively) tokens;

☐ each place $\in MP$ is labeled with a message, i.e., a function **mess**: $MP \rightarrow \mathcal{E}$ is defined ($\mathcal{E}$ is the set of messages specified for the E-service, according to the formalization provided in [6]).

Examples of *E*-service Nets are provided in the example of Figure 3, in which each grey area represent a different *E*-service.

The orchestration (i.e., coordination) of different *E*-services consists of correctly routing messages among *E*-services in the right sequence; this may require to manipulate messages (i.e., to compose new messages from more basic ones or to extract basic messages from complex ones). In turn such an orchestration task is not statically assigned to a single organization, but it is passed from an organization to another one as the process goes on. Therefore the orchestration schema allows to define how different messages are exchanged among *E*-services (i.e., *E*-service Nets) and how the enactment task is moved along organizations/orchestration engines.

The orchestration of different *E*-services can be represented as an *Orchestration Net*, which is a specific net connecting at least two *E*-service Nets, and specifying the routing of messages and the act of passing the task of the orchestration from an organization to another one. In Figure 2(b) a portion of orchestration is shown: when the output message β is received from an *E*-service and the orchestration task is assigned to $organization_\alpha$, the message is manipulated in order to produce two input messages α_2 and α_3 to send to two different *E*-services, and the task of the overall control (i.e., of the orchestration) is moved to a different *organization*$_\beta$. An "hexagonal" place is the graphical notation for an *orchestration place*.

An Orchestration Net (O Net) is a net where:

❏ *places are of three different types, specifically orchestration places, referred to as OP, input message places, referred to as IMP, and output message places, referred to as OMP; input/output message places belong to different E-service Nets;*
❏ *each place ∈ OP is labeled with an organization; the availability of a token in an orchestration place means that the task of the orchestration of the overall process is currently assigned to the organization labeling the place;*
❏ *for each transition t, there exist om ∈ OMP, im ∈ IMP and p, q ∈ OP such that (om, t), (p, t), (t, im) and (t, q) ∈ set of edges of the net; p can be equal to q, whereas om and im necessarily belong to different E-service Nets.*

The orchestration engine of the organization, which, at a given time, is executing the task of controlling and monitoring, is in charge of manipulating the messages and correctly routing them; then, if it is specified in such a way, the engine moves the orchestration schema (i.e., the representation of the net, in the form of a XML document) to the engine of the next organization which is assigned the orchestration task.

4   Explanatory Example

In the following, we consider an example stemming from the Italian *E*-government scenario. The considered process is a simplified version of the one for "providing aid to disabled persons" [9]. A citizen who has some disabilities (e.g., due to an accident) can apply for the provisioning of aid, in the form of a disability pension. In order to start the process, the citizen needs *(i)* a certificate, provided by the City Council he lives in, assessing its residence (permanent address), and *(ii)* to fill in an application form. The residence certificate is needed in order to identify and certify which local administrations will manage the process. Such documents need to be presented to the Local Health Authority, which, after negotiating an appointment with the citizen, examines him and prepares a report. Such a report needs to be sent to the Prefecture, which has to take the effective decision based on some business rules. Meanwhile, the citizen communicates to the Prefecture his intention to apply for a disability pension, and receives an acknowledgment of this communication. Finally, when the decision is made by the Prefecture, it stores the final record of the process; in case the disability pension has been assigned to the citizen, it prepares all the documents (e.g., the pension book needed to draw money in a bank or in a post office) and delivers them to the citizen. At this point the citizen can receive the pension each month.

Currently the process lasts about eighteen months, and most of the time is spent in sending documents among administrations; they are often sent through

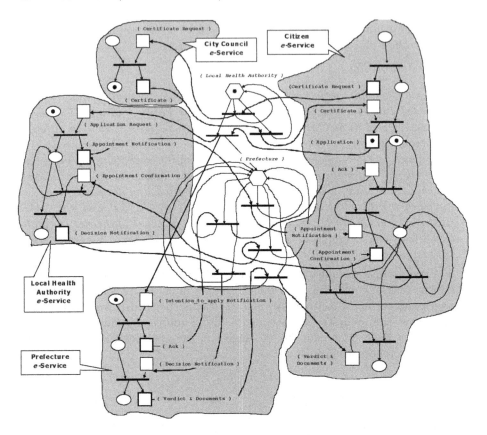

Fig. 3. The orchestration schema (*E*-service and Orchestration Nets) of the running example

ordinary mail, in some cases the citizen acts as a messenger among administrations. A radical solution would be to re-engineer the process, as for example to eliminate the activities of the Prefecture, and to let all the process be managed by the Local Health Authority; in such a case, the citizen would interact only with a single administration. Unfortunately, some issues hamper radical changes in the process, such as the fact that Local Health Authorities have neither resources and skills for managing the final document production activities, nor the legal responsibility, which in turn is assigned by law to Prefectures; moreover, modifying such laws is quite complex. Therefore the only viable solution is to support the current process through computer and network technologies, in order to speed as much as possible the interactions among the subjects involved. This in turn requires that each administration develop some *E*-services to be available on the Italian Nationwide Public Administration Network [9], and an appropriate *E*-service for the citizen, such as an application accessible through the Web and simple e-mail protocols. Such an application might be deployed on a portal, managed by the Government, or be delivered to citizens as a special supplement in newspapers, etc. However, independently of its deployment, the citizen application is an E-service like the others involved in the process.

A cooperative application supporting this process would require the orchestration of the different E-services (i.e., the Citizen_E-service, the LHA_E-service, the PRE_E-service and the CC_E-service); the task of such an orchestration, either due to technological constraints or to organizational ones, needs to be moved along the process, e.g., at the beginning is assigned to the Local Health Authority and passed to the Prefecture after it receives the notification from the citizen (through the Citizen_E-service). In Figure 3 the orchestration schema (i.e., the overall net) is shown. The four involved E-service Nets are highlighted, and in the central part of the picture the Orchestration Net is visible.

5   Related Work

In the workflow community, much attention has been paid to adaptive and extensible systems and to the separation of concern between interface and implementation of a process and/or activity. The eFlow system [10] is a process management system that supports adaptive and dynamic service composition, by separating the concepts of process schema, service node and service process instance, all of them described through an XML-based description language. In [11], different activities of a multi-enterprise process are decoupled into activity interfaces and activity implementations. In [12], an approach is proposed in which B2B protocols expose the public processes whereas WfMS's implement the private processes of an enterprise. All these proposals do not address the specific issues of E-service coordination, which is a task with specific peculiarities, different from the ones of workflow integration, as pointed out in [4].

Some languages have been proposed for specifying E-service conversations, that is possible sequences of exchanged messages [13,6]; moreover, WSFL [14] is a XML-based language for the composition of Web Services. All these elements are building blocks onto which to develop an orchestration theory, but any complete proposals, as of authors' knowledge, has not been presented in the literature.

Petri Nets have been proposed for modeling workflow components (e.g., [15]) and for demonstrate specific properties in inter-organizational scenarios (e.g., [16]).

In [17] the issue of service composition is addressed in the context of Web Components, as a way for creating composite Web Services by re-using, specializing and extending existing ones. The aims of the Service Composition Specification Language (SCSL) and the Service Composition Planning Language (SCPL) are similar to the Petri Net-based model proposed in this paper, even if they differ on specific features; moreover, the Service Composition Execution Graph (SCEG) can be considered as a kind of orchestration schema.

6   Conclusions and Future Work

The model proposed in the paper allows the definition of E-services as conceptual components, corresponding to running services, which can be composed and used during the execution of different processes. E-service composition at the conceptual level needs to be defined both in terms of data flows and control flows between the E-services. Such an orchestration of E-services is a novel and difficult task, which can not be addressed with classical workflow-based technologies and methodologies. Substitution of E-services with compatible ones and delegation to different organizations during the enactment require the definition of an orchestration model and the development of suitable orchestration engines, distributed among the different cooperating organizations. In this paper, a framework for E-services has been presented, with specific focus on the orchestration engines, and a model for specifying orchestration schemas has been proposed, based on specific classes of Petri Nets.

The model proposed in the paper is being implemented and will be experimented within the *VISPO (Virtual-district Internet-based Service PlatfOrm)* Project. In the project, several services are provided for participants in a virtual district, and the orchestration model proposed in the paper has the goal of providing a reference model for orchestration of processes used by organizations participating in the virtual district. The VISPO platform has the goal of allowing participation in the activities of the district by invoking a series of available E-services according to the rules defined in the orchestration schema. The orchestration engines will allow controlling the correct evolution of the process, and alerting the current process responsible if exceptions are raised.

During the implementation and experimentation phases, possible representation in appropriate languages (e.g., XML) need to be carried out. Moreover the design of the orchestration engines need to be defined, in order to address specific issues such as deadlocks, possible timeouts, etc. On the basis of analysis techniques to be based on the Petri Nets, development environments for composing E-services and designing their orchestration will be also provided.

Acknowledgments. The work of Massimo Mecella and Barbara Pernici is supported by MIUR, "Fondo Strategico 2000" Project *VISPO*.

References

1. A.K. Elmagarmid and W.J. McIver Jr (eds.), "The Ongoing March Towards Digital Government (Special Issue)", *IEEE Computer*, vol. 34, no. 2, 2001.
2. G. De Michelis, E. Dubois, M. Jarke, F. Matthes, J. Mylopoulos, M.P. Papazoglou, K. Pohl, J. Schmidt, C. Woo, and E. Yu, "Cooperative Information Systems: A Manifesto", in *Cooperative Information Systems: Trends & Directions*, M.P. Papazoglou and G. Schlageter, Eds. Accademic-Press, 1997.
3. U. Dayal, M. Hsu, and R. Ladin, "Business Process Coordination: State of the Art, Trends and Open Issues", in *Proceedings of VLDB 2001*, Roma, Italy, 2001.

4. J. Yang, W.J. Heuvel, and M.P. Papazoglou, "Tackling the Challenges of Service Composition in *E*-marketplaces", in *Proceedings of RIDE-2EC 2002*, San Jose, CA, USA, 2002.

5. M. Mecella, B. Pernici, M. Rossi, and A. Testi, "A Repository of Workflow Components for Cooperative *E*-applications", in *Proceedings of the 1st IFIP TC8 Working Conference on E-commerce/E-business*, Salzburg, Austria, 2001.

6. M. Mecella, B. Pernici, and P. Craca, "Compatibility of *E*-services in a Cooperative Multi-Platform Environment", in *Proceedings of VLDB-TES 2001*, Rome, Italy, 2001.

7. W. Reisig and G. Rozenberg, Eds., *Lectures on Petri Nets I: Basic Models*, Springer Verlag, LNCS 1491, 1998.

8. K. Jenses, *Coloured Petri Nets. Volume 1*, Springer Verlag, EATCS Monographs on Theoretical Computer Science, 1992.

9. C. Batini and M. Mecella, "Enabling Italian *E*-government Through a Cooperative Architecture", *IEEE Computer*, vol. 34, no. 2, 2001.

10. F. Casati and M.C. Shan, "Dynamic and Adaptive Composition of *E*-services", *Information Systems*, vol. 6, no. 3, 2001.

11. H. Schuster, D. Georgakopoulos, A. Cichocki, and D. Baker, "Modeling and Composing Service-based and Reference Process-based Multi-enterprise Processes", in *Proceedings of CAiSE 2000*, Stockholm, Sweden, 2000.

12. C. Bussler, "The Role of B2B Protocols in Inter-Enterprise Process Execution", in *Proceedings of VLDB-TES 2001*, Rome, Italy, 2001.

13. H. Kuno, M. Lemon, A. Karp, and D. Beringer, "Conversations + Interfaces = Business Logic", in *Proceedings of VLDB-TES 2001*, Rome, Italy, 2001.

14. F. Leymann, "Web Service Flow Language (WSFL 1.0)", IBM Document, May 2001. Available on-line (link checked October 1st, 2001): `http://www-4.ibm.com/software/solutions/webservices/pdf/WSFL.pdf`.

15. W.M.P. van der Aalst and M. Weske, "The P2P approach to Interorganizational Workflows", in *Proceedings of CAiSE'01*, Interlaken, Switzerland, 2001.

16. V. Atluri and W.K. Huang, "A Petri Net Based Safety Analysis of Workflow Authorization Models", *Journal of Computer Security*, vol. 8, no. 2/3, 2000.

17. J. Yang and M.P. Papazoglou, "Web Components: A Substrate for Web Service Reuse and Composition", in *Proceedings of CAiSE'02*, Toronto, Canada, 2002.

Composite Applications: Process Based Application Development

Anil K. Nori and Rajiv Jain

Asera Inc.
600 Clipper Drive
Belmont, CA 94002

Real Time Enterprises derive sustainable competitiveness through a completely coordinated forward movement of every quarter of their businesses - designing, buying, selling, planning and servicing. Managers have a complete, personalized, on the moment, all the time, and everywhere available, visibility across all their business functions to make durable decisions.

Clearly, building and sustaining real-time enterprise means deploying collaborative solutions across the business functions. But the real challenge is to build these solutions such that they are flexible, scalable, maintainable, and future-proof – and all this within a budget that is affordable and not a drain on the business.

The evolution from custom-built applications, to packaged applications, to today's need for more adaptable solutions is a tough challenge. The right answer is found neither in in-house custom applications nor standardized third party packaged applications; it is somewhere in the middle.

Right answer is "**composite applications**" which are built using processes (Web Services) from different packaged applications and assembling (configure) a business process to match how things are really done in the enterprise.

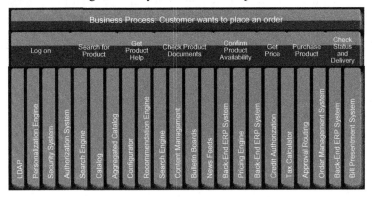

A Typical Composite Application

Take an example of the Commerce Solution for Real Time Enterprises. When deployed by an enterprise, one of the processes that match how business needs to be done with customers is "Self-Service Order Process". As illustrated in the figure, this process requires assembling a composite business process from the services provided by various packaged applications.

A. Buchmann et al. (Eds.): TES 2002, LNCS 2444, pp. 48-53, 2002.
© Springer-Verlag Berlin Heidelberg 2002

Following are some of the requirements of such a solution that are typical of any Real Time Enterprise solution –

Real-time aggregated information
Real-time aggregated information on the products, pricing, order status, etc. from multiple backend systems. Online catalog and online product information pulled from multiple backend systems and aggregated in real-time.

Seamless, configurable process
Rapid integration of multiple application web services into a seamless process configured according to the user's requirements. Enable business analysts to declaratively configure, control and change the processes and services leveraged in the solution.

Right Information to the Right People
One aggregated view of the customer. One selling interface for multiple divisions and channels leveraging this aggregated customer information, yet presenting personalized view of the process to every individual.

Rules-based Personalization and Entitlement
Enable personalization and entitlement of data and process to improve customers' experience and productivity. Through rules-based personalization, provide recommended views of the catalog. Tailor offers to the customers based on exhibited spending patterns or known preferences. Enable business analysts to easily create, publish and update communications targeted for key customers.

Globalization
Provide personalized delivery of data and process in the language and according to the cultural requirements specific to geographical region. Serve all the regions through single deployment.

Ability to Rapidly Change
Change is constantly required - whether it is for adjusting offers tailored to customers, publishing new product information, or drawing upon a new data source to aggregate additional information. Enable business users to select, publish and update tailored information to customers, and developer tools to easily upgrade the solution.

Extensibility of the process
Extend the solution - whether it is extending the process to a new end market, or extending order management in order fulfillment and logistics.

Efficient Maintenance
Solution management services, including administration services such as distributed user management and partner management, to enable business analysts to declaratively manage the offerings delivered to customers. These requirements of a Real Time Enterprise Solutions can only be met if they are built as Composite Applications.

Composite Applications Defined

Composite Applications are process-centric applications built by assembling inter-application flows. These applications are inherently designed for collaboration making them ideal for building Real Time Enterprise solutions. Since these applications are user-centric and configurable by business analysts, solutions built in this model are highly configurable, personalized, and changeable.

Further composite applications are standards-based, open and interoperable as well as Web Services-based, they making solutions highly extensible and future-proof.

Since composite applications are process-centric, and built as workflows – they are easy to visualize and develop, provide high level of reusability, provide flexibility to change, and can be modularly deployed in distributed environments, as well as they are best suited for integration with disparate applications.

Composite applications do not make any assumptions about their access mechanisms. Same composite application can be accessed by a user on a web browser or a mobile device as a set of personalized interaction process flow, or can be accessed by an automated B2B collaboration process flow e.g. RosettaNet PIP, or can be accessed via a published service interface like Web Service.

Composite Applications	Web-ified Applications
Configurable business processes	Pre-defined business processes
Designed for collaboration (many-to-many)	Designed for a single enterprise
Web Services-based	Data-base driven
Workflow based Applications	Monolithic Applications
Customer-centric	Enterprise-centric
Web-centric	Web-enabled
Configured by business analyst changing business processes	Customized by developers modifying code
Open, interoperable	Self-contained
Flexible, adaptable	Rigid

Properties of Composite Applications vs. Web-ified Applications

Composite Applications Architecture

Composite applications are built within multi-tier architecture. There are three core layers to composite application architecture:

– Delivery Processes
– Application Logic Processes
– Integration Processes

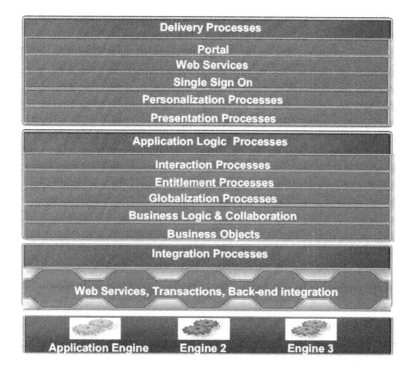

Composite Applications Architecture

Application Logic Processes

Adaptability and evolvability of business processes is the key requirement for any composite application. Business processes differ from one organization to the other, and these processes evolve over time. The business logic and collaboration layer provides a flexible environment to model the application flows to adapt to unique business processes of every organization.

Since composite applications are information-based, they do not make any assumptions about the sources and physical layout of data. To achieve this independence Business Objects provide a comprehensive data definition framework. Business Objects are defined in XML Schema to model composite application data as well as associated consistency and validation rules.

A seamless and personalized user interface across applications is an essential requirement for any composite application. Moreover the user interface must be adaptable to conform to every customer's site branding requirements through simple configuration changes. The presentation layer provides a robust environment to build these unified user interfaces.

Delivery Processes

Delivery layer is an important aspect of how composite applications are deployed in enterprises. Important characteristic for composite applications is their ability to adapt to the existing enterprise environments – for example a global enterprise has users with different cultural backgrounds, or different users may have different roles hence different needs and privileges, or users who perform multiple functions may need access to all of their applications via a personalized portal page.

The delivery layer provides services that deliver a unique user experience to each end user. One can use portal objects to deliver composite applications to portal interfaces, or business managers can use rules based personalization to target content and business processes to different user communities, or expose composite applications (or sub-processes within composite applications) as web services.

Integration Processes

Integration of enterprise resources is the key characteristic of composite Applications. Since disparate enterprise resources do not provide uniform integration interfaces, it is essential for composite applications to have a multidimensional integration framework that allows various levels and types of integration mechanisms. Integration processes do a seamless business integration of resources by doing - Process integration, Application integration, and Business-to-Business (B2B) integration.

Integration processes are built over standards based messaging interfaces allowing it to leverages off-the-shelf EAI and B2Bi solutions.

These processes can also be built on Web services that provide industry standards based mechanism to integrate with back-end as well as partner systems. Business processes are published as web services by describing them in a standard format (WSDL). Composite applications consume these web services by stitching them into the application flow. When the composite application runs then these web services are invoked by exchanging messages in a standard format (SOAP) over standard HTTP(s) transport protocol.

Summary

To be successful, a real-time enterprise needs business solutions that can be

- Integrated with the latest industry innovations as well as custom, legacy, and back-end systems, enabling enterprises to present themselves as one united, value-added entity while leverage existing IT investments
- Customized and personalized to support business processes across multiple functions, users, and locales around the globe. Changed rapidly to support an enterprise's business strategy to gain market leadership. To speed time-to-market, enterprises are looking for a way to customize the business processes, connect those applications, and deploy a seamless solution.

Define a business process...   **... power it with packaged and custom software...**

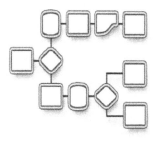
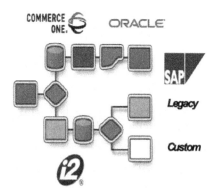

The Composite Applications model fuses best-in-class applications with any other existing systems. Composite applications provide a unified user interface, configurable workflows, and security and entitlement features across all applications and devices. The result is a highly personalized and customizable system that adapts rapidly to new business processes and requirements.

Design Methodology for Web Services and Business Processes

Mike P. Papazoglou and Jian Yang

Infolab, Tilburg University, PO Box 90153, 5000 LE, Tilburg, Netherlands
{mikep,jian}@kub.nl,

Abstract. E-business is shifting attention from component based to web service based applications. Most enterprises spend most of their time assembling applications by consuming web services rather than worrying about the design principles underlying them, their granularity or the development of components that implement them. In this paper we present a design methodology for web services and business processes. We discuss how business process should be described so that services can be properly identified and provide strategies and principles regarding functional and non-functional aspects of web service design.

1 Introduction

Many enterprises are spending a significant amount of their time assembling applications that provide web service functionality rather than worrying about the design principles underlying the web services, their granularity or the development of components that implement them. One question arises naturally: what is the proper way to design web services so that they can be efficiently used in business applications, can be managed, reused, priced and metered?

Implementing a thin SOAP/WSDL/UDDI [3,2,4] layer on top of existing applications or components that realize the web services is not enough to build reliable, manageable, and re-usable web services. There is still a list of issues that need to be addressed and researched in connection with design methodologies and engineering principles before web services become the prominent paradigm for distributed computing and electronic business.

We can certainly borrow several ideas from the area of component software development. Although it provides some technical insights such as reusability and plug-replaceability, specification, and design principles which can be useful to web service design, these two concepts are different in terms of the level of abstraction and (functional and non-functional) concerns.

What is missing is a sound design methodology and engineering principles for developing web service based applications. The methodology we propose herein is based on core web service infrastructure, i.e., WSDL and WSFL [1]. It consists of two parts: a *framework for business process analysis* and *service design principles*. The former provides the means for identifying web services and their relationships; the latter gives the guidelines for web service design from both functional and non-functional perspectives.

A. Buchmann et al. (Eds.): TES 2002, LNCS 2444, pp. 54–64, 2002.
© Springer-Verlag Berlin Heidelberg 2002

To illustrate the ideas in our web service design methodology, we use an application scenario from the business domain of e-travelling and in particular the specifications of the open travel agency [11]. OTA has specified a set of business processes for obtaining services relating to the travel industry. We will demonstrate how the design principles are applied in terms of this example.

2   Service Interface and Specification

When designing an application, developers develop a logical model of what an enterprise does in terms of business objects (such as product, customer, order, bill, etc) and the services the business requires from these business objects (what is the stock level, what is the delivery schedule and so on). The developer may implement these concepts as a blend of service interfaces and components (the business objects). Components are normally used to implement (realize) the service functionality. Frequently, the interfaces that the components realize are too low level and not representative of the actual business services provided. This implies that we are dealing with two largely complementary elements: the *service interface* and its corresponding implementation component (*service realization*), illustrated in Figure1. It is important to distinguish between these two elements because in many cases the organisations that provide service interfaces are not the same with the organisations that implement the services. A service is a business concept that should be specified with an application or the user of the service in mind, while the service realization may be provided by a software package, e.g., an ERP package, a special purpose built component, commercial off the shelf applications (COTS), or a legacy application. To a service client is irrelevant whether the services are provided by a fine-grained suite of components, or a single monolithic ERP. It is important that the developer who implements the service still thinks about granularity so they can change parts of the implementation with the minimum of disruption to other components, applications and services. The granularity of components should be the prime concern of the developer responsible for providing component implementations for services, whereas service designers should be more interested in the process operations and assembly potential of the provided services.

The only way one service can interact with another is via its interface. The interface simply provides the mechanism by which services communicate with applications and other services. Technically, the service interface is the description of the signatures of a set of operations that are available to the service client for invocation. The *service specification* must explicitly describe all the interfaces that a client of this service expects as well as the service interfaces (if any) that must be provided by the environment into which the service is assembled. As these service interfaces are provided by other services the service specification serves as a means to define how the service interface can be related to the interfaces of the imported services and how it can be implemented out of imported service interfaces. In this sense the service specification has a mission identical to that of the WSFL global model in that it is a composition meta-model that provides a description of how the web- service interfaces interact with each other

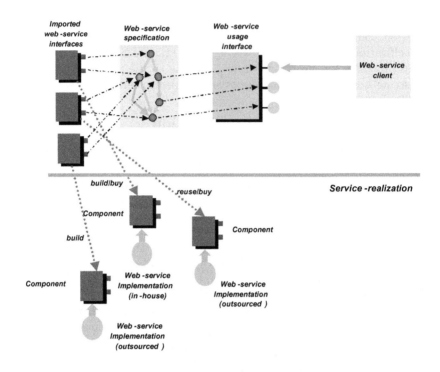

Fig. 1. Service Realization Strategy and Architecture

and how to define a new web service interface (`<PortType>`) as a collection (assembly) of existing ones (imported `<PortType>`s). A service specification, thus, defines the encapsulation boundary of a service, and consequently determines the granularity of replaceability of web service interface compositions. Just like components, services can be plug-replaceable, only if service specifications are self- contained and symmetrical [6]. As service development requires that we deal with multiple imported service interfaces it is useful to introduce this stage the concept of service usage interface. A *service usage interface* is simply the interface that a client of the service expects to see.

3   Describing Business Process Features

The key focal point of web service design is the business process. A business process leverages the `<port type>` element in WSDL to define its basic process activity interface. A business process can be modelled as a state machine where activities are modelled as web service invocations, which are sequenced by state transition events (control flow activities).

Determine objectives and describe the business process structure: The first step in the service design methodology is to determine the business process objectives and describe the business structure and the functions of the business process. The business process structure refers to the logical flow or progression of the business process. The functions of a business process are expressed in terms of the activities or the services that need to be performed by a specific business process. For instance, the registration of a new customer is an activity in a sales order process. The description of a process encompasses the following actions:

1. *Identify, group and describe the activities that together implement a business process:* The objective of this action is to identify the services that need to be combined in order to generate a business process and then describe the usage interface of the overall business process. The structure of a business process describes how an individual process activity (`<PortType>`) is linked with another in order to achieve a business process. To assemble a higher-level service by combining other web services, the service designer needs to:
   - Select the services to compose by looking at how these services and their operations within a business process relate to one another.
   - Connect the usage interface of the business process to the interfaces of imported services and plug them together.
2. *Describe activity dependencies, conditions or synchronisation:* A process definition can organise activities into varying structures:
   - *Hierarchical activity definitions:* in a hierarchical definition processes activities have a hierarchical structure. For instance, the activity of sending an insurance policy for a travel plan can be divided into three sub-activities: compute the insurance premium, notify insurance, mail insurance premium to the customer.
   - *Conditional activity definitions:* in process definitions that have a conditional activity structure activities are performed only if certain conditions are met. For instance, it may be company policy to send a second billing notice to a traveller when an invoice is more than two months overdue.
   - *Activity dependency definitions:* process definitions are incomplete without further indication of the activity structure. In any process definition, sub-activities can execute only after their parent activity has commenced. This means that sub-activities are implicitly dependent on their parent activity. In other cases there might be an explicit dependency between activities: an activity may only be able to start when another specific activity has completed. For instance, an itinerary confirmation cannot be sent to a traveller unless all flights have been reserved by an airline.
3. *Describe the implementation of the business process:* Write the application, e.g., provide a WSFL definition, that maps the operations and interfaces of imported services to those of another in order to create the usage interface of the business process (higher- level web service).

Describe business activity responsibilities (roles): The second step in the service design methodology is to identify responsibilities associated with business process activities and the service providers that are responsible for performing them. Each activity within a business process, e.g., a web services flow model such as WSFL, is associated with a particular web service provider who fulfils a defined role (responsibility) within the process. Each service provider is expected to properly fulfil the business responsibility of implementing the web service, or set of web services, which perform that activity within the process under the role that the provider is expected to undertake. To explicate this we use the OTA travel reservations example and assume that this business process is expressed in WSFL. For each activity, we would identify service provider responsible for the execution of the process step (for example, services offered by a travel agent or by an airline company) and define the association between activities in the flow model and operations offered by the service. In the travel reservations example, we may define the business process for handling travel reservations as a WSFL flow model. However, we do not bind the activities to particular service providers. Instead we identify the generic service provider (role) that is required for each activity (for example, some travel agent for the activity process book the trip, and some airline service for the activity order and issue the tickets). We would then define the WSDL web service interface of the flow model, that is, the WSFL <serviceProviderType> of the flow model. This interface has two facets: one facet defines the interface that a service client would use when requesting the processing of a travel reservation, that is, the operations that the web service provides for use by service requesters. For example, service would provide an operation that takes a trip order as input and passes it on (through a WSFL flow source) to the activities in the flow model for processing. The other facet identifies the operations that the service requires from the other service providers.

4   Service Design Principles

The service design principles that underlying the service design stages described above revolve around two well-known software design guidelines: coupling and cohesion. These guarantee that services are self-contained, modular and able to support service composability.

4.1   Service Coupling

It is important that the grouping of activities in business processes is as independent as possible from other such groupings in other processes. One way of measuring service design quality is *coupling*, or the degree of interdependence between two business processes. The objective is to minimise coupling, that is, to make (self-contained) business processes as independent as possible by not having any knowledge of or relying on any other business processes. Low coupling between business processes indicates a well-partitioned system that avoids the problems of service redundancy and duplication.

Coupling can be achieved by reducing the number of connections between services in a business process, eliminating unnecessary relationships between them, and by reducing the number of necessary relationships, if possible. Coupling is a very broad concept, however, for service design can be portioned along the following dimensions:

1. *Representational coupling:* The business processes should not depend on specific representational or computational details of one another. The central tactic stems from the idea of abstract classes in object-oriented design where composite classes and actions minimises dependencies on irrelevant representational and computational details [7]. These concerns lead to the exploitation of interoperability and reusability for service design. This solves several service options related to design, including:
   a) *Interchangeable/replaceable services:* existing services may be swapped by new service implementations – or ones supplied by a different provider offering better performance or pricing – without disrupting the overall business process functionality.
   b) *Multiple service versions:* different versions of a service may work best in parts of a business processes depending on the application's needs. For example, a stock exchange service may provide different levels of detail, e.g., financial details, charts, market projections, depending on the charging options.
2. *Identity coupling:* Connection channels between services should be unaware of who is providing the service. It is not desirable to keep track of the targets (recipients) of service messages, especially when they are likely to change or when discovering the best service provider is not a trivial matter.
3. *Communication protocol coupling:* A sender of a message should rely only on those effects necessary to achieve effective communication. For example, one-way styles of operation where a service end point receives a message without having to send an acknowledgement places the lowest possible demands on the service performing the operation. The service that performs the operation does not assume anything about when the effects of the operation hold, or even require that a notification be sent back indicating completion.

   Low coupling increases the degree of isolation of one business process from changes that happen to another; simplifies design understanding; and increases the reuse potential of web services.

4.2   Service Cohesion

Cohesion is the degree of the strength of functional relatedness of operations within a service. Designers should create strong, highly cohesive business processes, business processes whose services and service operations are strongly and genuinely related to one another. The guidelines by which to increase cohesion are as follows:

1. *Functional service cohesion:* A functionally cohesive business process contains services that all contribute to the execution of one and only one problem-related task. At the same time the operations in the services of the business process must also be highly related to one another.
2. *Communicational service cohesion:* A communicationally cohesive business process is one whose activities and services contribute to tasks that use the same input and output messages. Communicationally cohesive business

processes also have quite clean coupling, because their elements are hardly related to elements in other business processes.

3. *Logical service cohesion:* A logically cohesive business process is one whose activities all contribute to tasks of the same general category. These tasks are selected and invoked outside the business process.

High cohesion increases the clarity and ease of comprehension of the design; simplifies maintenance and future enhancements; achieves service granularity at a fairly reasonable level; and often supports low coupling. The fine grain of highly related functionality supports increased reuse potential as a highly cohesive service module can be used for very specific purposes.

5   Non Functional Service Design Guidelines

Non-functional service characteristics describe the broader context of a service, e.g., what business function the web service accomplishes, how it fits into a broader business process context as well as characteristics of the hosting environment such as whether the service provider ensures security and privacy, what kind of auditing, security and privacy policy is enforced by the service provider, what levels of quality of service are available and so on, e.g, non- functional characteristics of web services such as those described by the Web Service Endpoint Language (WSEL).

5.1   Service Provisioning Strategies

Service provisioning is central to operating revenue generating web services between organisations. It is a complex mixture of technical and business aspects for supporting service client activities and involves choices for service realization, service enrolment, auditing, metering, billing and managing operations that control the behaviour of a service during use. The provisioning requirements for web services impose serious implications for the design methodology of services.

5.1.1 Service realization strategies. The separation of specification from implementation allows web services to be realized in different ways. It becomes important then to plan effectively when deciding how to realize or provision services, consider the diversity of realization alternatives and make the right choice. There are important factors that need to be considered during this process and these are similar to the factors considered when realizing components [8]:

- *Gap analysis.* This technique decides the service realization strategy by incrementally adding more implementation details to an abstract service usage interface. During this process a service realization architecture can be used to express how the service usage interface is connected to and assembled from the interfaces of the web services out of which it is composed, see Figure 1.

Gap analysis is used to compare planned services, revealed by the service realization architecture, with available software service implementations. Figure 1 shows how imported service interfaces, which are part of a business process are realized in terms of already existing interfaces and implementations. The ticker arrows in this figure denote the different provisioning possibilities, such reusing, building or buying service interfaces and their underlying implementations. This figure also illustrates that service interfaces may be provided by one service provider while another provider, e.g., an ASP company, may offer their underlying implementation. A gap analysis strategy may be developed in stages and results in a recommendation to do development work, reuse or purchase web services.

The service realization strategy involves choosing from an increasing diversity of different options for services, in addition to service reuse, which may be mixed in various combinations including:

1. Purchasing/leasing/paying per use for services. This option is covered in some detail in the section on service metering and billing.
2. Outsourcing service design and implementation. Once a service is specified, the design of its interfaces or sets of interfaces and the coding of its actual implementation may be outsourced.
3. Using wrappers and/or adapters. Non-component implementations for services may include database functionality or legacy software in the form of adapters or wrappers.

5.1.2 Service billing strategies. From the perspective of the service provider a complex trading web- service is a commercialisable software commodity. For example, a service provider may decide to offer simple services (with no quality of service guarantee) for free, while it would charge a nominal fee for use of its complex (added value) web services. With complex trading web services the quality of service plays a high role of importance and the service is offered for a price. These types of services are very different from the selling of shrink-wrapped software components, in that payment should be on an execution basis for the delivery of the service, rather than on a one-off payment for an implementation of the software. For complex trading web services, the service provider may have different charging alternatives. These may include:

1. Payment on a per use basis. With this alternative a client is charged some nominal fee each time they invoke the service.
2. Payment on a subscription basis. With this alternative a client is charged a set amount of money for a given period of time.
3. Payment on a leasing basis. This alternative is similar to subscription; however, it is geared towards web services that may provide high value for a shorter period of time.
4. Lifetime services. These services are offered for a set amount of money for their entire lifetime.
5. Free services. An advantage of this model is that services could be offered to requesters for free for a period of time and then they can be moved into

some payment plan. Providers, who create services for free, would normally distribute their functionality with a simple SLA agreement that allows for a future charging mechanism to come into play.

6. Free with hidden value. This term refers to services that may actually get advantage from clients using them. For example, a client may use a web service for free but may have to pay a subscription fee when it wishes to see more services related to the free service.

A service design methodology should take into account several important aspects relating to the accounting process for service provisioning, such as service metering, rating and billing.

Service metering model: Use of a service by a client must be metered if the service provider requires usage-based billing. Then the service provider needs to audit the service as it is used and bill for it. This could typically be done on a periodic basis and requires that a metering and accounting model for the use of the service be established. The model could allow the establishment of a service contract for each new subscriber and tacking and billing for using the subscribed hosted services. To achieve this, the service-metering model could operate on the assumption that web services with a high degree of value are contracted via, for example, SLAs. The metering model can cover different payment possibilities such as fee-for-use model, the subscription model, and the lease model.

Service rating/billing model: Software organisations that are used to the traditional up-front license/ongoing maintenance pricing structure for software should come up with annuity-based pricing models for the web services they provide. The pricing (rating) model could determine subscriber rates based on subscription and usage events. For example, the pricing model could calculate charges for services based on the quality and precision of the service and on individual metering events based on a service-rating scheme. The billing model associates rating details with the correct client account. It provides adequate information to allow the retrieval and payment of billing details by the client and the correct disbursement of payments to the service provider's suppliers (who are in turn service providers offering wholesale services to the original provider).

5.2   Service Policy Management Models

As a wide range of services is provided across a network it is only natural that services would introduce policy management models that determine differentiated services according to business rules or application-level policies. There are many reasons why businesses might want to give different levels of service to different customers or why they might need different levels of priority to different business transaction models involving web services. Therefore, it is no surprise that such criteria are considered to be equally important to technical policies such as security or authentication.

Consider for example a stock quote service where different clients may be given different levels of data quality depending on how much they are prepared to pay. A free service would provide a mere stock quote trade price with some delay. Some clients, however, may be prepared to pay for a higher level of service providing more timely stock quote prices and other financial data, e.g., financial charting, stock growth trends, and so on. Moreover, there might be clients who would need some characteristics of data quality but no others. For instance, some investors may be interested in streaming market quotes and data while others may not. Therefore, service providers can mix different levels of service precision, granularity, timeliness and scope. Another possibility is to differentiate services based on technical quality details such as response time, performance bandwidth used, and reliability. If a service is designed to cover a fairly wide spectrum of service levels according to some set of policies then it is likely that this service would achieve much higher levels of use [10].

5.3   Service Programming Style

Services have two programming styles: RPC or document-based. Determining the service programming style is largely a design issue as different applications impose different programming-style requirements for web services. Consider for example an application that deals with purchase order requests, purchase order confirmations and delivery information. This application requires that request messages may contain purchase orders in the form of XML documents while response messages may contain purchase order receipts or delivery information again in the form of XML documents. This type of application uses data-oriented web- services. Moreover, there is no real urgency for a response message to follow a request immediately if at all. In contrast to this, consider an application that provides businesses with up-to- the-instant credit standings. Before completing a business transaction, a business may require to check a potential customer's credit standing. In this scenario, a request would be sent to the credit check web service provider, e.g., a bank, processed, and a response indicating the potential customer's credit rating would be returned in real time. This type of web service relies on an RPC programming style. In this type of applications the client invoking the web- service needs an immediate response or may even require that the web services interact in a back- and-forth conversational way.

5.4   Authorisation Design Considerations

Since web services should allow access to sanctioned clients, security is a first order business consideration. Normally, an integrated approach to security is required whereby all technical system aspects as well as business policies and processes are taken into consideration.

Increasingly authorisation capabilities are emerging as a major security requirement for e-business. An enterprise not only needs to know who the requesters accessing their services are; it also needs to control the what web services that requester has access to, what factors affect availability of the web- services to that customer, and what auditing is required to ensure the non-repudiation of transactions with that requester. Other factors in the decision making include policies that are active at the time of the service request.

With authorisation models, access to web services can be restricted to autho-rised requesters and applications in much the same way that Web sites restrict access to authorised clients and applications. Authorisation can usually take place for each operation within the web service. Alternatively, there may be oc-casions when authorisation for a web service (or business process) as a whole is more appropriate, for instance where a high granularity of security is not criti-cal [9]. There are different authentication models for client authentication. For instance, an authentication model may require that a client authenticates itself by presenting its encoded credentials or may require that XML signatures be generated for web service requests.

Once a web service design methodology has been applied, web service specifi-cation in WSDL can ensue on the basis of the following steps: (1) specifying the service interface; (2) making operation parameters; (3) messaging and transport; (4) implementing. An example of this can be found in [5].

6   Conclusion

In this paper we argue that without design methodologies and sound engineer-ing principles web services can not be properly developed to achieve what they promised: reusability and plug-replaceability, flexibility and extensibility. We then propose a methodology which provides a framework for identifying web ser-vices from business processes and principles in web service design which covers both functional perspectives such as coupling and cohesion, and non-functional perspectives such as provision, billing, pricing and metering. The design strat-egy is in line with the web service standards WSDL and WSFL, and software engineering principles.

References

1. "Web Service Flow Language (WSFL 1.0)",
   http://www-4.ibm.com/software/solutions/webservices/pdf/WSFL.pdf.
2. "Web Service Definition Language", http://www.w3.org/TR/wsdl.
3. "Simple Object Access Protocol (SOAP) 1.1", http://www.w3.org/TR/SOAP.
4. UDDI Project, "UDDI Technical White Paper", September, 2000,
   http://www.udddi.org.
5. Bilal Siddiqui, "Deploying Web services with WSDL",
   http://www-106.ibm.com/developerworks/library/ws-intwsdl/ .
6. D.F. d'Souza, A.C. Wills, "Objects, components and frameworks with UML", Addison-Wesley, Longman Inc., 1999.
7. D. de Champeaux, D. Lea, and P. Faure, "Object-oriented system development", Addison-Wesley publishing co., 1993.
8. P. Allen, "Realizing e-Business with Components", Addison-Wesley, 2001.
9. P. Cauldwell, et. al., "XML Web Services", Wrox Press Ltd., 2001.
10. CBDiForum "Design Pattern: Differentiated Service", www.cdbiforum.com, pp 3-8, December 2000.
11. Open Travel Alliance, OTA, "2001C Specifications", http://www.opentravel.org, 2001

E-service Based Information Fusion: A User-Level Information Integration Framework

Abdelsalam (Sumi) Helal and Jingting Lu

Computer and Information Science and Engineering Department,
University of Florida, Gainesville, FL32611, USA
helal@cise.ufl.edu
http://www.harris.cise.ufl.edu/projects/e-services.htm

Abstract. Managing fast-growing personal information is a time-consuming and laborious task that affects people's daily life. In addition, learning new skills is always an obstacle for end users, to fully take advantage of any new technology-based services. A framework is highly desired here to allow people to collect and fuse personal information without dealing with complex emerging technologies. In this paper, we introduce our e-service based Information Fusion framework for end-users. This framework enables end users to collect scattered information from diverse autonomous sources, and transparently create a repeatable process by which newer instances of the same information can be obtained in the future. By exploiting this framework, users won't need to repeat the manual information gathering task over and over again. We present our framework and provide some implementation details.

1 Introduction

With the fast pace by which we live today and with the information society we are becoming, people have more and more personal information concerning many aspects of their lives. This includes on-line brokering accounts, bank accounts, and credit cards, to mention just a few. People often spend substantial amount of time gathering and managing such information, every time this information or summary of it is needed. Usually, such information is scattered across different business sites. For example, many people have three or four bank accounts, more than one credit card, and several airline frequent flyer accounts. For regular online services, an end user needs to go to each individual web site to authenticate and manually fill in the necessary details to invoke a service and get the information (i.e. balance of a checking account). This is a time consuming process that will be repeated every time the end-user seeks a more up-to-date version of the information.

An alternative way to access information from different sources is using the emerging e-service technology. E-service is viewed as "any service or functionality that can be accessed by a business or a consumer programmatically on the Internet, using standard representation and protocols" [3]. It can greatly improve the efficiency of invoking and integrating services, including information. On the other hand, it in

A. Buchmann et al. (Eds.): TES 2002, LNCS 2444, pp. 65-75, 2002.
© Springer-Verlag Berlin Heidelberg 2002

volves fairly professional and complicated processes for end users, requiring them to have significant knowledge of e-service related specifications. Even for e-service specialists, it is their responsibility to modify the service requests correspondingly if a particular service interface is changed later on, or to deal with status query directly for checking back the execution status of a long-running service. Regardless of its efficiency, the plain e-service framework is clearly a complex and inconvenient way of invoking services and gathering information.

The major goal of our E-service Information Fusion framework is to tame this complexity and simplify the use model of the emerging e-service standards so that services can be used transparently by non-expert-users. This can be done through a framework that involves a methodology at the e-service provider side, and a carefully designed, user-friendly interface that facilitates the access and integration of information on the internet, at the end-user side.

1.1 Motivating Scenario

Let's meet a software engineer here, Kin lee, who has three bank accounts in three different online banks: Bank One, Bank of America and Hong Kong Bank. Every time he checks his three accounts' balances, Kin spends a good deal of time on going into each individual bank's website and filling multiple forms to finally get the bank balances. Fig. 1.1 depicts this balance-querying scenario.

Before he can receive the balance at Hong Kong Bank, Kin needs to make n interactions with the web site to input his context such as account and password, etc. Similarly, m interactions are needed at American Bank, and k interactions at Bank One. Hence, Kin need to do a total of $(n + m + k)$ interactions in order to retrieve all three balances and finally calculating net worth, himself. Apparently, he has to repeat the $(n + m + k)$ interactions every time he wants to check the balances. And we haven't mentioned yet that he needs to memorize and put the accounts and passwords information somewhere safe. This repeated tedious process could turn into a nightmare and a waste of time for future web users. This can only exacerbate the more web users opt to the electronic statement option of the various businesses.

We know e-services can be invoked in a standard messaging through the Internet, facilitating different businesses to build their applications on different systems and technologies they prefer. Thus Hong Kong Bank, for instance, may implements the "balance" service as an e-service and publishes it in a public e-service repository to let more potential users (both businesses and individuals) use the service easily. The process that Kin will follow if he wants to exploit the e-service version of "balance" service is as follows. He first needs to refer to a public e-service repository to find the Hong Kong Bank's e-balance service description file, then generates the appropriate request message containing his context, and finally invokes the e-service to get the balance result. All exchanged messages should be based on some standard message format. And if the service interface is changed later on, Kin will get an error message when he tries to invoke the service again. Thus he must retrieve the service's new description file to change the service request accordingly. Obviously, this process is more suitable for businesses since they can invest much on implementing the corresponding software framework, whereas it is not necessary and practical for Kin to master the e-service related emerging technologies. A user-level e-service interface is clearly needed here.

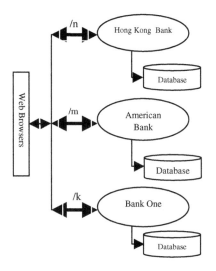 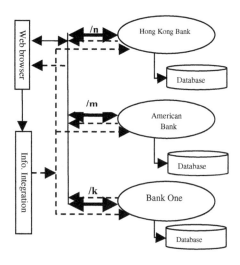

Fig. 1.1. Kin needs to do $(n + m + k)$ interactions to retrieve snapshots of balances from 3 different accounts every time. ("/n" represents n interactions,"/m" represents m interactions, "/k" represents k interactions*)*

Fig. 1.2. Kin made $(n + m + k)$ interactions to retrieve snapshots of balances from 3 different bank accounts. Kin did this once, and in doing so, he extracted the process i.e. the e-service standard request message to an "Information Integration" module. (Dashed lines show the direct way for Kin to subsequently invoke the e-balance service).

Fig. 1.2 depicts our framework. It shows a more efficient process to query three different banks for three different balances from an "Information Integration" module without manually inputting any data by Kin. This process involves $(n + m + k)$ interactions only the first time Kin queries the three banks. During these interactions, Kin transparently and reflexively extracts the user-service-based information gathering process such as the e-service standard request message. In the future, Kin will not visit each bank's web site and repeat the same interaction steps. Instead, Kin will use the information integration module to directly obtain the data he needs. In essence, the Information fusion framework creates a new meaning of e-service – "informational e-service", which encapsulates particular user-service-based information in an e-service invocation compared to regular e-services concept. As a result, Kin doesn't even need to search for the "balance" e-service description file in a public e-services repository to exploit the e-service. The information integration module handles all communication with the service provider and prompts Kin to input additional data only if necessary. This approach does not only save time, but also hide any changes made to the e-balance e-service interface, from Kin.

Furthermore, this framework provides a facility that can automatically evaluate all the embedded e-services binders at one time for users, reducing lots of user's intervention activities.

In effect, what Kin has accomplished is a user-level fusion of information from heterogeneous sources. Such problem has been a daunting task in the past. Today, with emerging e-service technologies such as XML, SOAP and WSDL, user-level integration is becoming possible.

Creating an information fusion engine that integrates users' scattered personal data, and transparently exploits e-services without requiring users to know or handle the technology and the implementation details is the motivation of our E-service Information Fusion Framework.

In the following subsections, we describe our e-service based framework that realizes the above pleasant vision. Section 2 introduces related works. In section 3, we discuss in details the design, architecture, and implementation of the e-service Information Fusion framework. Conclusion and future work are discussed in Section 4.

2   E-service Information Fusion

Our e-service Information Fusion framework aims at providing an Information Integration at the end-user level, hiding all data inputs, service implementations, and emerging standards from the users. The basic functionalities implemented by the E-service Information Fusion framework can be summarized as follows:

- Capture the context of a particular user-service-based interaction. Such context includes a service standard request message (SOAP message here) which contains a user's context and complies to the corresponding service interface definition, and a service URL from which the above request message can be captured and the e-service can be invoked later on.
- Provide an "e-service binder" which visually represents the new "informational e-services" and can be used by users through a tool to invoke a particular e-service directly.
- Provide a methodology for Information Fusion framework clients and service providers to follow. Such methodology will allow our framework to achieve information integration across heterogeneous and autonomous sources.
- Hide from users changes made to the e-service interface over time.
- Nicely convey long-running e-services to users
- Provides a facility to automatically evaluate all the embedded e-services binders at one time for users
- Provides simple manipulating functions on returned results, i.e. calculating summary of balance

2.1 E-service Information Fusion Architecture

Fig. 2.1 depicts the major components of the E-service Information Fusion architecture. We present the architecture through the steps that take place during three phases

Phase I. Using our methodology, the business provider creates e-services and publishes them in an *e-service repository* (Fig. 1.2 step 1). The business provider also links information that is dynamically generated (e.g. the service SOAP request including the particular user's context) to the e-service that computes this information. Our methodology is simple. It calls for structuring the applications behind certain information as e-services. It also calls for using a unique HTML representation to convey the fact that a piece of information in a dynamic web page has an underlying e-service implementation that is externalized to the end-user. Using our methodology, a business provider can decide on what information it wishes to externalize.

Phase II. A user accesses an online service for the first time, using a tool that follows our e-service framework. Such a tool is a standard browser connected to a

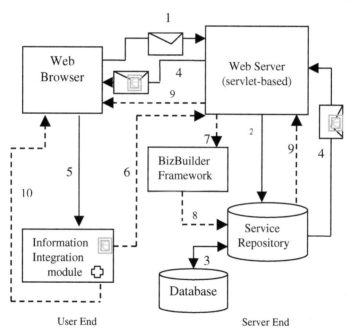

Fig. 2.1. E-service Information Fusion Architecture (Solid-line represents the process for invoking legacy services; Dash-line represents the e-service invocation process through e-service Information Fusion framework; ▣ represents "e-service binder"; whereas ⊕ represents simple manipulating functions).

"builder tool" that enables the user to "cut and paste" visual representation of the "informational e-services" that implement (compute) certain information. What the user sees during this browsing session is the data he needs, "shadowed" by visual indicators that information has externalized e-services available. A piece of information and the corresponding visual indicator will be unambiguously related be the way they are laid out next to each other.

The web server at a provider web site receives a user HTTP requests and extracts data from it (step 1). According to the invoked service name, a *service repository* will be searched to find the requested service (step 2). Since the service is implemented as e-service, at the point, the appropriate SOAP request is created for the use in a data-base, facilitating sending it back to the user when he cuts and pastes "e-service binder" to "builder tool" later on. The SOAP request is compatible with the corresponding e-service interface syntax, containing any authentication information and other parame-ters supplied by the user. The local service is finally invoked with the appropriate parameters, involving interactions with database (step 3). Along with the e-service results, part of the users' information (we name this critical *context*), the e-service URI, service name and provider name, all of which compose of a component named "e-service binder", will be presented back to the user's browser (step 4). The "e-service binder" is the visual cue that alerts the user that the "means" to obtaining this information again in the future can be cut and paste, and saved in the "builder tool" (we call this tool as Information Fusion Module) (step 5). The user can decide to cut and paste, and save, or may ignore the alert. By through the visual cut and paste op-erations, the corresponding e-service SOAP request message is being captured from the service side and saved along with e-service URL in context repository at the user end, accomplishing the "informational e-services" creation at users side. Getting complete SOAP request message from service implementers rather than generating the SOAP request at a user end is a good choice for making services implementation transparent from users.

Phase III. The Information Fusion module can be made to appear as web-presence (step 10). When users want to invoke the same service again, they only need to click the saved "e-service binder", and the binder will retrieve the corresponding e-service SOAP request message and service URL in context repository and communicate with the correct web server (step 6). The web server interacts with the BizBuilder frame-work (explained in section 3.3) to find the appropriate local service for the requested e-service (step 7). The corresponding service in the service repository is executed (step 8 and step 3), and the result is sent back to the user (step 9). Finally, the user can invoke multiple e-services. For instance, if the user "built" a global bank statement by copying and pasting multiple e-services, provided by three different banks, in phase II, the result would be a personal information integration record with multiple e-service references (and of course a set of hidden contexts) with some other kinds of personal data. The Information Fusion framework provides a facility to automatically evaluate all the embedded e-services binders at one time, reducing lots of users' intervention activities. Users can also define some predefined manipulating functions to apply them for same categorized results.

2.2 Information Integration Module

The Information Integration module sitting at user's end is a core component in the information fusion architecture. Fig. 2.2 shows the sub-components of the Information Integration module.

In a neat WYSIWYG interface, users "cut and paste" the "e-service binder" to an Information Integration builder to create a record with reference to e-services using their "e-service binders" (step 1). The corresponding SOAP request and service URL are also "pasted" into a context Repository (step 2). By this mechanism, the "e-service binder" becomes a visual representation of so called "informational e-services".

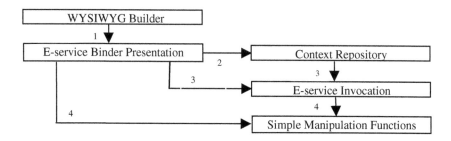

Fig. 2.2. The components of Information Integration module (⬚ represents defined simple manipulating functions, ▢ represents "e- service binder")

By just clicking the "e-service binder", a standard SOAP request which contains the user's information is retrieved from the context repository and titled with the services URL, is sent to the appropriate web server to invoke the e-service (step 3). After users get service results, they can further perform the defined simple functions based on the results (step 4), such as calculating balance summary. This module provides simple steps for users to follow to create their e-services binders presentation and context repository, and invoke e-services directly and complete the defined functions.

We use the BizBuilder framework [3], which facilitates the invocation of e-services at the service provider side. This framework can convert legacy services (Java services particularly) to e-services and facilitate their invocation. Due to space limitation, we are unable to describe its details. However, the reader is referred to [3].

3 Design of the Information Integration Module

Our design extends a spreadsheet-like software named *Jeks*, which provides rich mathematical functions for users to manipulate resulting data. For space limitation, we present only the Jeks-based design.

Jeks [6] is a GNU General Public License software created by Emmanuel Puybaret. It implements an extendable spreadsheet-like tool using Java swing Jtable, providing rich mathematical functions facilities. This spreadsheet-like interface is a nice work-space for our Information Fusion framework, since we can perform simple manipu-lating functions, especially aggregates. Furthermore, each individual cell is naturally a good placeholder for an independent "e-service binder". Fig. 3.1(a) illustrates the architecture of Jeks-based Information Integration.

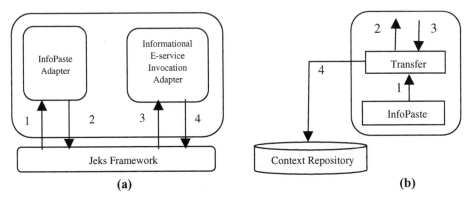

Fig. 3.1. (a) The architecture of Jeks-based Information Integration module, (b) The InfoPaste Adaptor.

There are two sub-adapters in the Information Fusion Adapter: InfoPaste and In-formational E-service Invocation. They interact with Jeks framework, users' context repository and services server to accomplish their purposes.

3.1 InfoPaste Adapter

InfoPaste adapter is responsible for transferring a service context from the e-service server to the user's building tool. We borrow from the HTTP protocol and redefine a variant protocol format for the particular "e-service binder" component. This can be specified as follows:

http://serivceURL#providername#servicename#information

ServiceURL is the web address of a servlet-based e-service. "providername" is the name of a particular service provider like "Hong Kong Bank". "Information" contains minimum critical user information such as account, which can be used for the service server as index to search for the corresponding user-service SOAP request message in database.

Users can get the above important information by "copy and paste" the "e-service binder" component from web browser to the Jeks tool, utilizing the regular "copy shortcut" functions for the HTTP protocol and employing the special InfoPaste Adapter. The difference between special InfoPaste and regular paste function in the Information Integration module lies in that InfoPaste can transfer the corresponding user-service-based context from the service's side to the user's side when it appears to do the same visual pasting as regular paste function.

Fig. 3.1(b) shows two sub-modules in the InfoPaste adapter architecture. When users "copy and paste" the "e-service binder" component from the presented web page to the Jeks tool, the InfoPaste sub-module is invoked (Fig.3.1(a) step 1); it parsers the "serviceURL", "servicename" and "information" data out and passes them on to the Transfer sub-module (Fig.3.1(b) step 1). The Transfer module communicates with services servers to request transferring the exact service SOAP request message (Fig.3.1(b) step 2). After receiving the HTTP SOAP request, the servlet-based service server extracts critical information including the invoked service name like "balance", and user-unique context like account. Then it indexes them to its database to find the SOAP request message in per user-service base and send it back to the user (Fig. 3.1(b) step 3). Transfer module extracts the exact SOAP request message from the server response and save it along with the "serviceURL" to Context repository (Fig. 3.1(b) step 4). The row and column value of a cell will make the connection between an "e-service binder" in the cell and the corresponding user-service-based SOAP request in context repository. Finally, InfoPaste module presents the "e-service binder" with service provider's name into the cell that the user chooses to save the binder into (Fig. 3.1(a) step 2). The user can "copy" and "InfoPaste" multiple "service binder" from diverse services server, and save them to a file along with other categorized personal data and predefined manipulation functions, forming a personal information integration record (or information sheet).

3.2 E-service Invocation Adapter

E-service Invocation Adapter is the major component, which accomplishes the e-service invocation process. Fig. 3.2 shows four sub-modules comprising the E-service Invocation Adapter. These are *EvaluateE-serivces, CheckE-Serivce, updateRequest and ServiceStatus.* Due to space limitation, we only briefly describe these modules.

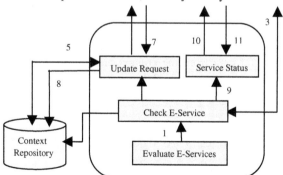

Fig. 3.2. The Architecture of E-service Invocation Adapter

EvaluateE-Services module. Evaluates all embedded e-service binders in a given spreadsheet. The user opens his information integration file (sheet) and simply clicks the button for this function (Fig. 3.1(a) step 3). This module will scan each cell which contains an e-service binder one by one, invoking the *CheckE-Serivce* module for each e-service binder.

CheckE-Service Module.   When invoked by *EvaluateE-Serivces* module for evaluation of one e-service binder in a cell (Fig. 3.2 step 1), *CheckE-Serivce* module retrieves the corresponding user-service-based SOAP request message and serviceURL from a context repository indexed by the row and column values of the cell (Fig. 3.2 step 2).   Then *CheckE-Service* sends the HTTP SOAP request to the service server to invoke the e-service and get the results back (Fig. 3.2 step 3). E-service Invocation Adapter can redirect the flow of action based on the returned results. If the e-service has been invoked without errors and the expected result is returned i.e. the balance, *CheckE-Service* can directly present the result back into the cell (Fig. 2.3(a) step 4).

One important achievement of the Information Fusion framework is graceful recover from errors due to change to the e-service definition. If this is to ever happens, the Information Fusion Adapter tries to reuse as much context as possible before it uses the new e-service definition to prompt the user for input (according to the new definition). After the new context is constructed, the Information Fusion recaptures the new SOAP request message generated by the service and updates the "e-service binder". In this case, the service will send back a SOAP request message containing a list for all missing or wrong-type parameters for the new e-service interface, with a particular method name such as *"mismatchedPara"*.

UpdateRequest module.   Recaptures the new user-service-based SOAP request in case an e-service interface is changed over time. For example, HongKong Bank at first implemented the interface of "balance" e-service with two input parameters: account and password; now they want users to provide one more input: social security number to enhance security.   The *UpdateRequest* module is invoked with all required additional data extracted from a service response by *CheckE-Service* module (Fig. 3.2 step 4), and the user is prompted to input additional data, achieving a change-tolerant end-user interface.

After *UpdateRequest* collects the desired new information, it merges the new data along with old but valid data from the context repository into a SOAP request and sends it over to the service server (Fig. 3.2 step 6). The e-service will regenerate the appropriate SOAP request message according to the information sent by the user, and returns it back (Fig. 3.2 step 7).   *UpdateRequest* stores the updated user-service SOAP request to the context repository (Fig. 3.2 step 8). Subsequent invocations of the e-service, will retrieve the correct SOAP request message.

ServiceStatus module.   ServiceStatus module is responsible for checking long-running service status for users.

4 Conclusion

We believe that achieving user-level information integration is becoming possible thanks to the emerging e-services technology. Our E-service Information Fusion Framework enables end users to construct their own information pages (or sheets) that integrate multiple autonomous information sources, all without having to learn or understand the complexities of the e-service technology themselves.

Early on during our research, we realized that the user interface design is very critical for the success of this framework. Specifically, our goal is to provide an easy "copy and paste "or "drag and drop" functions between a builder tool we are implementing and a general browser featuring contents from service providers that use our e-service based information fusion framework.

References

1. http://java.sun.com/products/hotjava/3.0/, java.sun.com
2. Kent Brown, "SOAP for Platform-Neutral Interoperability", http://xmlmag.com
3. R. Krithivasan and A. Helal, "BizBuilder - An e-Services Framework Targeted for Internet Workflow," Proceedings of the third Workshop on Technologies for E-Services (TES'01), Springer Lecture Notes in Computer Science series, VOL. 2193. In conjunction with VLDB 2001, Sept 2001, Rome, Italy
4. Richard Karpinski, "Inside UDDI", Transformation Today, June 7, 2001
5. Yasser Shohoud, "Introduction to WSDL", http://www.devxpert.com
6. Emmanuel PUYBARET, http://www.eteks.com/jeks/en/#WhatJeks

A Request Language for Web-Services Based on Planning and Constraint Satisfaction

M. Aiello[1], M. Papazoglou[1,2], J. Yang[2], M. Carman[3], M. Pistore[3], L. Serafini[3], and P. Traverso[3]

[1] DIT — University of Trento, Via Sommarive, 14, 38050 Trento, Italy
contact author, phone +39-0461-882055
aiellom@dit.unitn.it,
http://www.dit.unitn.it/~aiellom
[2] INFOLAB — University of Tilburg, PO Box 90153, NL-5000 LE Tilburg, NL
{mikep,jian}@kub.nl,
http://infolab.kub.nl/people/{mikep,jian}
[3] ITC-IRST, Via Sommarive,18, 38050 Trento, Italy
{carman,pistore,serafini,traverso}@irst.itc.it,
http://sra.itc.it/people/{carman,pistore,serafini,traverso}

Abstract. One of the most challenging problems that web-service enabled e-marketplaces face is the lack of support for appropriate service request languages that retrieve and aggregate services relevant to a business problem. We present an architectural framework for web-service interaction based on planning and constraint satisfaction, and a web-service request language (WSRL) developed on the basis of this framework. This framework is capable of performing planning under uncertainty on the basis of refinement and revision as new service-related information is accumulated (via interaction with the user or UDDI) and as execution circumstances necessitate change.

1 Introduction

The current phase of the e-business revolution is driven by enterprises that look to B2B solutions to improve communications and provide a fast and efficient method of transacting with one another. E-marketplaces are the vehicles that provide the desired B2B functionality. An e-marketplace is an electronic trading community that brings multiple customers, suppliers, distributors and commerce service providers in any geographical location together to conduct business over the Internet to produce value for end-customers and for each other.

A vertical e-marketplace, e.g., semiconductors, chemicals, travel industry, aerospace, etc, provides value by efficiently managing interactions between buyers and sellers in a specific industry. A vertical e-marketplace identifies a shared business vocabulary, standard business processes and product categorization tailored to a particular industry. Further, the e-marketplace establishes and uses the shared meaning of these products and business processes to facilitate trading partner integration needs. The business interactions between organizations that

A. Buchmann et al. (Eds.): TES 2002, LNCS 2444, pp. 76–85, 2002.
© Springer-Verlag Berlin Heidelberg 2002

make up a business process are standardized and formally described, e.g., modeled using UMM (UN/CEFACT Modeling Methodology N090), and published via e-business directories such as the UDDI. Vertical e-marketplaces provide to their members a unified view of sets of products and services and enable them to transact using diverse mechanisms, such as web-services, available in the e-marketplace. This allows companies to conduct electronic business, by invoking web-services, with all partners in a marketplace rather with just the ones with whom they have collaborative business agreements. Service offers are described in such a way that they allow automated discovery to take place and offer request matching on functional and non-functional service capabilities.

One of the most challenging problems that web-service enabled e-marketplaces face is the lack of support for appropriate service request languages that retrieve and aggregate services relevant to a business problem. To understand this we may use an application scenario in the business domain of e-travelling and in particular the specifications of the open travel agency [1]. OTA has specified a set of standard business processes for searching for availability and booking a reservation in the airline, hotel and car rental industry, as well as the purchase of travel insurance in conjunction with these services. OTA specifications use XML for structured data messages to be exchanged over the Internet. Business processes like these specify how agents in an e-travelling marketplace interact in order to satisfy a traveller's requests. Key capability for a service request language would be to satisfy a user request by transparently assembling service solutions from different serviced providers in the e-marketplace dynamically, by aggregating and composing services and by constructing an end-to-end holiday package comprising a number of optimized flight and accommodation choices.

In this paper, we concentrate on the use of planning mechanisms for use within the context of web-services. In particular, our research aims is to provide higher-level lightweight constructs for a service request language whose semantics are based on extended temporal languages used for model based planning and on linear constraint satisfaction. In that respect, we combine a goal language for expressing extended goals in non-deterministic domains [2] with a system-level planning language for interacting with composed web services [3].

The paper is organized as follows: in Section 2, we relate planning to web-services. In Section 3, we introduce a domain for e-travelling. In Section 4, we illustrate the proposed approach by defining a formal request language, its interpretation, execution model, and a possible implementation. We show an example of a request and its execution in Section 5.

2   Planning for Web-Services

The field of AI planning offers high potential for solving problems in the context of web-enabled applications by instilling planning and scheduling capabilities in distributed decision-making agents in order to manage resource-constrained domains [4]. Recently, different planning approaches have been proposed (see [5, 6,7]), most of which focus on gathering information and on applying deterministic planning. In our view AI planning provides a sound framework for developing a web-services request language and for checking the correctness of the plans that are generated by it. Our work concentrates on developing a service request language for e-marketplaces. This request language results in the generation of executable plans describing both the sequence of plan actions to be undertaken in order to satisfy a request and the necessary information and constraints essential to develop each planned action.

There are a number of requirements that web-service centered planning should satisfy. The plans should have an "open dynamic structure" and be situated in the context of execution. This implies that plans should deal with non-deterministic effects of the business domain and the set of potentially executable actions may change during the course of planning. Hence, plans should be amenable to refinement and revision as new information is accumulated (via interaction with the user or UDDI) and as execution circumstances necessitate change. For instance, once a travel plan has been generated and proposed to the user, the user may decide to change some of the parameters connected to an action, e.g., hotel booking, by dynamically reconfiguring the plan. As plans inevitably do not execute as expected there is the constant need to be able to identify critical constraints and decision trade-offs, and for evaluation of alternative options. In the planning parlance, this means that it should be possible to deal with interleaved plans, interactive plans, reactive plans that deal with exogenous events, e.g., information supplied by the UDDI, and contingency plans that deal with uncertain outcomes of non-deterministic actions. This need for dynamic planning capabilities is at direct odds with classical planning research that assumes complete knowledge of the conditions in which the plan will be executed, deterministic execution and actions with predictable outcomes and little space for incremental changes. In addition to these requirements, there is also the core requisite of being able to prove the correctness of the correspondence between a request (goal) and the plans generated by the request language as a response to this request.

To comply with the above requirements, we have chosen to: (1) to use a model based planner for non-deterministic domains, e.g., open travel, and a standard constraint satisfaction solver; and (2) work with a combination of an extended temporal language and a linear constraint satisfaction language for expressing the goals (requests). The service request language can.express requirements regarding the possible sequences of actions and the possible values of parameters for planned actions; while, the plans generated by the request language are capable of dealing with non-determinism, interleaving and constraints resolution.

3 The Domain of E-travelling

To describe the service-based interaction between a traveller, a travel agency and a tour operator, we use the business process specification found in [1]. This business process specifies the format of a user request and the replies of the service providers in an open-travel marketplace that may offer web-service functionality.

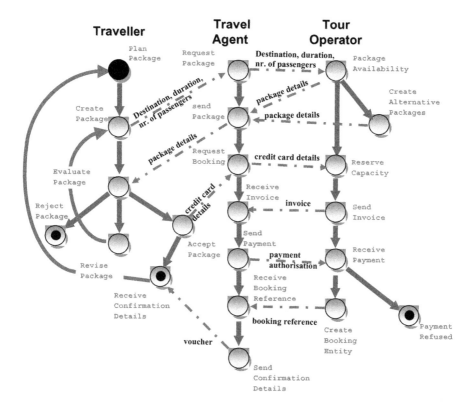

Fig. 1. The *Package Tours/Holiday Bookings* activity diagram.

We use an activity diagram to formally represent this standard business process, Figure 1. Solid arrows in this diagram represent flows of control while dashed arrows represent flow of messages. Each node in the diagram represents an activity. There are three agents whose activities are described: a traveller, a travel agent, and a tour operator. Following the UL convention we use solid filled circles to denote initial states and circles surrounding a small solid circle to denote end states. This formalism allows for cycles shown as outgoing arrows from end states.

In Figure 1, the business process is initiated when a traveller provides the parameters necessary for a holiday package (destination, duration, nr. passengers). This triggers a request activity at some travel agent, which in turn triggers a package availability request from some tour operator. Holiday package related information messages are exchanged until the traveller is able to choose between rejecting, modifying or accepting the package. Potential users (travellers) can come up with requests to book their holidays on the basis of the business process described by this activity diagram. For instance, a traveller may desire to travel to Rome for a specific time frame and may also require a plane ticket and optionally a hotel reservation for exactly the same period of time in the same city and for a given number of accompanying passengers.

Formalizing the OTA specification with an activity diagram is just one of many possible options. Here we are not concerned with which is the best formalism for modeling web-service interactions, rather we are interested in presenting an architecture for interaction with e-marketplace based web-services that is independent from the chosen modeling formalism.

4   Service Planning and Constraint Satisfaction

When users interact with e-marketplace based web-services, ideally they wish to specify only their goals and to obtain the desired results. Consequently, the basic premise of our approach is to equip the user with an expressive service request (goal) language so that he can specify his objectives clearly and unambiguously.

4.1   The Request Language

The services request language, described in this paper, is based on appropriate extensions of a formal planning language for expressing extended goals called *EaGLe* [2]. The *EaGLe* language is an extension of the well-known temporal logic CTL [8]. It inherits from CTL the possibility of declaring properties on the non-deterministic temporal evolutions of a system, and extends it with constructs that are useful for expressing complex planning goals, such as sequencing of goals, and goal preferences. *EaGLe* is defined over a set of activities A and constraint objects C as follows:

- $a(c)$ is a *basic well formed formula* (wff) if $a \in A$ and $c \in C$;
- $\neg a_1(c)$ | $a_1(c) \wedge a_2(c')$ | $a_1(c) \vee a_2(c')$ (c and c' are different constraint objects) and other logical combinations of basic wff are "basic" wff;
- **DoReach** $a_1(c)$|**TryReach** $a_1(c)$|**DoMantain** $a_1(c)$|**TryMantain** $a_1(c)$ are wff iff $a_1(c)$ is a *wff* if $a_1(c)$ is a basic wff;
- g_1 **And** g_2 | g_1 **Then** g_2 | g_1 **Fail** g_2 | **Repeat** g_1 are wff if g_1, g_2 are wff.

In the following we describe the most salient features of the *EaGLe* language (see [2] for a complete description and for the full semantics of the language).

EaGLe allows for expressing conditions that are *vital* to reach or to maintain (e.g.,"(**DoReach** $a(c)$)") or "(**DoMaintain** $a(c)$)", respectively), as well as *optional* or *desired* conditions ("(**TryReach** $a(c)$)" or "(**TryMaintain** $a(c)$)").

Moreover, it allows for expressing *concatenation* of goals (e.g., "$((a_1(c) \vee a_2(c'))$ **Then** $a_3(c''))$" expresses the fact that activity $a_3(c'')$ has to happen after at least one of the activities $a_1(c)$ or $a_2(c')$ has occurred) and for expressing *preferences* between goals (e.g., "**TryReach** $a_1(c)$ **Fail** **DoReach** $a_2(c'))$" expresses the fact that the preferred goal is to achieve activity $a_1(c)$ but that, if this is not possible, then it is vital to achieve at least activity $a_2(c')$.

EaGLe is an expressively rich language to express goals over activities and succession of activities, but it lacks the possibility of expressing quantitative information over individual activities, such as a timeout condition over a given activity. To overcome this limitation, we extend this language with the expressive power of linear constraints [9]. We associate with each activity a constraint object $c \in C$ that is composed of a number of variables that range over different domains and over which one can express linear constraints. More formally, if $c, c' \in C$ are constraint objects, $c.v_1, \ldots c.v_k$ a set of variables associated with the constraint object c, and $D_1, \ldots D_n$ a set of domains equipped with operators, then we allow formulas of three kinds: first, variable declarations $c.v \in D_j$; second, linear constraint within a constraint object c involving variables, operators, and constants defined for D_j such that any two c variables comparing in the same constraint range over the same domain; third, linear constraint across constraint objects c and c' involving c and c' variables, operators and constants defined for D_j such that any two c and c' variables comparing in the same constraint range over the same domain.

The combination of the *EaGLe* with the linear constraint language forms a sound foundation for introducing constructs necessary for a web-services request language (WSRL). This language is used in the first instance for experimentation purposes and we plan to extend its functionality for completeness in the future.

4.2   The Planning Framework

A user can specify a request in terms of the WSRL introduced in the previous section by supplying the destination, duration, and passenger number input parameters required to instantiate the formal business model and rules in Figure 2 and by attaching possible constraints to the request for a holiday package, e.g., flight prices, accommodation preferences, etc. An issue that arises is how to interpret the goal and how to plan an execution sequence that satisfies it. This is the responsibility of the planning framework illustrated in Figure 2. This figure gives a high-level view of the planning framework. In particular, it illustrates that when a user formulates a request in the WSRL this is posed against a formal description of an abstract business model and business rules (top-left), e.g., the activity diagram of Figure 1. The parts of the formalized business process that are related to the user's request are then translated automatically into a state transition graph suitable for direct execution by a planner module. The planner checks whether the request can be satisfied. If the request can be satisfied, it returns a generic (uninstantiated) plan for further processing. If the request cannot be satisfied, then it furnishes an explanation of why the goal failed and prompts for reformulation of the request. Note that, at this level, the planner traverses activity paths along the formalized business process that could satisfy the request but it is not concerned with the values of the constraint objects tied to these activities, e.g., actual ticket prices, destinations and so on. We refer to this type of plan as a *generic plan*.

If there is a succession of activities that may satisfy the goal, then the generic plan is instantiated by interacting with UDDI registered web-services. This results in a number of *instantiated plans* for each generic plan. The instantiated

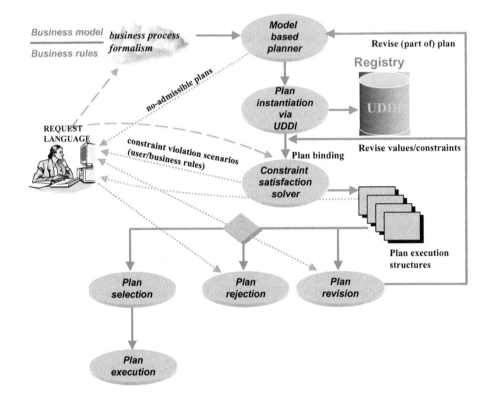

Fig. 2. Approach to planning for web-services.

plans provide values for the user's request such as different flight carrier possibilities, destinations, prices, duration, etc. For each instantiated plan a constraint satisfaction solver is invoked to check whether user specified constraints or web-service provider specified constraints are satisfied. If these constraints can be satisfied then the plan is considered as executable. If they are not, then the user is prompted again with information regarding the constraints that are violated for a particular instantiated plan. Finally, the constraint satisfaction module "approves" the set of *plan execution structures* that are ready for execution. At this point, the user has to make a choice. The user may select one plan from the set of plan execution structures, and commit to its execution. Alternatively, he may reject some or all the plans. The user may even choose to revise fragments of a set of executable plans. This results in a new planning phase at the level of the model based planner.

An experimental system for execution of service request and resulting plans is under construction. We have represented the formal model of the e-travel domain (activity diagram in Figure 1) in terms of NPDDL, a non-deterministic extension of the PDDL (the standard Planning Domain Description Language, see [10]).

The domain description and the goal (request), expressed in the $EaGLe$ language enriched with constraints, was then fed to a Model Based Planning (MBP) software module to check the validity of the generic plan [11]. This is an advanced prototype system for execution of plans that either executes a plan in its entirety or returns an explanation of why the plan failed. Solving the linear constraints of the constraint objects coming both from the user side and from UDDI supplied web-service instances was achieved via ECL^iPSe, a standard constraint satisfaction solver software module [12]. Communication between these two modules is at very preliminary stage, thus input data had to be simulated.

5   Example of Executing a Trip Request

At this stage we revisit the OTA e-travelling example and consider a traveller that wants to travel to a destination in Italy such as Rome, Milan or Venice. This traveller wants to use an airline carrier, leave on the 1st of June and return on the 10th, with two accompanying passengers. These are the destination, duration, and number of passenger input parameters required by the formal business process in Figure 1. The traveller also requires accommodation for the same period of time and the same destination. Furthermore, the traveller finds it vital to have a flight ticket, but would still go even if s/he did not have a hotel reservation. Obviously the passenger does not wish to reserve accommodation without a confirmed flight ticket. In WSRL the request may look as follows:

$$(\textbf{DoReach} \ (\text{Plan\_Package}(\alpha) \wedge \text{Receive\_Confirmation}(\alpha)) \quad \textbf{Then}$$
$$(\textbf{TryReach} \ (\text{Plan\_Package}(\beta) \wedge \text{Receive\_Confirmation}(\beta))))$$

This request can be read as follows: "it is vital (**DoReach**) that I perform the activities in which I plan the package α (fight) and receive a confirmation for it. Once this vital activity is achieved (**Then**), optionally (**TryReach**), I want to plan the package β (hotel reservation) and receive a confirmation for it."

α and β represent a set of constraints over the e-travel domain described in the following:

$$\alpha. \begin{cases} \text{what} & \in \text{Services} \\ \text{arrival date} & \in \text{Dates} \\ \text{departure date} & \in \text{Dates} \\ \text{where} & \in \text{Cities} \\ \text{traveller} & \in I\!N \end{cases} \qquad \beta. \begin{cases} \text{what} & \in \text{Services} \\ \text{arrival date} & \in \text{Dates} \\ \text{departure date} & \in \text{Dates} \\ \text{where} & \in \text{Cities} \end{cases}$$

α.what	$= \{\text{plane\_ticket}\}$	β.what	$= \{\text{hotel}\}$
α.arrival date	$= \{\text{May 1st}\}$	β.arrival date	$= \alpha.\text{arrival date} + 1$
α.departure date	$= \{\text{May 20th}\}$	β.departure date	$= \alpha.\text{departure date} - 1$
α.where	$\in \{\text{Rome,Milan}\}$	β.where	$\in \{\text{Rome,Venice}\}$
α.traveller	$= 3$	β.where	$= \alpha.\text{where}$

In the following we simulate the execution phases of this request in terms of the framework in Figure 2. We make the assumption that initial states generate constraint objects that are then attached to all traversed activities or message links in the activity diagram. The objects are consumed by the end states.

Planning. The e-travelling example of Figure 1 is modeled in NPDDL by describing activities as actions of a non deterministic domain. The NPDDL description together with the goal of the user expressed in WSRL are to the MBP, which returns a plan.

Instantiation via UDDI. The plan returned by the model based planner MBP is instantiated by interacting with the UDDI registry. The same generic plan can be instantiated against various web-service providers.

Constraint satisfaction solver. Subsequently, the constraint objects with declarations and constrains supplied by both the user request and by interactions with the web-services, e.g., that the flight to Rome is not available on 1st June, need to be satisfied. The ECL^iPSesoftware module is used for this purpose. Each instantiated plan that satisfies the constraints is kept as candidate for execution. If there are no solutions to the constraint satisfaction problem, the user gets notified about which constraints are violated.

Plan choice. The output of the previous step is a series of plan execution structures which the user chooses.

6 Concluding Remarks and Future Work

We have presented an architectural framework for web-service interaction based on planning and constraint satisfaction and a service request language developed on the basis of this framework. The design of the planning framework is based on coherent views of the issues arising when planning under uncertainty (as plans inevitably do not execute as expected) in dynamic environments where there is the constant need to be able to identify critical decision trade-offs, revise goals and evaluate alternative options. This framework recognizes that in an uncertain and dynamic world such as that of web-services a correspondence must be drawn between the formal representation of this world and the planer's model of it. Consequently, the planning framework draws a correspondence between the formal representation of a business domain model and the planer's model of it. It then instantiates plans on the basis of the plan model via interaction with the UDDI infrastructure; provides a natural account of why plans are violated; and when necessary dynamically reconfigures plans on basis of user interaction. These design considerations are reflected at the level of the request language that generates plans over web-services residing in an e-marketplace.

We have given full semantics of the constructs of the WSRL that subsume the planning composition language we proposed in [3]. There we introduced constructs at the systems-level to support web-service composition, whereas the WSRL includes constructs such as alternative activities, vital vs. optional activities, preconditions, postconditions, invariants, and constraint operators over quantitative values that can be employed at the user-level when formulating a goal. The novelty of this approach lies in the automatic generation and verification of plans over web-services residing in an e-marketplace once a user request is concretely expressed and formally specified. This framework provides generality and flexibility and can be used as a basis for effective planning for different types of applications dealing with interacting web-services.

A preliminary implementation of the ideas mentioned in this paper has been constructed (as explained in section 4.2) and further tests are underway. A number of issues remain open for future investigation. First, activity diagrams are not expressive enough to model complex web-service interactions. For instance, they lack the ability of expressing cardinality constraints (such as that there are many travel agents for each traveller, or that there is exactly one payment for one e-voucher). Second, the integration between the *EaGLe* section and the constraint section of the WSRL is at an experimental stage and needs to be improved in order to be able to obtain more expressive plans. Furthermore, constraint formalisms especially tailored at electronic commerce can be used in place of linear constraints such as dynamic constraints [13].

References

1. OTA Open Travel Alliance. 2001C spec., 2001. http://www.opentravel.org.
2. U. Dal Lago, M. Pistore, and P. Traverso. Planning with a language for extended goals. In *18th National Conference on Artificial Intelligence (AAAI-02)*, 2002.
3. J. Yang and M. Papazoglou. Web component: A substrate for web service reuse and composition. In *14th Int. Conf. on Advanced Information Systems Engineering CAiSE02*, 2002.
4. S. Smith, D. Hildum, and D.R. Crimm. Toward the design of web-based planning and scheduling services. In *Int. Workshop on Automated Planning and Scheduling Technologies in New Methods of Electronic, Mobile and Collaborative Work*, 2001.
5. D. McDermott. Estimated-regression planning for interactions with Web Services. In *6th Int. Conf. on AI Planning and Scheduling*. AAAI Press, 2002.
6. C. A. Knoblock, S. Minton, J. L. Ambite, N. Ashish, I. Muslea, A. G. Philpot, and S. Tejada. The ariadne approach to web-based information integration. *International the Journal on Cooperative Information Systems*, 2002. Special Issue on Intelligent Information Agents: Theory and Applications, Forthcoming.
7. C. A. Knoblock, K. Lerman, S. Minton, and I. Muslea. Accurately and reliably extracting data from the web: A machine learning approach. *Data Engineering Bulletin*, 2002. To appear.
8. E. A. Emerson. Temporal and modal logic. In J. van Leeuwen, editor, *Handbook of Theoretical Computer Science, Volume B*. Elsevier, 1990.
9. P. Van Hentenryck and V.J. Saraswat, editors. *Principles and Practice of Constraint Programming*. MIT Press, 1995.
10. M. Ghallab, A. Howe, C. Knoblock, D. McDermott, A. Ram, M. Veloso, D. Weld, and D. Wilkins. PDDL—The Planning Domain Definition Language. In R. Simmons, M. Veloso, and S. Smith, editors, *Int. Conf. AIPS98*, 1998.
11. P. Bertoli, A. Cimatti, M. Pistore, M. Roveri, and P. Traverso. MBP: A Model Based Planner. In *n Proc. IJCAI'01 Workshop on Planning under Uncertainty and Incomplete Information*, 2001.
12. ECLIPSE. Eclipse Constraint Logic Programming System, 2002. http://www-icparc.doc.ic.ac.uk/eclipse.
13. M. Iwaihara. Supporting dynamic constraints for commerce negotiations. In *WECWIS 2000*. IEEE, 2000.

Communication Flow Expressions in a Notification and Response System

Joann J. Ordille[1] and Thomas Petsche[2]

[1]Avaya Labs, 233 Mount Airy Road, Basking Ridge, NJ 07920
joann@research.avayalabs.com
[2]Avaya, 211 Mount Airy Road, Basking Ridge, NJ 07920
petsche@avaya.com

Abstract. We introduce communication flow expressions (CFEs), a general technique for specifying the who, how, when and where of communication. CFEs use a three-value logic including some new logical primitives that are useful in supporting communication. CFEs integrate the communication requirements of applications with the communication preferences of users. We describe the first application of CFEs in the Avaya Xui Notification and Response System.

1   Introduction

Techniques exist for specifying data flow, work flow or program flow, but mostly rudimentary techniques have been available for specifying communication flow. Oftentimes these rudimentary techniques equate specifying a recipient for a request with some method of contact such as sending email to a mailbox or a message to a pager. *Communication flow expressions (CFEs)* provide a more general technique for specifying the who, how, when and where of communication. Communication flow expressions specify the recipients for a request and how, when and where the recipients receive the request. They obey the preferences of the recipients for receiving communication. Communication flow expressions also specify what action to take when a particular recipient fails to respond successfully to a request.

Enterprise applications need to contact people. They have requirements for how the contact is done and what responses, if any, are collected. For example, an application may search sequentially for a manager to approve an exception to normal processing procedures for a customer. Another application may need to search in parallel for one expert to answer a question, or an entire team to perform emergency surgery. Applications may need to contact someone immediately in a crisis or they may want to remind someone of a task at an appropriate later time. Enterprise applications also have requirements about what to do when the contact is unsuccessful where success is something that they define themselves. For example, if an emergency team is not assembled, the application may transfer the patient to another hospital.

Recipients, on the other hand, have preferences about how and when they are contacted. For example, they may want particular people (e.g. a boss or family member) or people who represent particular interests (e.g. an executive from a Fortune 500

A. Buchmann et al. (Eds.): TES 2002, LNCS 2444, pp. 86-96, 2002.
© Springer-Verlag Berlin Heidelberg 2002

Company) to be given more flexibility in establishing real-time contact. Recipients may routinely delay contact about known tasks (e.g. weekly status or expense updates) until a convenient time or place. Oftentimes, the preferences of recipients are at odds with the implementation of a specific application. In those cases, recipients find creative work-arounds for satisfying their preferences, or find their enterprise's processes frustrating or even annoying.

Communication flow expressions capture and combine the requirements of applications and preferences of recipients. Communication flow expressions are active recipient lists. Each recipient is active, because recipients provide rules that replace their name in the communication flow with further details about when, where and how to contact them. The rules allow recipients to incorporate their personal communication flow into the communication flow expression for the request. Recipients can use the rules to pick different personal communication flows based on characteristics of the sender, the topic of the request or the demands of their schedule.

Communication flow expressions support notification requests that require minimal acknowledgements from the recipients as well as notification and response requests that require actions by the recipients with application-defined criteria for success. Communication flow expressions support contacting recipients via a variety of communication devices, such as cell phones, pagers, fax, email, wired phones and web applications. Since recipients are active in the communication flow, the flow responds to changes in the place and schedule of the recipient.

The Avaya Xui Notification and Response System is a low cost "any medium" notification and response system that enables communication for business applications quickly without changing the communications infrastructure or the applications. "Xui" is pronounced "Zoo-ey" and is derived from the notion that, since a GUI is a graphical user interface and a TUI is a telephone user interface, then an interface that can run on a variety of endpoints must be an xUI. The Avaya Xui is the first application of communication flow expressions.

2   Communication Flows

A communication flow is the path of a request from requester to recipients. Although we often think of this path as a simple connection between two parties, modern communication capabilities enable a variety of communication flows. Flows can contact recipients or devices used by a recipient in parallel or sequentially. Flows can wait for all recipients or just some of the recipients to respond to a request. They can take a different direction when a communication error occurs.

Communication flows are characterized by communication flow expressions, success specifications, and rules for specifying personal preferences. *Communication flow expressions* specify to whom, when, where and how to deliver a request. They also specify what to do when failures occur.

A novel feature of communication flow expressions is how they deal with failures. Failures occur for two reasons. First, there may simply be a failure to contact a recipient or a recipient may never respond to a notification. We call this case *notification failure* and the inverse *notification success*. Second, the recipient may be contacted and subsequently reject the request or answer it negatively. We call this case *response failure (saying "no")* and the inverse *response success (saying "yes")*. "No" and "yes" have a semantic component, because it is only the application that can determine whether or not the recipient has acceptably responded (said "yes") to a request for the purposes of continuing the communication flow.   For example, response success may occur when a recipient reviews a document and votes against its acceptance. The recipient has said, "Yes, I am done with the review," and the communication flow continues with the next reviewer. On the other hand, response failure may occur when a recipient reviews and rejects a request for a software revision. The recipient has said "No, we will not do this software revision," and the communication flow ends or continues with error processing.

Communication flow expressions are evaluated using a three-value logic. Notification failure (*maybe*), response failure (*false*) and response success (*true*) are the three values of the logic. Notification success is a transitory state that occurs before response success or response failure, so it is not represented directly. With many devices, it is only possible to know that a notification has been received when a response from the recipient is received.

An example suffices to show the benefits of the three-value logic used in communication flow expressions over a two-value logic. Suppose one wants to ask Joann to join a committee. If Joann refuses, Priya is to be asked instead. Using the simple two-value logic primitive *ELSE*, we get: (Joann ELSE Priya). Now suppose further that Joann uses the same logic to specify that she prefers to be contacted via cell phone, or if that fails via office phone, or if that fails to delegate the request to Jerry: (cell ELSE office ELSE Jerry). Problems are inherent in this formulation, because the requester undoubtedly wants to contact Priya based on the outcome of an actual response from Joann, and Joann only wants Jerry contacted if she fails to respond – not if she responds with no. It is impossible to get all these outcomes from the two-value logic. In our three-valued logic, Priya is only contacted if Joann says "No," and Jerry is contacted only if Joann fails to respond. We return to this example after describing our communication primitives in the next section.

Communication flow success specifications describe the conditions for response success and failure at each step in the communication flow. They support both a system-wide default success specification and a requester-defined success specification default for a particular communication flow. Alternatively, a requester can specify the success specification for each recipient in the communication flow using the Test Response Status Primitive described in Section 3.2.

3   Communication Flow Expressions

Communication flow expressions provide a flexible, general technique for specifying recipients for a request and how to direct communication in response to their replies. A recipient can be a sub-expression, a role ("Customer Service"), a person ("Jerry"), a device ("800-555-1234") or a program or agent ("My Calendar").

Primitives direct the flow of requests to recipients. Central to the communication flow expressions are primitives that combine directions for parallel or sequential communication with an evaluation of how the status of communication with a recipient affects the communication flow. Other primitives control when contact is made.

3.1   Parallel and Sequential Primitives

The following primitives can naturally be grouped into parallel/sequential pairs: AND/THEN, OR/ELSE, RACES/DELEGATES, and VOTES/POLLS. Parallel and sequential primitives differ in how the operands are evaluated. In parallel primitives, each recipient is contacted in parallel. Outstanding requests are canceled when they are no longer necessary to determine the truth value of the primitive. In sequential primitives, requests are made to each recipient in the order that they appear. When that recipient responds, a request is sent to the next recipient if necessary to determine the truth value of the primitive. Each primitive evaluates to true, false or maybe depending on the success of the communication with the recipients.

AND specifies that two recipients are contacted in parallel, and that the communication flow is successful (evaluates to true) when both recipients respond with success. If the request to one of the recipients fails, the AND evaluates to false and the request to the other recipient is cancelled if possible. In all other cases, the AND evaluates to maybe.

THEN is the sequential form of AND, that is, the recipients are contacted one at a time in the order they appear and the second recipient is contacted only if the first recipient responds with success. When the first operand returns maybe, the second operand is NOT evaluated in the case of the THEN primitive and the truth value of the THEN primitive remains maybe. This choice was made for THEN to provide a more natural semantic interpretation. In the case of the AND primitive, the second operand is evaluated and the primitive returns false if the second operand returns false.

OR specifies that two recipients are contacted in parallel, and that the communication flow is successful (evaluates to true) if at least one recipient responds with success. If both recipients respond negatively, then the primitive evaluates to false. In all other cases, the primitive evaluates to maybe. ELSE is the sequential form of OR such that the second recipient is contacted only if the first response is not successful.

The AND/THEN, OR/ELSE primitives are all focused on contacting enough recipients to determine the success or failure of a communication flow expression. Sometimes, it is also useful to accept the first of many possible responses. This is not possible with the existing primitives, because they count votes until success is achieved or made impossible. The parallel primitive RACES succeeds or fails according to the status of the first of its operands to respond. If the first respondent succeeds, RACES succeeds. If the first respondent fails, RACES fails. The request to the second respondent is cancelled if possible. For example,

```
Cell RACES Office RACES Email RACES Web
```

succeeds or fails according to the first response received from a recipient via any of the following media contacts: cell phone, office phone, email or web portal.

Unlike the other primitives discussed, RACES provides equal weight to a success or a failure response from one operand. AND/THEN responds immediately to the failure of an operand, but waits for results from both operands before returning success. OR/ELSE responds immediately to the success of an operand, but waits for both operands before returning failure. RACES responds immediately to the first response from an operand, and returns the result of that operand. It is particularly useful, as shown in the above example, for contacting an individual via multiple devices and allowing the individual to answer the request with success or failure via just one of those devices. RACES cannot be specified by the other primitives. DELEGATES is the sequential form of RACES. DELEGATES only evaluates the right operand if the left operand returns notification failure (maybe).

Returning to the example in Section 2, Joann can specify her preferences as:

```
cell DELEGATES office DELEGATES Jerry
```

while the generator of the request specifies:

```
Joann ELSE Priya
```

Jerry only responds if Joann fails to respond. Priya is only contacted if Joann or Jerry, when Joann is unavailable, says "No."

It is possible to generalize the sequential and parallel communication flow primitives for lists of recipients. The parallel and sequential forms of the AND/OR primitives are special cases of two more general primitives that allow parallel or sequential voting by a list of recipients. For example, the successful AND primitives are votes by two recipients where 100% vote yes, and successful OR primitives are votes by two recipients where at least 50% vote yes.

VOTES contacts a list of recipients in parallel and returns success (true) if a count or percentage of success responses is reached. Each recipient can be a communication flow expression, and the count or percentage represents the number of successes that must be received for the VOTES to succeed. For example,

```
{Tom, Joann, Jerry} VOTES 50%
```

contacts Tom, Joann and Jerry in parallel. If at least two respond with success, VOTES results in success.

VOTES fails (returns false) when enough recipients return false responses to prevent the specified count or percentage from being reached. In the other cases where success cannot be reached, VOTES results in maybe. In the above example, if at least two of Tom, Joann and Jerry respond with failure, VOTES results in failure. On the other hand, a true, a false and a maybe results in a truth value of maybe. POLLS is the sequential form of VOTES.[1]

3.2   Status Interpretation and Temporal Primitives

The success of a request to a recipient involves notification success and response success. Notification success occurs when the recipient is contacted successfully. Response success, by default, occurs when a recipient responds in a way that satisfies the definition of success for the application. For the Avaya Xui web API, the default for response success is to reply to a web form without including the value of "false" or "no" for the submit button. A "false" or "no" for the submit button is the default response for response failure.

Some applications may require an application specific definition of response success. For example, an application requests a credit line increase for a customer from

---

[1] Note that VOTES/POLLS follows the truth table of THEN (rather than the truth table of AND) when one of two operands returns maybe.

several banks in parallel. Success is defined as the approval of at least a $10,000 increase in the customer's credit line.

The Test Response Status primitive allows applications to provide a response success specification as a logical expression of comparisons of attribute-value pairs from the response. The logical expression is specified between question marks after the recipient whose response is to be tested. The comparisons can include equality, inequality, range and regular expression matching. In cases where the success specification is the same for all recipients in a communication flow, but different from the system default, a request-wide default can be supplied. When the primitive is applied to expressions containing multiple recipients or subexpressions, it is applied to each recipient in the more complicated expression.

The following CFE specifies the response success status for the example above without using the default facility:

```
Bank1? (credit_increase >= $10,000) and
(status="approved") ? OR Bank2? (credit_increase >=
$10,000) and (status="approved") ? OR Bank3?
(credit_increase >= $10,000) and (status="approved") ?
```

This can be shortened to:

```
(Bank1 OR Bank2 OR Bank3)? (credit_increase >= $10,000)
and (status="approved") ?
```

The first bank to approve at least a $10,000 increase completes the request with the CFE value of true. Outstanding requests to the other banks are canceled.

An interesting area for future work allows success specifications to perform aggregation and other advanced processing on the attributes of the response and then test the results for success or failure.

In addition to the primitive that tests the response status, the BETWEEN, BEFORE and AFTER primitives specify that the request is to be sent to the recipient during some time interval. The temporal interval can specify times of the day, absolute dates and times, dates and times relative to the current time, e.g. +05:00 hours, days of the week, or daily, weekly, monthly, or yearly intervals.

Multiple temporal constraint primitives can be associated with a recipient. In that case, the largest temporal interval satisfying all the primitives is used. For example,

```
Joann BETWEEN 08:00-17:00 BETWEEN 14:00-19:00
```

is equivalent to

```
Joann BETWEEN 14:00-17:00
```

When a temporal constraint primitive is applied to expressions containing multiple recipients or subexpressions, it is applied to each recipient in the more complicated expression.

4   Personal Preferences

Recipients can specify rules for how to translate their name in a communication flow to a personal communication flow expression. Recipients can specify conditions on attributes of the request, such as the title and requester attributes, to control which personal communication flow expression is used for a particular request. For example, recipients can choose certain topics, as they are expressed in the title, or requesters for immediate attention via cell phone. They can choose other kinds of requests for later attention via email or the web.

5   Avaya Xui Notification and Response System

The Avaya Xui Notification and Response System is the first application of communication flow expressions. The Xui is a system that delivers notifications and accepts responses to a recipient via any user interface (TUI, GUI, etc., hence xUI). It is a low cost "any medium" notification and response system. Most other systems are limited in media and function (e.g., they only send email notifications to a cell phone or pager). While systems are beginning to appear that send notifications and collect some limited forms for responses via different media, e.g. Attention! [1], we do not know of another system with the power of the Xui to collect, understand and process responses. The Xui system enables communication for business processes quickly without changing the communications infrastructure.

Applications submit requests to the Xui in a single format and receive responses in a single format. They do not need to know which media will be used for communication. The communication flow is adapted to the device or devices available. Senders use communication flow expressions to specify who to contact and when to contact them. Recipients specify rules for refining communication flow expressions with details of how, i.e. which devices to use, and when to contact them.

Fig. 1 depicts the Xui Notification and Response System. An application submits a request to the Xui via an interface-specific application program interface (API) such as a web or a unified messaging interface. Each application interface provides services for submitting or canceling a request and returning results. These services update lists of pending and completed requests in the Xui Request Manager.

The Xui Request Manager uses the communication flow expression services of the Communication Flow Manager to determine how to deliver the request to the appropriate recipients and to determine how to respond to the success or failure of each communication attempt. The Communication Flow Manager contacts the directory system to obtain information about recipients, their preferences and the devices to be used in contacting the recipients. The Xui Request Manager follows the directions of the communication flow in performing each media specific communication with a recipient. If contact via a particular medium cannot be made after a specifiable duration or number of attempts, an error is returned to the Xui Request Manager.

The Xui mediates all requests to the recipients specified in the communication flow expression. This allows the Xui to record responses, communicate those responses to the Communication Flow Manager, and through the Communication Flow Manager to take different paths through the communication flow based on the differing content of those responses. In the case of the Xui web API, all requests are represented as web pages and those requiring responses include forms for accepting the response. The requests are rewritten to direct responses to a URL on the Xui web server, so completion status can be recorded before being rerouted to its final destination. This final destination is the originally designated receiver of the POST on the web form. The routing and return processing of the Xui can be adapted to various methods of specifying requests and responses, such as those in unified messaging systems [2] or XML-based APIs [3].

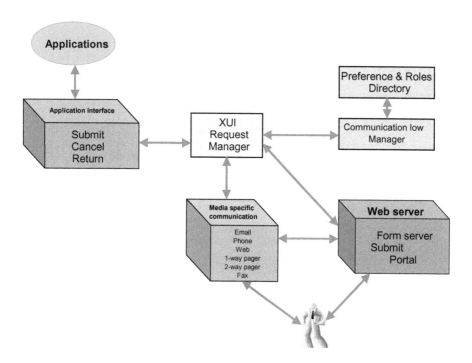

Fig. 1. The Avaya Xui Notification and Response System includes an API, a Request Manager, media-specific methods for communicating with recipients, a web server for handling submissions of request responses, and a Communications Flow Manager which interprets communication flow expressions with the recipient, rule and communication flow information from a directory system.

5.1 Sample Application

The Communication Flow Manager and the Xui Notification and Response System provide a powerful framework for building applications. One of the first applications we built, called *Xui Request Submission*, allows a requester to ask a question, specify the types of response desired, and receive a collated set of responses from recipients via email. A simple extension of this application would use the Xui facilities to forward the collated response to the requester via his/her personal communication flow.

Figure 2 shows the form for making a request via the Xui Request Submission application. Joann is sending a request to schedule a meeting to YangQian and Petsche. If they agree to the meeting time and place, then the request is forwarded to their manager to see if he can also attend. The generated request is sent to recipients via different media contacts as appropriate. It includes a yes button and a no button for answering the request. Figure 2 also shows the compiled results of the request. Petsche could attend the meeting but YangQian could not, so their manager was not contacted.

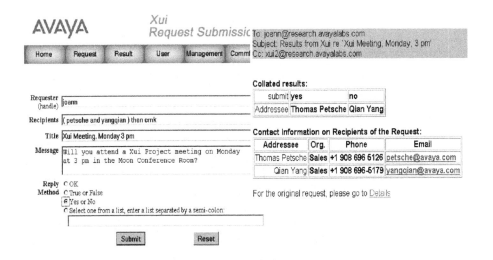

Fig. 2. The Xui Request Submission Application accepts a request to schedule a meeting on the left and reports the collated results of the request to the requester in email on the right.

In another example, the requester offers shares of stock in block allotments on the IPO of a new company to preferred customers for a 2-hour period. Temporal constraints are applied to a named communication flow, PreferredCustomers. Preferred-Customers translates to a parallel conjunction of recipients. The requester provides a series of options in the request to his/her best customers, see the request submission form in Figure 3. The email version of the request is shown on the right in Figure 3. Collated responses are returned as soon as all recipients respond or the 2-hour period of the offer expires. If a recipient fails to respond in the 2-hour period and then attempts to view or respond to the request, an appropriate message is displayed and the reply is neither solicited nor accepted.

Other applications are also in development. For example, XuiTalks announces talks to an organization, and reminds recipients periodically unless they respond that additional reminders are unnecessary. XuiExpert sends requests for information to appropriate experts in parallel and cancels outstanding requests once an answer is received.

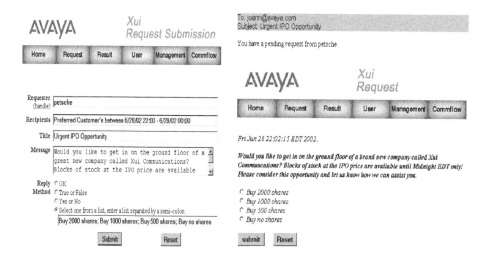

Fig. 3. The Xui Request Submission Application accepts a request to purchase stock in an IPO on the left and delivers 1the request to a recipient via email on the right.

6   Related Work

The growth of wireless services, such as using WAP [4] to push and receive responses to web forms on cell phones, has created a plethora of notification and response services that only contact one device. Communication flow expressions automate the preference-based selection of devices, and the Avaya Xui automates the media translation across multiple types of devices.

The Session Initiation Protocol [5] provides a registry where users can be associated with particular devices by registering a SIP Uniform Resource Locator (URL) for the device. A number of SIP proxies exist the support the ability to contact the list of URLs recorded in the registry for a given user in parallel or sequentially to establish communication with the user. Communication flow expressions provide more sophisticated parallel and sequential processing which take into consideration the results of a communication, and will work with both SIP and with other protocols for establishing a communication path.

Cardelli and Davies provide service combinators for accessing content on the web where each access succeeds by returning content or fails for some reason [6]. Communication flow expressions and service combinators naturally differ, because they address the needs of different application domains. They have interesting similarities, because they both provide vehicles for experimenting with models of high level communication services. Service combinators support parallel and sequential access similar to a two-valued version of the CFE OR/ELSE primitives. CFEs provide a three-valued logic and more options for parallel and sequential processing including some new logical primitives. Service combinators provide an interesting treatment of failures due to inadequate quality of service to address real-time response issues inherent in interactive retrieval of web content.

7   Conclusions

The speed, flexibility and power of communication flow expressions and the Avaya Xui in building applications has impressed us. Generating applications has been very quick, less than a day in most cases. The system has also proved to be a fruitful model for discovering new communication flow primitives and services.

References

1. Attention Software, Attention!, http://www.attentionsoftware.com/.
2. Rosenberg and Zimmer, "Unified Messaging/Communication," The Unified View, http://www.unified-msg.com/, July 2001.
3. World-Wide Web Consortium (W3C), "Extensible Markup Language (XML) 1.0, 2nd edition, T. Bray and others, editors, W3C, October 2000.
4. WAP Forum, "Wireless Access Protocol 1.2.1," June 2000.
5. Handley, M., H. Schulzrinne, E. Schooler, and J. Rosenberg, "SIP: Session Initiation Protocol," RFC 2543, March 1999.
6. Cardelli, L. and R. Davies, "Service Combinators for Web Computing," IEEE Transactions on Software Engineering, Vol. 25, No. 3, May-June 1999, pp. 309-316.

A Coverage-Determination Mechanism for Checking Business Contracts against Organizational Policies

Alan S. Abrahams, David M. Eyers, and Jean M. Bacon

Computer Laboratory
University of Cambridge
{Alan.Abrahams, David.Eyers, Jean.Bacon}@cl.cam.ac.uk

Abstract. The EDEE system provides a framework through which businesses may store the data pertaining to business events, contracts and organizational policies, within a single repository using the unifying notion of an occurrence. A collection of stored queries (cf. SQL views) is maintained. Each query describes the occurrences promised and prohibited under the provisions of the contracts and policies of an organization. This paper proposes a mechanism for both the static and dynamic derivation of the overlaps between queries. We show, through worked examples, that by determining these covering relationships we can discover inconsistencies between business contracts and organizational policies.

1 Introduction

Prudent business enterprises operating in e-service environments need to check proposed business contracts against their organizational rules, to ensure that their intentions do not violate internal regulations. The E-commerce application Development and Execution Environment, or EDEE, system [2] unifies storage of data pertaining to real business events, prospective actions and business policy through the notion of occurrences and queries over these occurrences.

In this paper, we propose a framework for storing contracts and policies, and for checking their consistency. We view both contracts and policies as sets of provisions. A provision specifies a promise, prohibition, permission or power; only the former two are demonstrated in this paper. Each provision embeds a query which describes the promised or prohibited occurrences. Our system facilitates dynamic addition of provisions, and through automatic derivation of overlaps between stored queries, can ascertain conflicts.

The notions of covering relationships between queries, and dirtying relationships between data and queries, are used to find run-time overlaps. We say that a query is *covered* by another stored query if the results of the former are a subset of the results of the latter for any data-set. Some questions of coverage are decidable statically, but others depend on application semantics: some covering relations change when new data is added, in a context-specific manner. We say a query is *dirtied* by new data (*input dirt*) if the new data changes a *criterion* (cf.

A. Buchmann et al. (Eds.): TES 2002, LNCS 2444, pp. 97–106, 2002.
© Springer-Verlag Berlin Heidelberg 2002

text of a WHERE clause in an SQL SELECT statement) of the query. For example, upon the addition of the new supplier, Steelmans, to the database, the query 'payments to **suppliers**' is dirtied as the results must now also include any 'payments to **Steelmans**'. Any such payments would be what we term *output dirt*. The materialized view literature [9] talks of dirt in the sense of our output dirt. Whereas materialized views would only change when any actual payments to Steelmans were added, covering relationships may change even in the absence of any payments stored in the database.

This paper shows how conflicts may be detected at the time contracts are added to the database, or when inserted data dirties queries and thus brings provisions into conflict. The example we present shows that a potential conflict between a promise to pay and a prohibition against a particular type of payment can be flagged as soon as the *promise* is entered, rather than merely at the time of payment. This conflict might be resolved by breaking the promise, violating the prohibition, or voiding one or both. Such conflict resolution is treated in [1].

2   Related Work

Current contract-driven inter-enterprise workflow architectures, such as COS-MOS [12] and CrossFlow [11] focus on service advertisement and invocation, but do not ascertain consistency between contractual terms and business policies. Initiatives such as the OASIS ebXML Collaboration Protocol Profile (CPP) and Agreement (CPA) specifications [7] again provide service advertisement and conformance-checking framework specification for the negotiation of organizational inter-operation. CPAs capture the technology-specific parameters agreed by parties. These include message formats (e.g. OBI), encryption techniques (e.g. SSL), and communication protocols (e.g. HTTP). There is no notion of the rights and duties of the parties, nor any provision for fulfillment monitoring. CPAs define specific business process arrangements, rather than a framework for managing the potentially conflicting policy sources which may govern a single business entity.

Previous contract assessment approaches, such as [4,6], apply Petri Nets or Finite State machines to determine contract status. Contracts are reduced to directed graphs that capture the business procedure, but leave provisions implicit. To allow inspection and analysis, provisions need to be explicitly captured within the business database. Explicit storage of provisions can then be exploited for consistency checking, contract performance assessment, and management review of which provisions pertain to items or occurrences. The goal of the OASIS Provisioning Technical Committee [5] is to propose standards for service provisioning. Their notion of a 'provision' is in the sense of 'providing resources'; the intention is to facilitate resource allocation by setting up, amending, and revoking system access rights (cf. access control policies) to electronic services. This can be contrasted to the normative, contractual sense of 'provision', which specifies desirable and undesirable situations in terms of conventions for interpreting various happenings, and attitudes towards the conventionally described occurrences. By dividing the problem into specifying inter-operation between separate provisioning systems, and specifying inter-operation between a provisioning system and its managed resources, they do not focus on the introspection required within any given provision management system to manage conflict situations.

It is instructive to contrast EDEE with traditional expert systems approaches to business logic. The occurrence database is the working memory of the system; production rules in EDEE are maintained in a list of queries over this database. These queries are explicitly stored criteria describing sets of items and occurrences. As such, they are more similar to SQL views, than to the throw-away queries executed by an SQL engine.

The EDEEQL extension of SQL [2] leads to an occurrence structure with a simple tabular form able to store business events and provisions of contracts and policies. It avoids the need to specify schemas explicitly for each occurrence class, thus increasing the dynamic configurability of the system. This particular storage approach has been chosen for semantic rather than performance reasons. The representation allows us to determine when parties participate in the same occurrence, but unlike full graph-based representations (for example, the Hydra database system [3]), we cannot directly locate more distant associations.

An underlying database system manages storage and retrieval of occurrences and queries. The coverage checking mechanism proposed in this paper optimizes the execution of these stored queries. Due to the common goal of incremental state re-computation, it has many similarities to the RETE [8] and TREAT [13] expert system optimization algorithms. The most striking difference is that our approach places an emphasis on dynamic compilation and analysis of coverage. This allows us to go beyond the fact/pattern matching in RETE and TREAT to also perform pattern/pattern matches as well.

3   Application Scenario

We introduce an application scenario, describe how operational data, provisions and queries are stored, then illustrate via a worked example how conflicts between provisions and internal regulations are determined.

In our scenario, SkyHi Builders is a construction company. Steelmans Warehouse a supplier of high-grade steel. SkyHi, having recently won a tender to build a new office block, enters into a contract with Steelmans. We select a hypothetical clause from this contract, **Clause C.1** SkyHi promises to pay Steelmans £25,000, and a clause from the SkyHi's risk management procedures (i.e. internal policy), **Clause P.3** Payments of more than £10,000 to suppliers are prohibited.

3.1   Storing Operational Data

Let us say SkyHi, a customer of Steelmans, has paid Steelmans £25,000 for a specific shipment. Let `being_supplier1` and `paying1` denote instances (hence the 1 added to create a unique identifier) of occurrences of type *being a supplier* and *paying* respectively. Table 1 shows the occurrence, role, participant schema

Table 1. A tabular schema for storing various occurrences

Commentary	Occurrence	Role	Participant
Steelmans *being a supplier* for SkyHi	being_supplier1	supplier	Steelmans
		supplied	SkyHi
SkyHi *paid* £25,000 to Steelmans	paying1	payer	SkyHi
		paid_amount	£25,000
		payee	Steelmans

Table 2. Schemas for storing prohibitions and promises

Occurrence	Role	Participant
prohibiting1	prohibited	Query10
promising1	promised	Query19

(Query10 = occurrences of paying with over £10,000 in role paid ∩
occurrences of paying with a supplier in role payee. See figure 1),
(Query19 = first occurrence of SkyHi paying Steelmans £25,000. See figure 2)

employed in EDEE to store this operational data. For readability we have included values like `Steelmans` in our tables instead of foreign key references. Similarly we show occurrence primary keys in forms such as `being_supplier1`, instead of foreign key references into a table describing the occurrence type (`being_supplier`). Finally we omit repeated key values in adjacent rows.

3.2   Storing Provisions of Contracts and Policies

To store contractual provisions – e.g. "X *prohibits* that [Y be paid]" and "X *promises* that [X pay Y]" – in a relational database we need to handle their embedded propositional content [2,10].

Consider Clause P.3 from the application scenario presented above. Clearly, we cannot store simply "Steelmans prohibits [paying1]" because paying1 is a concrete instance and might not yet have occurred anyway. We instead store the prohibition as `prohibiting1` in Table 2, and indicate the prohibited occurrences using a pointer to a database view (query) describing the set of prohibited occurrences, which is `query10` in Figure 1. Note that this query would be empty in the case that no prohibited occurrences exist.

Similarly, the promise in Clause C.1 of our scenario cannot be stored via "SkyHi promises paying1", because we need to store a description of a payment. The promise is thus stored as `promising1` in Table 2 with the promised occurrence represented by the pointer to `query19` in Figure 2. `Query19` asks for the *first* payment since it is exactly one payment that is promised. It may be empty in cases where the promise is broken or voided and no payments are made.

Storing provisions therefore requires the storage of views or queries which describe the promised or prohibited occurrences. Conflicts can be detected from

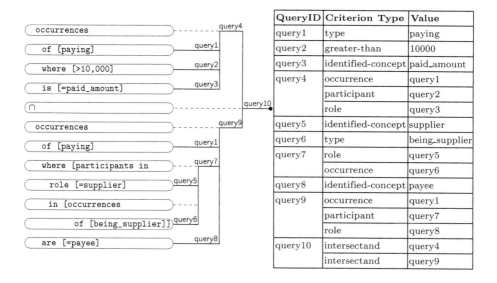

QueryID	Criterion Type	Value
query1	type	paying
query2	greater-than	10000
query3	identified-concept	paid_amount
query4	occurrence	query1
	participant	query2
	role	query3
query5	identified-concept	supplier
query6	type	being_supplier
query7	role	query5
	occurrence	query6
query8	identified-concept	payee
query9	occurrence	query1
	participant	query7
	role	query8
query10	intersectand	query4
	intersectand	query9

Fig. 1. Parse tree and storage schema for query that returns all occurrences where more than £10,000 is paid to a supplier

the overlaps between these stored descriptions. The next section describes how the semantics of a query may be stored in a database.

3.3   Storing Queries

To make queries that return occurrences more concise, we use our own language, EDEEQL[2]. Queries may be stored in occurrence-role-participant tabular form by assigning a query-identifier for each criterion's occurrence entry, and storing its type and value in the role and participant columns respectively. The criterion-value may be constant or a reference to an embedded query. The EDEEQL parser takes the textual form of the query and converts it to its tabular semantic form.

Take for example the query that returns all occurrences where more than £10,000 is paid to a supplier (query10, in the Participant column, for the row with prohibiting1, in Table 2 above). Figure 1 illustrates the parse tree for query10, and shows its nested sub-queries (Currency representation is omitted for simplicity). The second query we need to store is "select the first payment of £25,000 by SkyHi to Steelmans" (Query19 in the Participant column, for the row with promising1, in Table 2 above). The complete parse tree for this query, excluding the repeated query sub-expressions shown earlier, is given in Figure 2. Storing queries explicitly is helpful for finding covering-queries since we can analytically determine which queries, among a large number of stored queries, cover a certain item or query. We describe the mechanism for finding covering-queries, in the next section.

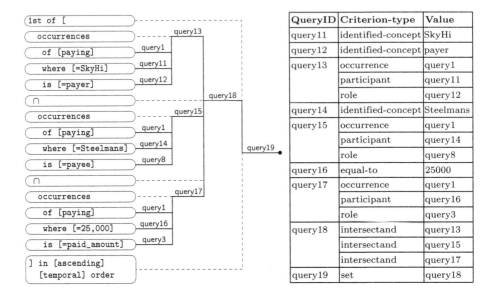

QueryID	Criterion-type	Value
query11	identified-concept	SkyHi
query12	identified-concept	payer
query13	occurrence	query1
	participant	query11
	role	query12
query14	identified-concept	Steelmans
query15	occurrence	query1
	participant	query14
	role	query8
query16	equal-to	25000
query17	occurrence	query1
	participant	query16
	role	query3
query18	intersectand	query13
	intersectand	query15
	intersectand	query17
query19	set	query18

Fig. 2. Parse tree and storage schema for query that returns the first payment of £25,000 by SkyHi to Steelmans

4   Finding Overlapping and Inconsistent Provisions

Assume a prohibition, `prohibiting1`, and the associated query describing the prohibited occurrences are stored in an empty database as shown in Table 2 and Figure 1. We then record that Steelmans is a supplier of SkyHi by inserting the occurrence, `being_supplier1`, as described in Table 1 (assume the payment, `paying1`, is not ever inserted). Upon insertion, the coverage-checking algorithm examines each of the unique items `Steelmans`, `being_supplier1`, `supplier`, `SkyHi`, and `supplied` in the set of triples added for this occurrence[1]:

1. **By Rule 4** item `supplier` is covered by the query `[=supplier]`.
2. **By Rule 1** item `being_supplier1` is covered by the query `occurrences of [being_supplier]`.
3. **By Rule 9** queries `[=supplier]` and `occurrences of [being_supplier]` dirty the query `[participants in role [=supplier] in occurrences of [being_supplier]]`. Substitution of the input dirt for the dirtied criteria (shown <u>underlined</u>) yields the partial re-evaluation query: `[participants in role [=supplier] in [=being_supplier1]]`. Evaluation of this partial re-evaluation query yields the output dirt `Steelmans`.
4. **By Rule 9 and step 3** Item (`Steelmans`) dirties query `occurrences of paying where [participants in role [=supplier] in occurrences of`

---

[1] Each of the rules mentioned here is defined in detail in the Appendix.

Table 3. Dirtied queries and their output dirt after addition of occurrence of `being_supplier1` to a new data-store

Dirtied Query	Output Dirt
query5	supplier
query6	being_supplier1, ...
query7	Steelmans

(query5 = [=supplier]), (query6 = occurrences of [being_supplier]),
(query7 = [participants in role [=supplier] in occurrences of [being_supplier]])

[being_supplier]] are [=payee]. Substitution of the input dirt (shown underlined) for the dirtied criterion yields the partial re-evaluation query: occurrences of paying where [=Steelmans] are [=payee]. Evaluation of this partial re-evaluation query yields no output dirt. The coverage-checker thus stops.

We conclude that the new occurrence, `being_supplier1`, is not prohibited, since the only query that covers it is, `occurrences of [being_supplier]`, which is not in the `prohibited` role in any prohibition. We nevertheless record which queries were dirtied by this new data and cache the output dirt, since we can use this dirt in future partial re-evaluations. The dirtied queries and their output dirt is shown in Table 3. The incremental nature of the algorithm is important as tens of thousands of occurrences may be stored in the database. Re-executing every stored query on each occurrence addition is infeasible, particularly since most results will be unchanged. The cache of dirtied queries facilitates creation of more specific partial re-evaluation queries. Even if the actual dirt cache was cleared to conserve resources, we can still rely upon the query optimizer to only re-evaluate the minimal set requiring re-evaluation. For large data volumes, a query execution approach is likely to be more efficient than a theorem-proving or logic programming approach, as the query execution approach incorporates query optimizers which take into account data profiles (predicate selectivity) when executing a query, whereas theorem provers and logic programs typically do not concern themselves with such execution efficiency issues.

Say SkyHi promises to pay to Steelmans £25,000. Assume this payment has been contemplated, but not effected; no occurrence of `paying` has been added to the data store. As shown in Table 2 and Figure 1, the promise can be represented by embedding the stored query, `query19`, in an occurrence of *promising*. Now, comparing the description of the promised occurrences (`query19`) to other stored queries, proceeding from its most deeply nested sub-expressions upwards:

1. **By Rule 3** [=25,000] (query16) is covered by query [>10,000] (query2)
2. **By Rule 7** occurrences of paying where [>10,000] is [=paid_amount] (query4) covers the query occurrences of paying where [=25,000] is [=paid_amount] (query17)
3. **By Rule 5** [=Steelmans] (query14) is covered by any query which covers Steelmans. As seen earlier, [participants in role [=supplier] in

occurrences of [being_supplier]] (query7) covers Steelmans. This fact
is stored in the last row of the "dirtied query and dirt" cache shown in Table
3. Therefore query7 covers query14.

4. **By Rule 7, and step 3** occurrences of paying where [participants in
role [=supplier] in occurrences of [being_supplier]] are [=payee]
(query9) covers occurrences of paying where [=Steelmans] is [=payee]
(query15)

5. **By Rule 6, step 2 and step 4** Query18 is covered by Query10

6. **By Rule 8 and step 5** The set criterion (Query18) covers Query19

7. **By Rule 2, step 5 and step 6** Query19 is covered by Query10.

We have thus shown that what is promised (the description of the promised
occurrences = Query19) in this context is covered by what is prohibited (the
description of the prohibited occurrences = Query10). We have thus detected a
dynamically appearing *conflict* between a provision embedded in a contract, and
an organizational policy. [1] describes mechanisms for resolving such conflicts.
Research into increasing the efficiency of our implementation, and confirming
through performance tests that the system is comfortably suited to real-world
business workloads, is ongoing.

5   Conclusion

We have proposed a coverage-determination mechanism for queries within e-
service environments. We discussed the data and query storage techniques employed by the EDEE system, and through a worked example, demonstrated how
our approach efficiently determined conflicts which appeared dynamically between business contracts and organizational policies.

Acknowledgments. This research is supported by grants from the Cambridge
Commonwealth and Cambridge Australia Trusts, the Overseas Research Stu-
dents Scheme (UK), and the University of Cape Town Postgraduate Scholar-
ships Office. We are grateful to Microsoft Research Cambridge for funding a
continuation of the research.
   Thanks are due to Dr Ken Moody for helpful comments on the draft.

References

1. A.S. Abrahams and J.M. Bacon. The life and times of identified, situated, and
   conflicting norms. In *Sixth International Workshop on Deontic Logic in Computer
   Science (DEON'02), Imperial College, London, UK*, May 2002.
2. A.S. Abrahams and J.M. Bacon. A software implementation of Kimbrough's disquotation theory for representing and enforcing electronic commerce contracts.
   Group Decision and Negotiations Journal, Forthcoming.
3. R. Ayres and P. J. H. King. Querying graph databases using a functional language
   extended with second order facilities. In *Advances in Databases, 14th British National Conferenc on Databases, BNCOD 14, Edinburgh, UK, July 3-5, 1996, Proceedings*, pages 189–203. Springer, 1996.

4. R.W.H. Bons, R.M. Lee, R.W. Wagenaar, and C.D. Wrigley. Modelling inter-organizational trade procedures using documentary petri nets. In *Proceedings of the Hawaii Internaional Conference on System Sciences*, 1995.
5. OASIS Provisioning Services Technical Committee. An introduction to the provisioning services technical committee. `http://www.oasis-open.org/committees/provision/Intro-102301.doc`, 2001.
6. A. Daskalopulu, T. Dimtrakos, and T.S.E. Maibaum. E-contract fulfillment and agents' attitudes. In *Proceedings ERCIM WG E-Commerce Workshop on the Role of Trust in E-Business, Zurich*, October 2001.
7. OASIS ebXML Collaboration Protocol Profile and Agreement Technical Committee. Collaboration-protocol profile and agreement specification. `http://www.oasis-open.org/committees/ebxml-cppa/documents/ebcpp-2_0.pdf`, 2002.
8. C. Forgy. Rete: A fast algorithm for the many patterns/many objects match problem. *Artificial Intelligence*, 19(1):17–37, 1982.
9. A. Gupta and I. S. Mumick. Maintenance of materialized views: Problems, techniques, and applications. *Data Engineering Bulletin*, 18(2):3–18, 1995.
10. S.O. Kimbrough. Reasoning about the objects of attitudes and operators: Towards a disquotation theory for the representation of propositional content. In *Eight International Conference on Artificial Intelligence and the Law (ICAIL 2001), St Louis, Missouri*, May 2001.
11. M. Koetsier, P. Grefen, and J. Vonk. Cross-organisational workflow: Crossflow ESPRIT E/28635 contract model, deliverable D4b. Technical report, CrossFlow consortium, 1999.
12. M. Merz, E. Griffel, T. Tu, S. Muller-Wilken, H. Weinreich, M. Boger, and W. Lamersdorf. Supporting electronic commerce transactions with contracting services. *International Journal of Cooperative Information Systems*, 7(4):249–274, December 1998.
13. D. P. Miranker. TREAT: A better match algorithm for AI production system matching. In *Proceedings of the 6th National Conference on Artificial Intelligence, Seattle, WA, July 1987*, pages 42–47. Morgan Kaufmann, 1987.

A Coverage Checking Rules

Below are the rules used for determining coverage relationships between queries in our example (the complete list is available on request).

Rule 1. An item is covered by queries with matching `type` criteria.
Rule 2. Transitively, a query is covered by any coverer of its coverers.
Rule 3. A numeric equal-to query Q, is covered by an equal-to, less-than or greater-than query if its `equal-to`, `less-than`, or `greater-than` criterion is, respectively, equal to, greater than, or less than Q's `equal-to` criterion. A numeric less-than query Q, is covered by numeric less-than queries where the `less-than` criterion is greater than the `less-than` criterion of Q. A numeric greater-than query Q, is covered by numeric greater-than queries where the `greater-than` criterion is less than the `greater-than` criterion of Q.
Rule 4. Any participant, occurrence, or role is covered by concept-identification queries where the `identified-concept` criterion is identical to the participant, occurrence, or role identifier.

Rule 5. A concept-identification query is covered by any query that covers its `identified-concept` criterion.

Rule 6. An intersection query Q, is covered by any intersection query P, if each of P's `intersectands` covers some non-zero number of Q's `intersectands`.

Rule 7. For two participant queries[2], P covers Q if P's `role` criterion covers Q's and P's `occurrence` criterion covers Q's. Similarly for occurrence queries[3].

Rule 8. An ordinal (sequence) query is covered by its `set` criterion. e.g. `1st [payments]` is covered by `payments`.

Rule 9. A query, Q, dirties any participant or occurrence query that has Q as its `participant` criterion, `occurrence` criterion, or `role` criterion.

---

[2] EDEEQL syntax is: `participant_query = PARTICIPANTS IN ROLE role_criterion IN occurrence_criterion`

[3] EDEEQL syntax is: `occurrence_query = OCCURRENCES OF occurrence_criterion WHERE participant_criterion IS | ARE role_criterion`

Managing Business Relationships in E-services Using Business Commitments

Haifei Li, Jun-Jang Jeng, and Henry Chang

IBM Thomas J. Watson Research Center
1101 Kitchawan Road, Route 134, Yorktown Heights, NY 10598, USA
{haifeili, jjjeng, hychang}@us.ibm.com

Abstract. With the rapid advancement of e-service technology, there is a need to manage business relationships among business entities such as service providers, service consumers, and internal departments. In this paper, we have proposed a novel approach to business relationship management using business commitments and associated business commitment hubs. Business commitments are commitments related to business issues such as service levels in service agreements, and terms and conditions in procurement contracts. The concept of business commitments has captured the essence of business relationships in e-services. Based on case studies, we have envisioned the need of establishing a business commitment hub to centrally manage the external relationships with trading partners and the internal relationships with internal departments. A language called Business Commitment Language (BCL) has been proposed to specify business commitments. These business commitments are used to monitor and control the execution status of e-services. Conceptually, the business commitment hub has two related subsystems: the active subsystem and the dashboard subsystem. The active subsystem responds to business events received from business entities. The dashboard subsystem visually displays the key data and the execution status of business commitments.

1 Introduction

Recently there have been many interests in studying e-services in e-commerce research community. An e-service [3] is usually established between two business entities that are either trading partners or internal departments. A relationship is said to be setup once an e-service has been established. There are many aspects of relationships between business entities, such as legal aspect, social aspect and economic aspect, and each of them requires serious academic research work. One approach to model the economic aspect is through business commitment. In this paper, business commitment is defined as commitment related to business issues. A language called BCL is proposed to specify business commitments from a viewpoint of a single business entity. Since a business entity may utilize multiple e-services to run its business, there is a

A. Buchmann et al. (Eds.): TES 2002, LNCS 2444, pp. 107-117, 2002.
© Springer-Verlag Berlin Heidelberg 2002

need to manage them in a uniform way. We call the system managing business commitments "business commitment hub."

During the execution of a typical e-service, there are many data exchanged between a service provider and a service consumer. In order to isolate the business commitment monitoring from the low-level details of e-service implementation, a concept called "KSI" (Key Status Indicator) is proposed. A KSI is an important parameter of the e-service that can manifest its status. An e-service may have multiple KSIs, which are the subject that business analysts want to monitor. The design of BCL follows the ECA (Event Condition Action) paradigm. The ECA is a common design pattern used in active database/system research community. In an ECA system, once an event has occurred, the condition is evaluated. If the condition is evaluated to be true, actions are to be taken. BCL expands the traditional ECA system in several ways. First, the concept of KSIs is introduced. The condition part is a logical expression based on KSIs and commitment variables. Commitment variables are threshold values that can be dynamically set by business analysts. Second, the concept of commitment profiles is introduced. A commitment profile provides values for condition matching variables and commitment variables. A profile provides a way to separate the logic part of a commitment from the data part of the commitment. Third, the action part of ECA is expanded to action set where a collection of related actions can be executed either sequentially or in parallel. In order to support the language, an architecture has been proposed for "business commitment hub." During the build-time, the business commitment hub accepts a BCL document and configures various components. During the run-time, the hub receives events, evaluates conditions, and takes corresponding actions. In the meantime, the KSI and execution status of business commitment are visually displayed in a dashboard.

Most work on SLAs/contracts is solely for external parties (e.g., trading partners). WSLA [1] and tpaML [2] are two specifications related to one-to-one service provider/service consumer relationship. The approach proposed in this paper is applicable to both external and internal parties. Therefore, it is possible to have an integrated view of business relationships to be managed, thus leading to an optimal solution of business relationship management. Traditional contract management or service level management [4] deals with trading partners individually; therefore a global view is missing. The final result is a sub-optimal solution. There is a need to collect the relationships among trading partners and interactions among internal parties, and to manage them globally. In this paper, we introduce a way to build a business commitment hub, which centrally manages business commitments from/to multiple parties. In particular, the concept of business commitments is presented, its corresponding language called BCL (Business Commitment Language) is explained, and an architecture based on BCL is proposed.

2 Business Commitments

According to Merriam-Webster's collegiate dictionary, commitment is *"an agreement or pledge to do something in the future."* Business commitments are broadly defined as commitments related to business issues. Commitments can be between trading partners (called external commitments), or between internal parties within a business (called internal commitments). The definition of business commitments captures not only the current stable states ("agreement") but also the future actions ("to do something") and constraints (not to do something); therefore it is an appropriate concept to describe certain types of business relationships and interactions that may require both agreements and actions from participating parties. A set of business commitments establishes the agreement of a business commitment hub to its customers (both external and internal) regarding how their artifacts are to be managed. In our opinion, the concept of "business commitments" nicely fits into the business commitment hub that likely manages multiple e-services and multiple parties.

2.1 Business Commitments, Contracts, and SLAs

It is critical to discuss the distinctions among Business Commitments, Contracts, and Service Level Agreements (SLAs). Informally, contracts are legal documents specifying the duties and obligations of parties involved in a deal. Contract is a generic term for agreements with a legal flavor. For example, the implication of signing a contract is that "if party A breaks the contract, party B may take party A to a court." An SLA is a contract between a service requestor and a service provider that specifies the minimal acceptable levels for the service. SLA is one type of contracts with a business and quantitative flavor (reflected in the term "level" in SLA). The concepts of business commitments, contracts, SLAs are related, but with different focus. Business commitment is the best concept to fit our needs because of its explicit focus on actions. These actions will be taken to configure, control, and monitor the execution of e-services.

2.2 BPCL Creation

Apparently, most business commitments are derived from contracts and/or SLAs. Some business commitments come from contracts and their relationships that are influenced by the perspectives of the owner of a business commitment hub. It implies that a business commitment hub should monitor and control not only the execution of individual contracts, but also the relationships among these contracts. In BCL, the relationships among contracts are captured as *inter-contract clauses*.

Figure 1 shows procedures for creating a BCL. We assume that Party1 is the owner of a business commitment hub and it negotiates the management agreements with multiple (three in this example) parties. The result of the negotiation between Party1 and Party4 is SLA1 (assuming Party1 and Party4 have negotiated a service agreement). The results of the negotiation between Party1 and Party3, and the negotiation between Party1 and Party2 are Contract2 and Contract3 respectively (assuming these two negotiations are about general business contracts). Party1 may have its internal SLAs/Commitments that describe the obligations of various internal departments. Since SLA1, Contract2 and Contract3 are results of separate negotiations, they are fed into a process called Inter-Contract Analysis to generate possible inter-contract clauses. Inter-contract clauses are combined with internal SLAs/Commitments, SLA1, Contract2 and Contract3 (these are all from Party1's perspective) to form the BCL. The procedures described in Figure 1 are manual. How to automate these procedures is an important topic but beyond the scope of this paper.

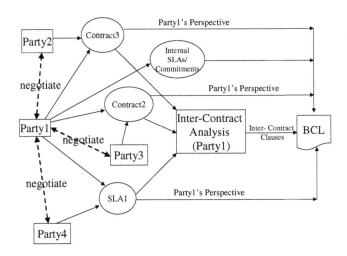

Fig. 1. Steps for Creating a BCL

3 Key Status Indicator and Commitment Profile

One of the major concepts embodied in BCL is *Key Status Indicator* (KSI). A KSI is an important data from an e-service that manifests the execution status of an e-service in the business sense. KSIs are a group of the subjects that a business commitment hub monitors and controls. It is obvious that not all the data within an e-service is a KSI. KSIs should be defined by business analysts who intimately understand the related e-services.

Key Performance Indicator (KPI) is a term used in areas like balanced scorecard [5], business intelligence, and supply chain management to describe the important data/parameters that can be used to measure (i.e., indicate) the performance of an enterprise. One key characteristic of KPI is that an indicator must be measurable. Otherwise, it is very difficult, if not impossible, to manage it. This key characteristic is inherited by the definition of KSI. Our definition of KSI is more specific and is closely tied to e-service.

Once KSIs extracted from e-services have been determined, business analysts can build useful relationships among e-services through KSIs. When an enterprise involves more than two parties and more than one e-services, the monitoring and controlling of the relationship are critical. One hypothetical business commitment could be: "if KSI1 from e-service 1 is greater than KSI2 from e-service 2, notify the business commitment hub."

Commitment profile is introduced to separate the logic part of a commitment from the data part of the commitment. The purpose of separation is to be scalable in composing a large BCL document. The logic part is a logic expression over KSIs and parameters. The data part provides values for these parameters. The logic part should be easy to understand, and the data part is simply a collection of data called commitment profiles. The data part can reside in a database table or other separate XML documents. Therefore, the core part of BCL can be small and easy to understand. Each profile has two components: identifying information and threshold information. Identifying information is formally called ConditionMatchingVariable, and the threshold information is formally called CommitmentVariable. As suggested by the names, the value for ConditionMatchingVariable is used as conditions to retrieve the value for CommitmentVariable. These CommitmentVariables participate in the evaluation of the logic part of the commitment. The evaluation results determine whether actions should be taken.

Let's consider an example from a widely studied domain in e-commerce. In a supply chain, a buyer needs to monitor the customer lead time (CustomerLeadTime) when it purchases a particular product from a particular customer. The buyer usually sets an upper limit for the threshold value of CustomerLeadTime. The symbol $CLT is used to denote that particular upper limit, and the symbol #Supplier and #Product are used to denote the supplier name and the product name respectively. If products are delivered to the buyer, the buyer needs to monitor the CustomerLeadTime. If the CustomerLeadTime exceeds $CLT, the dashboard should be informed and updated, and an email should be sent to the purchasing manager at the buyer side.

The above example illustrates several important ideas. At first, the commitment could be associated with an e-service like productDelivery. Even though the details of the e-service are not provided, it is possible to extract associated data from the e-service through wrappers. CustomerLeadTime is a KSI and can be calculated based on a formula. Second, a commitment is directional. This commitment is from the supplier to the buyer, and the buyer needs to monitor the execution status of the commitment. However, commitments always exist in pairs. Another (although implicit) commitment from the buyer to the supplier is that the buyer needs to pay money within a certain time period. The supplier monitors the status of the payment, and takes certain actions if the commitments are violated. Third, a commitment comes with certain actions. In the above case, there are two associated actions: dashboard notification and email notification. These actions are taken when the commitment is violated, but some actions may be taken regardless of the circumstances, such as a status report of the average CustomerLeadTime at the end of each month. The given actions are relatively simple, but more sophisticated actions are needed to handle a complex situation. Forth, information for commitment profile is easy to identify and understand. In the above example, #Supplier and #Product are condition matching variables and $CLT is commitment variable.

4 Structure of BCL

A BCL document contains a set of inter-related parts.

1. Party: party information. The descriptive information about parties participating in the business commitment hub.

```
<xsd:complexType name="PartyType">
  <xsd:sequence>
    <xsd:element name="PartyIdentifier"
      type="bcl:PartyIdentifierType"
        maxOccurs="unbounded"/>
    <xsd:element name="Contact"
type="bcl:ContactInformationType"/>
      <xsd:element name="RolePlayer" type="xsd:string"
        minOccurs="0" maxOccurs="unbounded"/>
  </xsd:sequence>
  <xsd:attribute name="name" type="xsd:string"/>
</xsd:complexType>
```

The party information contains identifier information, contact information, zero to many role players. There is one primary party that owns the business commitment hub. There are one to many parties that are participating in the activities of business commitment hub.

2. KSI: key status indicator. These are important parameters that indicate the execution status of e-service.

```
<xsd:complexType name="KSIType">
  <xsd:sequence>
    <xsd:element name="KSIName" type="xsd:string"/>
    <xsd:element name="KSIType" type="xsd:string"/>
    <xsd:element name="KSICategory"
      type="bcl:KSICategoryType"
      minOccurs="0" maxOccurs="unbounded"/>
    <xsd:choice>
      <!--got the value from a business process  -->
      <xsd:element name="ProcessAssociation"
        type="bcl:ProcessAssociationType"/>
      <!-- computing value based on other KSIs -->
      <xsd:element name="Computation"
type="bcl:FunctionType"/>
      <!-- deriving value from a basic KSI -->
      <xsd:element name="ValueDerivation"
      type="bcl:ValueDerivationType"/>
    </xsd:choice>
  </xsd:sequence>
</xsd:complexType>
```

As illustrated above, there are three different ways to get the value for KSI: directly from a business process, computing the value based on other KSIs, and deriving value from a basic KSI.

3. BusinessEvent. Events provide an entry point for evaluating the logic expressions inside each individual business commitment.

```
<xsd:complexType name="BEType">
  <xsd:sequence>
    <xsd:element name="EventName" type="xsd:string"/>
    <xsd:element name="EventType" type="xsd:string"/>
    <xsd:element name="ProcessID" type="xsd:string"/>
    <!-- event source: either Sender (directly come
      from a sender) or Timer (come from a timer) -->
    <xsd:choice>
      <xsd:element name="Sender" type="xsd:string"/>
      <xsd:element name="Timer"
        type="bcl:TimerType"/>
    </xsd:choice>
    <xsd:element name="Receiver" type="xsd:string"
      minOccurs="0"/>
    <xsd:element name="EventAttributes" type =
    "bcl:EventAttributesType" minOccurs="0"
      maxOccurs="unbounded"/>
  </xsd:sequence>
</xsd:complexType>
```

There are two event sources in our event model: Sender (directly come from a sender) and Timer (come from a timer). Any information specific to an event is stored within *EventAttributes.*

4. BusinessCommitment: The main parts of BusinessCommitment are BCIdentifier, triggering event, commitment level, validity, (logic) expression, initiator, receiver and actions. Actions are a set of action(s) to be taken when the logical expression is evaluated to be true. A commitment is directional, so it is necessary to indicate the initiator and the receiver. There are two possible values for commitment level: individual level (commitment for each transaction instance) and process level (based on the aggregated result over a certain period of time).

```
<xsd:complexType name="BCType">
  <xsd:sequence>
    <xsd:element name="BCIdentifier"
      type="xsd:string"/>
    <xsd:element name="TriggeringEvent"
      type="xsd:string"/>
    <xsd:element name="CommitmentLevel"
      type="bcl:CommitmentLevelType"/>
    <xsd:element name="Validity"
      type="bcl:PeriodType"/>
    <xsd:element name="Expression"
      type="bcl:LogicExpressionType"/>
    <xsd:element name="Initiator" type="xsd:string"/>
    <xsd:element name="Receiver" type="xsd:string"/>
    <xsd:element name="Action" type="bcl:ActionType"
```

```
          minOccurs="0" maxOccurs="unbounded"/>
      </xsd:sequence>
    </xsd:complexType>
```
5. *Actions*: Sequential and parallel execution of actions.
```
    <xsd:complexType name="ActionType">
      <xsd:sequence>
      <xsd:element name="ActionCategory"
        type="bcl:ActionCategoryType"/>
        <xsd:element name="ProcessID" type="xsd:string"/>
        <xsd:element name="ActivityName"
          type="xsd:string"/>
        <xsd:element name="Parameter"
          type="bcl:NameValueType"
          minOccurs="0" maxOccurs="unbounded"/>
        <xsd:element name="ExecutionMode"
          type = "bcl:ExecutionModeType"/>
      </xsd:sequence>
    </xsd:complexType>
```
ExecutionModeType is defined as an enumeration. Two valid values are "Sequentially" and "InParallel" in our model.

6. *Commitment Profile:* condition matching variables and commitment variables.
```
    <xsd:complexType name="CommitmentProfileType">
      <xsd:sequence>
      <xsd:element name="ConditionMatchingVariable"
        type="bcl:NameValueType" minOccurs="0"
        maxOccurs="unbounded"/>
      <xsd:element name="CommitmentVariable"
        type="bcl:NameValueType" minOccurs="0"
        maxOccurs="unbounded"/>
      </xsd:sequence>
    </xsd:complexType>
```

5 Architecture of a Business Commitment Hub

Figure 2 shows the architecture of a business commitment hub. During the build-time, the BCL is composed by business analysts, and is passed to the Configuration component. The Configuration component parses the BCL document and configures Actuator, Condition Evaluator, and Business Commitment Engine during the build-time. This part is shown as dotted lines in the figure. During the run-time, e-services send data to wrappers, which convert the data in e-services into KSI data and events. The KSI data and events are inputs to Business Commitment Engine (BCE). The BCE processes received events and calls Condition Evaluator to evaluation condition. Based on the result returned from the Condition Evaluator, the BCE calls Actuator to finish the work. Data generated from Actuator is sent to the Dashboard through pub/sub (publication/subscription) mechanism.

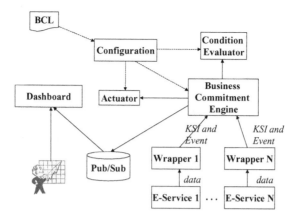

Fig. 2. Architecture of a Business Commitment Hub

6 Case Studies

6.1 Insurance Hub

In the insurance industry, small businesses may buy insurance policies through independent agents. These independent agents then contact with insurance carriers that actually issue the insurance policies. Since it is time consuming for an independent agent to deal with many insurance carrier that potentially have different policies, it is cost effective if an insurance hub can aggregate the result returned from multiple insurance carriers, and provide a uniform interface to independent agents.

During the business interactions between an insurance hub and insurance carriers, it is possible that the insurance hub may find that the policy rules provided by insurance carriers do not match the real world situation. The insurance hub may send a rule set revision request to insurance carriers. Since policy rule changes require human interventions, insurance carrier may take hours, even days, to process the rule set, and send the results back to the hub. From the viewpoint of insurance hub, it is beneficial if each insurance carrier can return the result with an agreed upon period of time. The value for the time period could be a part of SLA/contract between the insurance hub and carriers.

Two commitments can be derived from the above description. One is from carrier to insurance hub: the carrier must return the result within a specific time period and the insurance hub monitors the result. The other is from the insurance hub to carrier: at the end of each reporting period, the hub reports the average turnaround time to the carrier.

6.2 Supply Chain Management

In a large manufacturing enterprise, the manufacturing facility may be separated from the stocking center for the efficiency reason. The manufacturing facility deals with channels, which are actual customers of the manufacturing enterprise. The stocking center orders raw materials from suppliers. The interactions among these four entities are modeled as e-services. The business relationships among them are modeled as business commitments on top of these e-services. There are potentially many commitments, but three commitments are picked for the illustrative purposes.

The first commitment is called customer serviceability. It is a commitment from the manufacturing facility to channels. Depending on the channel/customer class, the on-time percentage should be 95%. Delivery is said to be on-time if it is finished within the pre-defined delivery time, such as 3 or 4 days. The second commitment is called supplier replenishment, which is from supplier to the stocking center. Depending on the supplier name, part name or part family name, the stocking center may require that cycle time should be less than 2 days, standard deviation should be less than 4 hours, and error tolerance should be less than 2 hours. The third commitment is called forecast accuracy. Depending on part name or part family name, the forecast accuracy should be greater than 80%.

It is easy to identify what KSIs, condition matching variables, and commitment variables are. For example, in the third commitment, ForecastAccuracy is a KSI, PartName or PartFamilyName is a condition matching variable, and 80% is the value for a commitment variable like $FA. During the run-time, the value for $FA can be dynamically modified, thus effectively change the commitment on the fly.

7 Conclusion

In this paper, we have presented an approach to manage business relationships in e-services using business commitments. We argue that business commitment is the appropriate way to managing business relationships. We have proposed a language, and architecture to build a business commitment hub. Two case studies, one from the insurance industry, and the other from the supply chain management, are provided to validate our design.

References

1. Ludwig, H., Keller, A., Dan, A., and King R.: A Service Level Agreement Language for Electronic Services, Proceedings of the 4th International Workshop on Advanced Issues of E-Commerce and Web-based Information Systems (WECWIS 2002), Newport Beach, CA, (2002)
2. Dan, A., Dias, D. M., Kearney, R., Lau, T. C., Nguyen, T. N., Parr, F. N., Sachs, M. W., and Shaikh, H. H.: Business-to-business integration with tpaML and a business-to-business protocol framework, IBM Systems Journal Vol. 40, No. 1, (2001)

3. Kuno, H., "Surveying the E-Services Technical Landscape", Proceedings of the Second International Workshop on Advance Issues of E-Commerce and Web-Based Information Systems (WECWIS 2000), Milpitas, CA, (2000)
4. Sturm, R., Morris, W., and Jander, M., "Foundations of Service Level Management," SAMS publishing, Indianapolis, IN, (2000)
5. Kaplan, R. S., Norton, D. P., "The Balanced Scorecard: Translating Strategy into Action," Harvard Business School Press, Boston, MA, (1996)

Ad-Hoc Transactions for Mobile Services

Andrei Popovici and Gustavo Alonso

Swiss Federal Institute of Technlogy Zürich, Switzlerland
{popovici,alonso}@inf.ethz.ch

Abstract. New developments in battery technology, networking, and devices allow the creation of new business models based on mobile computing and not requiring any fixed infrastructure. Mobile electronic commerce is today limited in size but future mobile networks will grow dramatically. In such environments, the participating nodes must be self organized to collaboratively implement all the services a fixed network would provide. In this paper we present the design and implementation of a system that supports the development of adaptive electronic services. We focus our attention on the problem of transactional interaction between nodes, which is an essential requirement in electronic commerce. To support, this feature, our system allows us to dynamically incorporate the transactional support in mobile nodes and provides the foundation for a self-organizing transaction system. The paper discusses then how groups of collaborating nodes can execute electronic transactions on an infrastructure-less, ad-hoc environment. We conclude with a preliminary performance evaluation.

1 Introduction

The widespread use of computing and communication devices is increasingly challenging the way services are provided to consumers. Traditionally, most electronic services have been built around a fixed infrastructure. However, the emergence of handheld and ubiquitous computing renders services that rely on a fixed network infrastructure inadequate in many scenarios. This new type of environments are require the participating nodes to collaborate to implement the functionality a fixed network would provide. They also exhibit the ability to *adapt* the behavior of the participating nodes to the current context (e.g., nearby services, physical location, oranizational unit, etc.).

The design of the infrastructure for electronic services is clearly lagging behind in addressing these new capabilities and constraints. Most existing systems depend on a fixed infrastructure. This dependency is very strong, both at the design and the conceptual level. For instance, all existing solutions for transactional interaction are based on a centralized component [5]. Thus, current products cannot work in a server-less environment where nodes may dynamically move from one application domain to another [15].

As a first step towards eliminating this limitation, we have designed a system capable of providing transactional support to groups of self organizing nodes.

A. Buchmann et al. (Eds.): TES 2002, LNCS 2444, pp. 118–130, 2002.
© Springer-Verlag Berlin Heidelberg 2002

The challenge is to provide transactional functionality without having to rely on any infrastructure and while allowing the nodes to change their transactional behavior depending on the group they join. The first requirement, avoiding a fixed infrastructure, implies that the nodes need to be able to organize themselves as a TP-Monitor. This objective can be achieved by making each node an entirely autonomous mini-TP-Monitor. The second requirement, the ability to adapt to different environments, implies that the transactional functionality cannot be hardwired into the node. What is needed is the ability to, at runtime, attach or detach to a node the mini-TP-Monitor functionality.

In this paper, we present a system capable of doing this. In our system, all nodes are members of a spontaneous network (e.g., Jini [2]). This addresses the problem of service discovery and brokerage in a server-less environment. When several nodes get together, one node makes available to the other nodes a small piece of code (less than 300 KBytes) that contains all the necessary transaction management logic. This code is based on the CheeTah system [15]. This solves the problem not having a fixed infrastructure for transactional processing. To provide adaptability, we use the PROSE system [17]. PROSE allows us to systematically modify the behavior of a running application by dynamically combining the (network-specific) transaction processing with the original application logic inside a Java Virtual Machine. We have taken advantage of this feature to redirect incoming and outgoing remote calls to a node through the TP-Monitor code so that the calls can be made transactional in an automatic and transparent manner. This same mechanism could also be used to support functionality like security or network awareness.

The paper is organized as follows: Section 2 presents a scenario in which the use of ad-hoc transactional functionality is explained, as well as a short description of the principles behind PROSE and CheeTah. Section 4 discusses the architecture of the system and how CheeTah can be used as a transactional extension within PROSE. Section 5 presents a brief performance evaluation. Section 6 concludes the paper.

2 Motivation

2.1 Ad-Hoc Transactional Services

One of the most promising applications of the Internet is electronic commerce. This is also likely to be the case for spontaneous networks, where smaller and increasingly pervasive devices will engage in commercial transactions among themselves, with base stations, and with remote nodes reached through a combination of wireless and wired infrastructure.

Because nodes are mobile, there is a clear need for self-organization and adaptability. For example, a device might use electronic services in different locations where each location requires different behavior. One of the essential behavior adaptations is transactional functionality. An example of such an exchange is shown in Figure 1.a. The participating nodes could be in an open air trade fair where suppliers, manufacturers, retailers, and customer meet to see

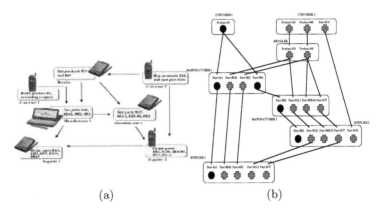

Fig. 1. (a) Example of ad-hoc transactional interaction, (b) its transactional structure.

the latest products available. Customers may want to buy some of the products after seeing them and consulting an online electronic catalog made available at the fair. Upon receiving an order, the merchants can contact each other to order parts and locate supplies. With the appropriate devices, these orders can be registered and confirmed on site and later uploaded to the company's computers. More importantly, the transactional functionality guarantees overall correctness by ensuring that all parts for a product are ordered and the orders confirmed, that there are enough supplies of parts and products for the confirmed orders, etc. Since the system is ad-hoc, customers can consult and order from different vendors and vendors can contact different suppliers in a fully dynamic manner. New nodes (customers and merchants) can participate by simply entering the fair grounds. Nodes can also leave without affecting other nodes (except that, of course, their services are no longer available).

The same scenario applies to nodes changing location. Assume there is a base station at each location (e.g., different fair grounds). Nodes that arrive to that location and want to execute transactions could receive the necessary code from the base station and then proceed as above. This code allows them to execute transactions with the base station and with any other node in that location. When they leave, this code is discarded. Upon arrival at a different location, a different version of the transactional code could be used in a similar manner. If there is no base station, the download could be done from some other node in that location.

To provide a secure environment for all services of a spontaneous network, it is essential to allow transactions of arbitrary complexity. The objective is that, once all nodes have the necessary software layer added to them, the interactions should be limited only by what transactional correctness allows.

2.2   Eliminating the Infrastructure: CheeTah and PROSE

One of the challenges of this scenario is to be able to guarantee transactional correctness without a centralized component. Based on *composite systems*, a solution to this problem has been recently developed (Cheetah [15]) and is now commercially available (Transactions Anywhere [3]). A composite system is a collection of autonomous service providers that interact transactionally following arbitrary configurations. Service providers reside at different locations and publish the services they are willing to provide. Components can offer increasingly complex services by combining and building upon the services provided by other components.

CheeTah is essentially a small TP-Monitor that resides in each node of the composite system. CheeTah aims to treat each remote call as a subtransaction of a global root transaction. Thus, a service designed to use CheeTah must wrap the application logic with invocations to the mini TP-Monitor inside each node. The management of the nested transactions is transparent to the application code, and (this is the relevant part) entirely local to the node. CheeTah is very lightweight, less than 300 KBytes of code, and very flexible. However, the idea behind CheeTah was that applications running over the Internet will be developed using CheeTah and each node would have its own CheeTah server. In a spontaneous service community, we cannot assume that all nodes have CheeTah and, thus, we need a way to treat CheeTah as a runtime component that can be dynamically added to a given node. This implies having a method to systematically change the functionality of *all* service calls inside *all* nodes so that CheeTah is invoked before and after each service call. Such changes *cut across* the system, i.e., they cannot be easily located in a particular module or class.

Aspect oriented programming (AOP) [11] is one of the approaches proposed to address this problem. AOP allows the description of extensions to an existing application when these extensions cannot be easily expressed using traditional object-oriented techniques like inheritance. The description of such extensions is based on the concept of *aspects*, the part of a software system that affects the behavior of several components. An aspect defines a collection of points in the execution of a program. In AspectJ [20,13], e.g., these points could be the invocations of some method(s) of a set of classes. In addition, each aspect contains the code to be inserted at (i.e., before or after) these execution points.

For providing transactional functionality, we need a solution that is capable of expressing cross-cutting adaptations at runtime. PROSE [17] is a dynamic AOP platform for Java, capable of detecting the events of interest and execute the additional actions (the extension) at runtime. Extensions are automatically applied every time a given event takes place (e.g., calling a method, modifying a field, etc.). PROSE is secure since it can use signatures to guarantee the integrity and authenticity of the code being added. It is also extremely flexible in that it allows to dynamically add and remove extensions to one or more Java-enabled nodes without affecting the underlying application.

In this paper, we show how to use PROSE to dynamically glue CheeTah to services exported by nodes joining a spontaneous network. This design allows us to consistently change the transactional behavior of a node as it forms new groups or enters different spaces.

3   Related Work

The explicit participation of the operating systems in the adaptation of under-lying applications has been explored in the Odyssey system [14]. This form of adaptation is known as application-aware adaptation. This technique has been used, for instance, to hide the effects of mobility using replication and cache consistency techniques. Conceptually, this work is related to our approach since also advocates an active implication of the infrastructure in the adaptation of applications. The same need to shift a part of the adaptation logic away from the application has lead to approaches that propose new software architectures to support adaptive systems [8,10,16].

Agent systems like [6] define integrated infrastructures with support for dis-tribution, coordination and dynamic behavior. Such systems are self-organized in the sense of providing the infrastructure for cooperative and distributed prob-lem solving. Dynamic behavior features allow an agent to load a new program at run-time. The new program defines additional functionality that extends the agent's capability to react to messages. Our approach is related to dynamic agents in that it allows run-time instantiation of new components. However, it does not propose a new distributed computing model or a new service infrastruc-ture. Its main focus is to allow *existing* service communities (we used Jini [2] as a prototype) to dynamically adapt to meet common goals. Thus, transactional correctness becomes possible due to CheeTah's ability to deal with arbitrary ser-vice configurations, while dynamic aspect-orientation [4,9,17,18] allows services to be extended transparently.

4   Transactional Extension of Mobile Services

4.1   Basic Architecture

The problem of context-aware adaptation [19] usually addresses the problem of nodes physically present in a certain area or location. We assume that net-work connectivity (specifically, multicast-domains) is equivalent to co-location [7]. Thus, co-located nodes use the network infrastructure to publish services using a common service discovery and brokerage system [2,12]. We further as-sume that all nodes are Java-based, and that they publish their services in the spontaneous network. Service invocations contain local operations (performed on a node-local database) and remote invocations to other nodes, discovered after joining a service community. In our architecture, the service discovery and brokerage functionality is provided by Jini [2] and service invocations are RMI based.

To illustrate self-organization in a service-community, consider a sub-inter-action of the example scenario, in which three services are communicating (e.g., a merchant is ordering sub-parts from two different retailers). This situation is depicted in Figure 2.a. In a first phase (discovery), nodes publish the descriptions of the provided services while other nodes discover the services of interest (step 1). After having established the partners, an invocation that spans all three nodes A,B, and C is triggered by node A (step 2).

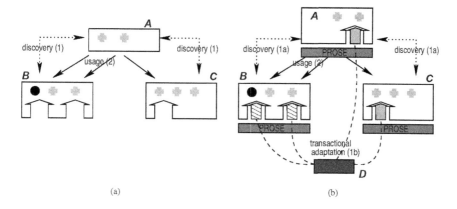

Fig. 2. (a) Service invocations in a pure spontaneous network (b) Service invocations in a spontaneous network with adapted nodes.

The self-organization part is represented by the adaptation of the nodes A, B, and C to the transactional requirements of the service community. This is achieved using PROSE extensions. These extensions are obtained from node D (Figure 2.b). Adaptation must be performed on *all* nodes of the service community expected to interact. In the fair-ground example, node D could be an available base-station, pre-configured to distribute fair-ground specific PROSE extensions. In a more dynamic setup, D may be one of the nodes, elected by other nodes to distribute the community-specific PROSE extensions. In the general case, one extension can be propagated from node to node as needed, while several extensions may be received from distinct nodes.

Extensions are distributed using the standard Java mechanism for downloading code. After discovery (step 1a), the insertion and removal of extensions is done by PROSE (step 1b). All participating nodes have PROSE running on them. With PROSE running, self organization and adaptation is achieved by exchanging extensions among the nodes. For transactional interaction we use CheeTah as an extension. The extension remain activated (and thus the service invocations are treated as transactions) until (i) the nodes leaves the service community (network disconnection), (ii) the transactional extension is replaced by a newer version, or (iii) the nodes autonomously decides to discard the extension.

When one node has received and activated several extensions, their effects may be overlapping or conflicting. In particular, when considering two different CheeTah extensions, we require that they intercept disjoint sets of remote service invocations. This avoids version incompatibilities.

4.2   Extensions

Extensions are compiled and signed Java classes. An extension describes where to do adaptations and what to do. Figure 3 contains an example of an extension. For reasons of space we cannot get into the details of extension coding, but this example should give a first impression of the mechanisms used. A more detailed description of PROSE extensions can be found in [17].

```
1  class BeforeRemoteCall extends AspectExtension {
2    Crosscut createRoot = new FunctionalCrosscut() {
3      // if we are the root, create a transactional context
4      public void ANYMETHOD(ServiceB thisObj, REST params)
5      {
6        if ( lookup(TX_CONTEXT) == null)
7        {
8          txCtx = ROOT_CTX;
9          cheetahTM.bind(currentThread(),txCtx);
10        }
11      }
12    { setSpecializer(ClasseS.extending(Remote.class)). AND
13            (MethodS.BEFORE) ); }
14  }
15 }
```

Fig. 3. A Java class containing the code for a runtime extension.

The extension is called BeforeRemoteCall. It contains one object (createRoot) which defines what to do (transform an invocation into a CheeTah transaction) and where to apply this action (before incoming remote calls of services of type B).

The method on line 4 instructs PROSE to execute its body for every method invocation (wildcard ANYMETHOD) of services of type ServiceB. The predefined class REST, is a wildcard that denotes arbitrary parameters list. Thus, the special signature matches invocations of the form ServiceB.*(*). This is however not enough, as we want CheeTah to be activated just before remote calls. This specialization is achieved on line 13 where a combination of building blocks specifies that services should extend the Remote class (thus, only methods of remote services will be intercepted by PROSE) and that the extension should be executed before the actual business logic in that method (through MethodS.BEFORE).

The body of this method represents the extension action to be executed at all code locations that match the conditions described above, that is, before incoming remote calls from other services. The extension instructs CheeTah to create a transaction context if the current invocation is not within the scope of a CheeTah transaction already (line 6). It then associates the newly created transaction with the current thread of execution. This way, all subsequent invocation to other services will be part of the newly created transaction. To activate this extension, an object of type BeforeRemoteCall must be passed to PROSE. This is done using the PROSE.addExtension method.

In PROSE it is possible to perform more accurate and complex interceptions than those used in this example. For instance, it is also possible to intercept method calls based on the type of parameters passed. The range of the interception can be widened by using wildcards, since in an ad-hoc environment the methods are not necessarily known. For scenarios where more knowledge about the application is available, the interceptions can be made much more precise, by including method signatures, parameter types, etc.

4.3   Inserting and Withdrawing Extensions

In our system, each node runs on top of a JVM with PROSE activated. PROSE is exported itself as a Jini service, which makes possible the remote invocation of the addExtension method. To add the extension shown in Figure 3 to a an arbitrary number of services, the following code fragment has to be executed each time a node joins the spontaneous service community. Since our prototype is based on Jini, which supports service discovery, a concrete implementation of this action is straightforward.

```
1 proseProxy = getRecentlyDiscoveredNode(PROSE.class);
2 proseProxy.addExtension(new BeforeRemoteCall());
```

On line 1, the stub of the remote PROSE system is retrieved. On line 2, a new instance of the BeforeRemoteCall extension is created and then sent to the newly discovered node (e.g., node B) via its proxy. Immediately after the extension is activated on the remote node, PROSE will modify the execution for a potentially large number of method boundaries.

4.4   The CheeTah Runtime Extensions

With PROSE in place, ad-hoc transactional interaction is accomplished by using CheeTah as an extension. In an RMI call, we distinguish between the *caller* node (which performs the marshalling of parameters and unmarshalling of result and is responsible for the *outgoing remote call*) and the *called* node (which performs the unmarshalling of parameters, the method execution, and the marshalling of the results, and is responsible for the *incoming remote call*).

The transactional interaction is implemented by intercepting remote calls and determining whether they correspond to a root transaction (it is an remote call within a thread that is not associated with any transaction), or a sub-transaction (it is an remote call from a thread that already belongs to some transaction). With this information, CheeTah can take over and control the execution of the RMI calls as if they were nested transactions.

As an example, assume a node N_1 calls method m of a remote node N_2. By intercepting the call, the local CheeTah extension can check whether it is associated with any transaction. If it is not the case, then it associates this call with a root transaction t_1. As part of the same RMI call to N_2, the CheeTah extension sends the root identifier (t_1) and node identifier (N_1) so that N_2 notices (i) that it is running a sub-transaction and (ii) the location of the parent. Since the signature of the call cannot be modified (otherwise we may not be able to reconstruct the original call at the other end), the information CheeTah needs to propagate is sent as *hidden parameters* of the $N_2.m(arguments)$ RMI call.

At N_2, the invocation of m is intercepted. The local CheeTah extension at N_2 extracts (and removes) the hidden parameters and sees a root transaction identifier. Accordingly, N_2 starts a local transaction t_2 as a sub-transaction of t_1. The sub-transaction t_2 is associated to the thread where the invocation of m runs. In this way, all RMI calls made during the execution of m can be intercepted and treated as sub-transactions of t_2. For these calls, N_2 associates the root identifier (t_1) and its own node identifier (N_2). This is all the information a CheeTah local extension needs to detect the structure of a nested transaction [15].

When calls complete, CheeTah must be activated again to gather information regarding all sub-invocations of a thread. This information is used for atomic commitment purposes and it includes the number of sub-transactions invoked [15]. As in the forward phase, the CheeTah extensions exchange information among themselves using a hidden *result* annotation. When a CheeTah extension sees that a call that just completed corresponds to a root transaction, this extension starts the 2-Phase-Commit protocol used to commit the results. The commitment protocol is performed among the extensions and does not involve intercepting calls.

All this behavior is implemented by adding two specific extensions to each node. The first extension is a RemoteCallContext extension. It provides the mechanism that allows a local CheeTah extension to communicate with a remote CheeTah extension without modifying the signatures of the calls being intercepted. On the caller side, this extension intercepts invocations to a node's communication layer (RMI) and sends the parent transactional data using mechanisms similar to the marshalling of arguments. On the called side, the information is extracted by intercepting the unmarshalling of arguments, thereby providing the data for the child transaction. Transactional information is also extracted when RMI calls return. This information allows to detect the termination of a sub-transaction.

The second extension is a TransactionalExtension. It relies on the existence of the extension RemoteCallContext. When this second extension is attached to a running node, it intercepts all remote invocations. If the extension, when notified of an incoming call, does not have any record of the node participating in a transaction, it immediately starts a root transaction. Otherwise, it associates the execution with a sub-transaction. Space constraints inhibit elaboration on the mechanisms used within CheeTah, specially those related to concurrency control and recovery; see [15] for details.

4.5   Transactional Behavior in a Service Community

Once all nodes of the service community have been dynamically extended, computations involving several nodes become transactional CheeTah enforces a correctness criterion [1] for arbitrary, dynamic configurations of autonomous components. Thus, each participant can be involved in multiple transactions simultaneously, while preserving global correctness.

One important issue not discussed so far is how the system behaves if nodes leave the ad-hoc community while they are participating in a transaction. This problem is not particular to our system but a general problem of any distributed transaction. Thus, we rely on the functionality available in CheeTah for this purpose. If, for example, a non-root participant leaves the community, its caller will notice the failure of the sub-transaction corresponding to its last call. The caller application may try an alternative solution, e.g., to invoke another node providing the same service. When noticing a failed remote-call, the adaptivity layer implemented with PROSE will eliminate the subtransaction corresponding to the failed method from the overall transaction. The global transaction will not be aborted, due to the properties of nested transactions. While this heuristic does not cover all possible failure cases, it provides a natural way to treat failures of participants. It may further happen that a participant leaves while it is in doubt about a transaction. While the time-window for such an event is small, the mini-tp-monitor implanted in the node will use an accepted policy of heuristic abort. Similarly, if the root node leaves the ad-hoc-community, the rest of the participants will remain in doubt until a time-out is reached. Then again, heuristic abort will be applied in each in-doubt participant. Such a heuristic requires manual intervention but it is a common approach in many database management systems.

5   Performance Analysis of the Transactional Extensions

5.1   Description of the Experiments

The feasibility of using PROSE in real applications depends on the demands in terms of throughput and response time of the particular scenario. The scenarios we tested are similar to those described in Section 2. We have abstracted out some of the details of the application to test several configurations and to identify all potential bottlenecks.

In each experiment, a varying number of nodes implement services following the structure of a composite system. That is, a call to one of the services provided by one node triggers further calls to the services of other nodes which, in turn, may call yet other nodes, and so forth. Each service is implemented as a series of remote invocations (which become subtransactions once CheeTah is activated) and a number of local operations, including access to a database through a JDBC interface. All service invocations are implemented as RMI calls. In each experiment we vary the depth and width of the nested transaction involved. As it was done with CheeTah [15], we perform a worst case analysis in that all nodes in the system are equally loaded, i.e., a transaction goes through every node. This setup is not realistic since, in practice, transactions are likely to run in disjoint subsets of nodes. However, this artificially high load and conflict rate gives us a good idea of what can be achieved with the transactional extensions. If, under the worst case scenario assumption, the performance observed is acceptable, we can be sure that, under normal loads, the performance will also be acceptable. Note, nevertheless, that the type of ad-hoc network we have in mind is not likely to be used for high load, high volume transaction processing.

For the experiments, we used Pentium III 600 MHz Linux nodes. In a wireless LAN, the limited bandwidth is the determining factor in terms of throughput.

Thus, to avoid the network bottleneck, we assume sufficient bandwidth by performing the experiments on a 100 Mbps Ethernet LAN. For data storage, we used an Oracle 8.0.3 RDBMS. The number of concurrent clients is determined by the configuration used in the experiment. Each configuration was characterized by the height of the root invocation hierarchy (how many levels until the leaves are reached, the leaves being the access to the local database) and its width (the number of sub-transactions per parent transaction). Figure 4.a shows an example of a configuration with depth 3 and width 1. Such a configuration is denoted 3x1. Figure 4.b is a 2x3 configuration, with the root invoking three other services (width is 3) and a total depth of 2. The configurations considered in the experiments include: 1x1, 1x2, 1x3, 1x4, 2x1, 3x1, 4x1, 2x3, 2x4.

(a)   (b)

Fig. 4. (a) 3x1 configuration with 2 levels and width 1,(b) 2x3 configuration with 2 levels and width 3.

Following the worst case scenario analysis idea, in all experiments we used a varying number of clients that connect to the very same node. This node acts as the root for all transactions, which adds further overhead. In this way, we can measure how far a given service can be loaded. Note that the node acting as the root has a significant load since, for instance, it has to initiate the commit protocol and create the context for all root transactions. From the transactional point of view, the extension added used the compensation mechanism provided by CheeTah.

Table 1 shows the results of the experiments for the different configurations. The two rows summarize the response time and throughput for CheeTah running as a PROSE extension.

Table 1. Response time (in seconds) and transactions per minute for CheeTah running as an extension.

Configuration	1x1	2x1	3x1	4x1	2x2	2x3	2x4
Average Response Time	0.1	0.17	0.22	0.24	0.22	0.26	0.33
Transactions/minute	615	344	271	251	275	233	181

In terms of throughput, the depth of the transaction plays a significant role in the overall performance (as was observed by Pardon and Alonso [15]). As the results for configurations 1x1, 1x2, 1x3, and 1x4 show, the deeper the transactions, the smaller the throughput and the larger the response time. Since a deeper transaction involves more RMI calls, these results are to be expected. In all cases, the overhead incurred by the dynamic interception mechanism, implemented with PROSE, ranged between 1.3% and 2% of the response time.

6   Discussion and Conclusions

Although the results presented are preliminary, they prove to a great extent the feasibility of the idea. One important issue not discussed so far is how the system behaves if nodes leave the ad-hoc community while they are participating in a transaction. This problem is not particular to our system but a general problem of any distributed transaction. Thus, we rely on the functionality available in CheeTah for this purpose. If, for example, a participant leaves while it is in doubt about a transaction, the mini-tp-monitor implanted in the node will use an accepted policy of heuristic abort. Such a heuristic requires manual intervention but it is a common approach in many database management systems.

Obviously, we do not expect to get the same high performance as that reached in the experiments. However, the experiments do show that dynamic adaptation is possible even in the case of transactional functionality. From a practical point of view, the initial prototype has allowed us to gain some experience and will form the basis to explore more elaborate application scenarios. Despite its limitations, it provides an interesting starting point to explore a part of the design space of future information systems. For instance, the scenarios we have in mind will be limited by the interactive nature of the applications and the low bandwidth of wireless settings. These two aspects will be much stronger constraints that PROSE and CheeTah so we are certain that the overhead introduced by our approach is acceptable in practice. Hence, since transactional interactions on ad-hoc networks are a key requirement for many applications, we believe the prototype described provides a realistic solution for this service. As the next step, we are currently porting the entire system to hand-held devices and will soon start the testing phase.

References

1. G. Alonso, A. Fessler, G. Pardon, and H.-J. Schek. Correctness in general configurations of transactional components. In *Proceedings of the ACM Symposium on Principles of Database Systems (PODS'99)*, Philadelphia, PA, May 31 - June 2 1999.
2. K. Arnold, A. Wollrath, B. O'Sullivan, R. Scheifler, and J. Waldo. *The Jini Specification*. Addison-Wesley, Reading, MA, USA, 1999.
3. Atomikos.   Peer-to-peer distributed transaction processing and distributed databases (iCatch). www.atomikos.com, 2002.
4. J. Baker and W. Hsieh. Runtime Aspect Weaving Through Metaprogramming. In *1st International Conference on Aspect-Oriented Software Development, Enschede, The Netherlands*, April 2002.

5. K. Boucher and F. Katz. *Essential guide to object monitors.* John Wiley & Sons, 1999.
6. Qiming Chen, Parvathi Chundi, Umeshwar Dayal, and Meichun Hsu. Dynamic-agents for dynamic service provisioning. In *Proceedings of the 3rd IFCIS International Conference on Cooperative Information Systems, New York City, New York, USA, August 20-22, 1998*, pages 95–104. IEEE Computer Society, 1998.
7. P. Couderc and A.-M. Kermarrec. Enabling context-awareness from network-level location tracking. *Lecture Notes in Computer Science*, 1707, 1999.
8. C. Efstratiou, K. Cheverst, N. Davies, and A. Friday. An Architecture for the Effective Support of Adaptive Context-Aware Applications. *Lecture Notes in Computer Science*, 1987, 2001.
9. N.D. Hoa. Dynamic Aspects in SOFA/DCUP. Technical Report 99/07, Charles University, Prague, June 1999.
10. E. Kiciman and A. Fox. Separation of Concerns in Networked Service Composition. Position Paper Workshop on Advanced Separation of Concerns in Software Engineering at ICSE 2001, Toronto, Canada, May 2001.
11. G. Kiczales, J. Lamping, A. Menhdhekar, C. Maeda, C. Lopes, J.M. Loingtier, and J. Irwin. Aspect-Oriented Programming. In Mehmet Akşit and Satoshi Matsuoka, editors, *ECOOP '97 — Object-Oriented Programming 11th European Conference, Jyväskylä, Finland*, volume 1241 of *Lecture Notes in Computer Science*, pages 220–242. Springer-Verlag, New York, NY, June 1997.
12. T. J. Lehman, A. Cozzi, Y. Xiong, J. Gottschalk, V. Vasudevan, S. Landis, P. Davis, Bruce K., and P. Bowman. Hitting the distributed computing sweet spot with TSpaces. *Computer Networks (Amsterdam, Netherlands: 1999)*, 35(4):457–472, March 2001.
13. Cristina Videira Lopes and Gregor Kiczales. Recent Developments in AspectJ. In Serge Demeyer and Jan Bosch, editors, *Object-Oriented Technology: ECOOP'98 Workshop Reader*, volume 1543 of *Lecture Notes in Computer Science*, pages 398–401. Springer, 1998.
14. B. D. Noble, M. Satyanarayanan, D. Narayanan, J. E. Tilton, J. Flinn, and K. R. Walker. Agile Application-Aware Adaptation for Mobility. In *Sixteen ACM Symposium on Operating Systems Principles*, pages 276–287, Saint Malo, France, 1997.
15. G. Pardon and G. Alonso. CheeTah: a Lightweight Transaction Server for Plug-and-Play Internet Data Management. In *Proceedings of VLDB 2000*, Cayro, Egypt, September 2000.
16. S. R. Ponnekanti, B. Lee, A. Fox, P. Hanrahan, and T. Winograd. ICrafter: A Service Framework for Ubiquitous Computing Environments. *Lecture Notes in Computer Science*, 2201, 2001.
17. A. Popovici, T. Gross, and G. Alonso. Dynamic Weaving for Aspect Oriented Programming. In *1st International Conference on Aspect-Oriented Software Development, Enschede, The Netherlands*, April 2002.
18. L. Duchien R. Pawlak, L. Seinturier and G. Florin. JAC: A Flexible Solution for Aspect-Oriented Programming in Java. In *Reflection 2001: Meta-level Architectures and Separation of Crosscutting Concerns*, pages 1–24, Kyoto, Japan, September 2001. Springer Verlag.
19. B. Schilit, N. Adams, and R. Want. Context-Aware Computing Applications. In *IEEE Workshop on Mobile Computing Systems and Applications*, Santa Cruz, CA, US, 1994.
20. Xerox Corporation. The AspectJ Programming Guide. Online Documentation, 2001. http://www.aspectj.org/.

Advanced Web Session Provider for Suspensible E-services

Jing Li, Xin Zhang, and Zhong Tian

IBM China Research Lab
2F, HaoHai, #7, 5th Street, Shangdi, BEIJING, 100085, CHINA
{lij, zxin, tianz}@cn.ibm.com

Abstract. Long running transactions and interaction intensive applications are quite common today on the Internet. The services offered by these applications are often challenged with user mobility and interruptability. In many cases, users of these services need to be able to finish their transactions from different clients just as their other business activities require them moving from places to places. Advanced Web Session Provider takes advantage of session management to facilitate service developers to meet such requirements. It extends the traditional session management so that sessions can be re-identified and restored for user after a service is suspended intentionally. It is not tied to any profiling facilities so that different privacy policy can be used when resuming and transferring sessions. The server-based session migration brings the general mechanism to sustain the above features in service development.

1 Introduction

The emerging Internet and Intranet landscape are populated by rich services of immense scale that offer to a diverse spectrum of clients. These services are available via Internet/Internet that completes tasks or transactions and are accessible at a particular Uniform Resource Locator [1]. On the Web, the Customers experience will be what defines a brand and differentiates it from the competition. According to Forrester Research, 90% of online shoppers consider good customer service to be critical when choosing a Web merchant [2]. But, of the top 50 consumer retail sites on the Web, Gartner Group's eTail eService Functionality Study, rated 4% poor, 73% fair, 23% average, and none good or excellent [3]. User requirements are not fully realized and satisfied by service providers.

Users today are even more mobility. The ubiquitous network connectivity and access points have revolutionized usage patterns of e-business applications. Users may use one or more e-services to perform their tasks. As more businesses moving online, many sophisticated tasks require lots of user interaction that can only be fulfilled over an extended period of time, and even at different places. A shopping application may provide a way to persist a shopping cart so that a user can continue shopping another day, another place. "Save as draft" is often requested by users for professional work like purchase order processing, or invoice reconciliation. The suspensible service with user mobility capability turns out to be an almost universal requirement.

A. Buchmann et al. (Eds.): TES 2002, LNCS 2444, pp. 131-140, 2002.
© Springer-Verlag Berlin Heidelberg 2002

Most solutions today try to meet these requirements by saving the persistent data to a backend database, or to a proprietory cookie. Developers need to extract the application recovery data from the database or cookie to initialize a continued conversation with users, and do some clean-up work. In this paper, an Advanced Web Session Provider(AWSP) is proposed to facilitate the online service developing with the mobile and interruptable features, especially in long running transaction.

2 AWSP Overview

Generally, a web session can be seen as a series of requests to a server, originating from the same user at the same browser across a period of time. Sessions can be used to maintain the state of user requests and to keep track of each user. But the usage of session somehow restricts user's web experience. The traditional session has a stiff life cycle and is only valid for one browser, which impedes the service suspensiblility and user mobility. (More discussion in 4.1)

AWSP extends the traditional session so that session owns extensible lifecycle and is free from binding with one fixed browser. In addition, multiple session states can be assigned to one user. AWSP also provides a programming model to facilitate the development. The user mobility discussed in this paper will focus on the sever side service enablement rather than device support. A scenario of the advanced-session enabled application will be presented in the following section.

3 Scenario of Suspensible Procurement Service

This scenario combines the mobile user, interrupted interaction and one-user-multiple-state into one story(please see figure 1). Peter works as one buyer. He often places orders via company's online procurement service. Now he is working on purchase order(PO) 101X using his desktop in office. He inputs a lot of data into the online PO before he finds one line item perhaps with wrong part Number. He calls Eric to double-check. But Eric needs to check some documents before answering Peter. While waiting for the confirmation from Eric and leaving the unfinished PO 101X alone, Peter begins another PO 103X. An staff review meeting will start in another building in 15 minutes. Peter has to save both his unfinished POs and go to the meeting with his notebook PC. During the coffee break, Peter logins again with his notebook to resume his two tasks. He picks the PO 103X and submits it. After the meeting, Peter receives confirmation from Eric on his way back to office. He logins again with his desktop to see the task of PO 101X. Then Peter continues the PO 101X from the confirmed line item and completes the whole PO.

In this scenario, each PO processing has its own session. Hence, Peter has two sessions simultaneously. AWSP provides two new operations(park and reclaim) on session to support this scenario. To support the new operations, the session should have a persistent lifecycle and be reclaimable.

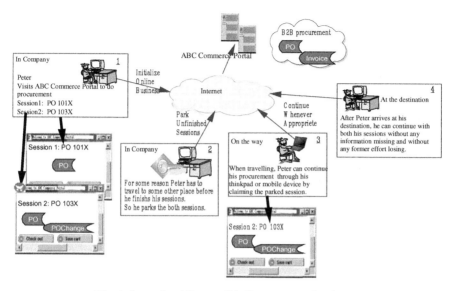

Fig. 1. Scenario of Suspensible Procurement Service

4 AWSP Design & Implementation

4.1 Extend Session Lifecycle

As an elementary function for web-based service composition, session management is now a fundamental component in most web application server product. Two major capabilities are defined and provided in most session management components:

- Session Tracking
- Recognize the new request as the sequential step to former requests from the same client.
- Session Object Management
- To manage the session context, provide application a proprietary space for sharing data in the same session.

Traditional web session tracking makes use of one identifier assigned by server to the session. The identifier is put to the client and presented in the client's requests. Generally, three techniques are used for session tracking [4]:

- Cookies, the most commonly used method, stores the identifier in the client browser and transfer the identifier between client and server in http head section.
- URL rewriting, ensures that following request URLs contain the identifier by rewriting URLs in former response pages at the time they are returned to client.

– Hidden form fields, presets the value of the hidden form field to the identifier that
will be transferred to the server once the user submits the form request.

Though there are multiple choices for session tracking, they share the same defi-
ciency: the session is tightly bundled to client browser. When a session is initialized,
the client has to keep interacting with the server to ensure the session be in the active
state, otherwise the session may expire due to the timeout before the client wants to
end the session. (Please refer to figure 2 to see session's lifecycle.) If a browser is
closed during a session, the client identifier will be lost, thus the session is ceased
even though the server-side session state is still valid. Though some mechanisms such
as persistent cookies can retrieve the old session identifier when browser is reopened,
they have the limitation that they are only applicable to the single browser on the
exact machine[5].

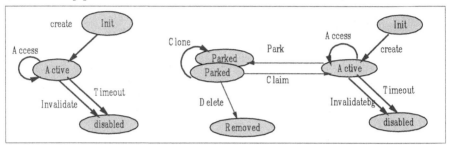

Fig. 2. Current Session Lifecycle   **Fig. 3.** Extended Session Lifecycle

Targeting at the above problems and to enable a more flexible web interaction
mode, AWSP enhances the session capability by means of extending the session lifecycle, as in figure 3. In this extension, sessions are not necessary to be always kept
active during its period of validity. Sessions can be parked and removed. Parked sessions are inaccessible to application to manipulate the session context stored in the
session object. The transitions exist between the active state and parked state via operation *Park* or *Claim*. For example in the given scenario, Peter saves both his partial
processed purchase orders for attending a meeting by simply parking his current session and then he can continue either of them anytime he wants by reclaiming the
parked session into active state.

An extended session lifecycle manager of AWSP is to mange the session state
transition. And a persistent session datastore is to manage parked session objects for
long term usage and hence to reduce the memory load. The transition between active
session(normally in-memory session) and parked session(also called persistent session for its preserving in persistent datastore) is controllable and awareness to the
user. The parked session is reclaimed not by the session identifier, which is transiently
available according to our former analysis, but by a user-aware identifier. Normally,
for applications that initialize a session after authentication, the user id used in the
authentication can be assigned as the identifier. Once the user logins with the same
user id, he can manage his parked sessions and reclaim one to continue. For applications that need no authentication, a user-aware identifier should be negotiated between client and server before session start.

The advanced session provided by AWSP can be used to construct service with a more flexible interaction mode. A user can make a "pause" when he needs an interruption, or simply "save" a session when he needs to shift his working place, in a way, mobile. As one user can perform the save operation for multiple times in different sessions or different session stages, he can own multiple session states in one service, just like owning multiple saving archives in a single game. With these suspensibility features, services can exhibit more affinity with online users.

4.2 Session State Management

Normally session state refers to server side session context in current session mechanism. Session object management for consistent access among different requests is a very important function for web application. To support the discontinuous interaction mode, AWSP extends the session object management module to maintain the parked session in a persistent storage and manage its consistency with corresponding in-memory active session. Besides the server side session context, the client UI state should also be preserved and re-rendered during the session transition between active state and parked state.

4.2.1 Server Side Session Context Management

A way to preserve a session state is to simply save the active session object in the parked session space. And the serialization interface will probably be used when the session object needs to be dumped in/out between memory and persistent storage. But the case turns to be much more complex when the following circumstances are considered:

− Some session related data may not be stored in session object. Some session related states are managed in its own mechanism and hosted in the network, such as stateful EJB.
− Some session data is not suitable to be persistent. For example, the database connection may dedicate to a short term session but is not suggested to be occupied for such a long time.
− Some data can be preserved, but it may not be valid after restoring. Sometimes changes taking place in backend system may make the preserved data invalid. For this kind of data, it is either unneccessary to preserve at all or neccessary to check its validation when restoring the session state.

For these possibilities, AWSP defines a pluggable interface to enable the session context be handled in application specific way during the state transition. The pluggable interface is defined as three special varibles in the session object, shown in table 1. The value of these variables can be either an instance or a name of the class that have implemented corresponding methods.

Extended Lifecycle Manager(ELM) is the module of AWSP to manage the session context. It defines Park and Claim operations to handle the transition of session state. The park operation is invoked when an active session is to be transferred to parked

Table 1. Pluggable Interface in Session Object

Variable Name	Description	Methods
AWSP_PRE_PARK	The preprocessor method for park	prePark
AWSP_DO_PARKCLAIM	The park and claim method	park, claim
AWSP_POST_CLAIM	The postprocessor method for claim	postClaim

state. During parking, the AWSP_PRE_PARK interface is firstly checked. If it is registered, the application-defined prePark method is triggered. The prePark method can trim the content in the session object according to the application's requirement, such as pruning some useless data or replacing a reference with its real data content. And the prePark method also makes the decision on which data shall be preserved at current scenario. Then, the session object is to be saved to persistent session datastore. The save procedure can either be conducted in a generic way or by an application-specific method. The default save procedure parses the session object for all data objects stored in it and utilizes their serialization interfaces to extract data and save into datastore. The default save procedure is applicable for most application. For storage efficiency or other consideration, the application can register its park method in AWSP_DO_PARKCLAIM interface so as to perform the save procedure in its own way. Thus the park method will be triggered to reorganize data objects into a single entity to be saved. The Claim operation has the symmetrical logic as the Park operation, as shown in figure 4.

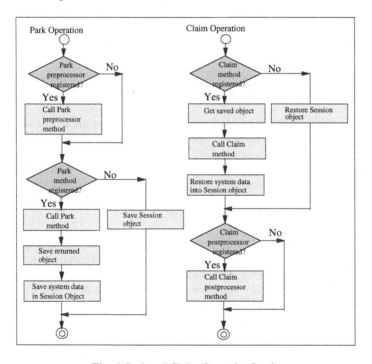

Fig. 4. Park and Claim Operation Logic

4.2.2 UI Rendering

Considering the long term interruption and user mobility, re-rendering client UI becomes a worthwhile function that helps to continue interaction from a proper point. There are four methods supported by AWSP to achieve UI persistency during session state transition.

− Assign a constant URL as restore UI for an application each
− As the simplest way, a pre-defined URL is requested and displayed to client no matter where the user was when parking. It's easy to achieve, but less user friendly.
− Re-send HTTP request
− To re-send the last HTTP request before parking to get the UI page regenerated by applications. It may work well for some cases though it has potential problems. If it happens that the requested page is to trigger some operations to make changes to your persistent data in backend database, the re-sending request may cause an unwanted data conflict in the database.
− UI capture and restore
− To capture the former generated UI result and redisplay it as a static html page when restored. This is the most user-friendly way as the user can view just the leaving page as he pauses the session last time. However, it is inefficient and less dynamic. For some applications that may change its behavior according to its backend system or database frequently, such as B2B applications, the former captured page is no longer valid since the server data has been changed.
− Assign UI restore URL for each section of application
− By dividing application into minor sections and assigning each section with a UI restore URL, the UI can be restored to a meaningful page that the user wants. As in an auction scenario, the car one user bid yesterday may not still available today, so the user may have to view the auction goods list before the next time he/she wants to continue. The meaningful page for the user in the example is the auction goods list page. Through this way applications may adapt their appearance to the up-to-date server side states.

Application can choose the applicable way from the above by setting application profile. Among the four options, the last method is recommended because that it holds a good balance between dynamic demand for agile business and stability requirement for service quality.

4.3 Architecture

The architecture of AWSP can be seen is Figure 5. Based on Websphere Application Server session management module, AWSP functions as an extension to WAS session management[6][7]. It provides a succinct programming interface and programming model that enables applications a fast construction for service interruptbility and user mobility. The major components include:
− Persistent Session Manager: to manage the parked session in datastore. It differentiates from other persistent mechanism in that it is aware by client, and it is identified by user-aware id that can be easily reclaimed at users' demand.

- Easy Session Access: to be a wrapper on WAS session. It provides a more easy access interface, and extends more interface for operating some system defined interface in the in-memory session object.
- Extended Lifecycle Manager: as the kernel module, it performs operations between in-memory session and persistent session, to provide a long-term lifecycle view.
- Configuration: to manage the profile of application/services related properties, include park mode, UI restore strategy.
- Management Interface: The management interface provides two views. For application user, it provides the function to list all the parked session the user has, to indicate which session the user is currently in, to restore the selected parked session, and to switch from one session into another. For the system administrator, the management interface provides a global view on persistent session store, and provide utilities for house keeping work on the persistent session store.

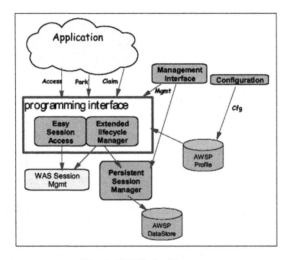

Fig. 5. AWSP Architecture

5 Programming Model

AWSP currently has its implementation in WAS environment. Its programming interface is provided in Java API and servlet. It doesn't need much effort for applications to enable the advanced session feature with AWSP. There is only a minor change on application structure and a little of variations on application code.

Typically, the application structure will shift its login procedure to integrate the session management function so that a user can manage his multiple states in that application. As in figure 6, when a login request is submitted, new valid session may not be created immediately, but rather the session management page should be displayed. The session management page lists the currently existing parked sessions for the user. The authenticated user can either choose a former parked session to claim it or follow the create session link in the session management page to initialize a new valid session. By choosing to claim a parked session, the parked session context will be dumped into memory session space and be activated to serve the user. The client UI will be rendered according to it's UI management strategy in the profile. By choosing to create session, a new valid session will be generated by initializing it with application's profile. It makes no difference between "New Session" and "Claimed Session" for application. The only distinction is that "Claimed Session" has a corresponding parked state.

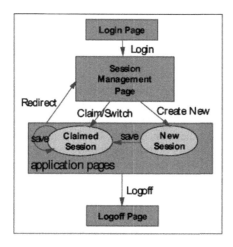

Fig. 6. Application Structure

- Login servlet
- In the Login program, after authentication, a special session should be generated which is only valid in the management pages.
    - HttpSession session = CSPSession.presetSession(request, response);
    - CspSession cspsession = new CSPHttpSession(session);
    - cspsession.setAppName(appName);
    - cspsession.setIdxID(userID);
- Then it can redirect to the session management page.
- Management servlets
- Default management servlets are provided by AWSP which can be reused mostly. The management API interface is also provided basing on which application can develop its own management program for better integrated user interface.
- Initialize new session
- When choosing to create session at management page, the code needed to initialize the session should be added before entering other application page.
    - HttpSession session = request.getSession();
    - CSPSession.initSession(session);
- Park and claim session

- The park and claim servlets are built-in servlets in AWSP. The claim operation is triggered through management page. Application can insert links to park servlet at any position that enables the user to execute the park operation. Application may register its own methods to control the session data transformation between the parked state and active state.
- Delete session
- Deletion is also an AWSP built-in servlet. User can select this operation in management page when the parked session is no longer useful.

6 Conclusion

Service developing requires more complex web user interaction. AWSP fills a gap between the current session management and artistic interaction requirement. It extends the traditional session lifecycle, brings new features from the sessions inner implementation and defines new operations. It takes advantage of the advanced session to address the user mobility and discontinuous interaction issue. The easy-to-use programming model that AWSP provides is believed to be a more general and flexible solution. Besides the new operations already defined by AWSP for extended session lifecycle, more operations like clone, split, merge, transform, etc., will be explored for session collaboration. It is the future work of AWSP, and hoped to diversify the web user interaction with more flexibility.

References

1. Akhil Sahai, Vijay Machiraju, "Enabling of the Ubiquitous e-Service Vision on the Internet", e-Service Journal 1.1 (2001) 5-19.
2. Christopher M.Kelley, James L. McQuivey, Christine Ham, "Driving Sales with Service", Forrester Research
3. Cox, Beth. "The Law of Averages: CRM on the Web". Internet.com 11 Aug. 2000. 15 Oct. 2000, http://ecommerce.internet.com/opinions/print/0,,3551_435911,00.html
4. "Building servlets with session tracking", Ibm.com/developerWorks.
5. "Persistent Client State HTTP Cookies: Use with Caution", Netscape.com. http://home.netscape.com/newsref/std/cookie_spec.html
6. "Java Servlet Specification", sun.com. Http://java.sun.com/products/servlet/
7. Steve Eaton. "Maintaining session data with the WebSphere session manager", http://www-106.ibm.com/developerworks/library/it/it-0801art26/index.html

PLM_{flow}–Dynamic Business Process Composition and Execution by Rule Inference

Liangzhao Zeng[1], David Flaxer[2], Henry Chang[2], and Jun-Jang Jeng[2]

[1] School of Computer Science and Engineering, University of New South Wales [***]
[2] IBM T.J. Watson Research Center, USA
zlzhao@cse.unsw.edu.au, {flaxer,hychang,jjjeng}@us.ibm.com

Abstract. With the proliferation of the Internet and the wide acceptance of e-commerce, increasing numbers of business processes and services are offered by distributed and heterogeneous service providers. This
has created the need to explicitly employ workflow management systems
(WFMS) to coordinate and control the flows of services. One of the fundamental assumptions of existing WFMS is that workflow schemas are
predefined. Such an assumption becomes impractical for dynamic business processes that must be altered and composed on the fly to meet
changing business conditions. PLM_{flow} proposes a dynamic workflow
system that is capable of supporting non-deterministic processes such
as those found in collaborative product design scenarios, where decisions
made by collaborative partners necessitate the dynamic composition and
modification of running workflows. Instead of building complex static
workflows to accommodate an explosive number of possibilities, we ad-
vocate a business rule inference based system to dynamically generate
and execute workflows. As a result, end users can focus on the business
goals to be achieved, instead of having to create detailed control and
data flows for the work at hand.

1 Introduction

In last few years workflow management has increasingly gained relevance as
the technology of choice for business process reengineering, e-commerce and
business-to-business integration. As a result, many enterprises and organizations
have moved towards the automation of their business processes using WFMSs.
One of the fundamental assumptions in WFMS is that workflow schemas (i.e.
tasks, control flow and data flow) are predefined. In order to automate business processes workflow designers need to understand business processes and
use workflow modeling tools to define workflow schemas. When an end user
wants to execute a business process, she creates a workflow instance by selecting a workflow schema and providing necessary input data. WFMS executes the
workflow instance and returns the results to the end user.

One of the most significant weaknesses of predefined workflow schemas is their
lack of flexible mechanisms to adequately cope with ever-changing environments.

[***] This work was conducted while the first author worked in IBM

A. Buchmann et al. (Eds.): TES 2002, LNCS 2444, pp. 141–150, 2002.
© Springer-Verlag Berlin Heidelberg 2002

Modification of business processes is necessary to meet changes in application requirements, technology, policies, and organization. However, such modification procedures are time consuming and costly. Moreover, enterprises are changing constantly: entering into new markets, introducing new products and fine-tuning themselves through mergers, acquisitions, alliances and divestitures. We assert that predefined workflow schemas may become increasingly impracticable for many enterprises.

In this project, we propose a solution to dynamically create workflow schemas. This is achieved through using of business rules and rule inference. Business rules are statements about how business is conducted, i.e., the guidelines and restrictions with respect to business processes in an enterprise. We argue that business rules should be independent of individual business processes. This is different from traditional WFMSs where the business rules are implicitly embodied in the predefined workflow schemas. A business rule based framework is an agile solution that provides the flexibility to adapt business changes. When business rules are separated from businesses processes, any changes in business logic can be captured by modifying business rules and deploying them to business processes on the fly. In this paper we propose a novel framework called PLM_{flow}, which is an outgrowth of a research project dedicated to advancements in Product Lifecycle Management. PLM_{flow} enables dynamical business process composition and execution by business rule inference. The salient features of PLM_{flow} are:

- A set of business rule templates for modeling business logic. We define a set of business rule templates that cover all aspects of business logic in business processes.
- A non-deterministic workflow engine that creates workflow schemas through a combination of backward-chain inference and forward-chain inference. Use of this workflow engine allows end users to focus on their business goals instead of having to provide the detail control flows and data flows. The workflow engine is also able to detect and resolve conflicts among business rules.

The remainder of this paper is organized as follows. Section 2 describes business rule templates. In section 3, we give details on workflow engine. Section 4 gives a brief overview of related work. Finally, section 5 provides some concluding remarks.

2   Business Rules

We propose business rules to describe business logic and policy of an enterprise. In the following subsections, we present a process event model, and then give the details on business rule templates. Business rules are defined as ECA (Event-Condition-Action) rules that are stored in a rule base and are executed by a rule inferring engine.

2.1   Event Model

An event is defined to be an instantaneous and atomic occurrence at a point of time. For example, in a service instance, an event may be initiated from a state change or a data change that is produced by actions. Similar events are grouped into an event type, and are further classified into subtypes, resulting in an event type hierarchy. For example, events that come from end users are grouped into a user event type, which are further classified into more specific groups, such as USER/INITIAL or USER/CANCELLATION. Different event types are distinguished by different event type names. There are several event types including: user events, temporal events, task events, state events, action events and data change events.

2.2 Syntax and Semantic for Conditions

A rule condition is a threshold that determines whether a rule should be fired. Rule conditions are built from atomic conditions using Boolean operations AND ($\wedge$), OR ($\vee$) and NOT ($\neg$). An atomic condition is a Boolean function $f(op, t_1, t_2, ..., t_n)$, where op is an operation that returns true or false, t_i is a term of either a constant or data name. A data name is regarded as value of the data. For example, data name A represents value of A (i.e. $Value(A)$).

2.3 Business Rule Templates

There are two categories of business rule templates that we present as follows:-
1. **PLM Flow Schema Management Rules.** PLM Flow schema management rules are used to dynamically create PLM Flow schemas. There are two kinds of PLM Flow schema management rules, namely backward-chain rules and forward-chain rules.

- *Backward-chain rules* indicate the precondition of executing a task. The precondition can be data constraints, which means some data must be available before the execution of tasks. The precondition can also be flow constraints, which means execution of task requires other tasks to be finished first. In some cases, FlowConstraints() may have AND (i.e. $\wedge$) or OR (i.e. $\vee$) operation. For example, FlowConstraints() = {Task_A } $\vee$ {Task_B}, which means either Task_A or Task_B need to be finished first.
  Expression: Event(*)|(ServiceSchema==*)
  {Precondition(FlowConstraints()| DataConstraints())}
  Example 1 (*Backward-chain Rule*).
  Event(*)|(ServiceSchema == 'CostAnalysis')
  {Precondition (FlowConstraints() = {'TestPlanning'})}
  In this example, the rule indicates before executing the task of CostAnalysis, the task of TestPlanning need to be finished first. □

- *Forward-chain rules* indicate some actions may need to be executed as the execution result of service instance.
  Expression: Event(*)|(Condition)
  {AppendPLMFlow(ServiceSchema)|Drop(ServiceSchema) }

Example 2 (*Forward-chain Rule*).
Event (TASK, *, costAnalysis, *, FINISHED)|(cost > $2000)
{AppendPLMFlow (audit_2)}

In this example, the rule adds the task of audit_2 into PLM Flow schema if the task of costAnalysis is finished and the cost is greater than \$2000. □

2. **PLM Flow Execution Rules.** PLM Flow execution rules are used to manage PLM Flow instances. There are three kinds of rules as follows:

- *Service provider selection rules* are used to select service providers are selected during the runtime.
  Expression: Event(Selection, {ServiceSchema1...ServiceSchemaN})|(C){f}
  Here, we assume that for each task, the system discovers a set of service providers and each service provider has multiple SLAs to perform the service. The action f is a Multiple Criteria Decision Marking (MCDM) function that evaluates the SLAs and returns a 3-tuple response ⟨ServiceSchema, ServiceProvider, SLA ⟩. The details about MCDM function are given in [7].
- *PLM Flow instance management rules* are used to manage instances.
  Expression: Event(*)|(C) {Suspend|AddAction|DeleteAction|Migrate}}
  The event is corresponding to task event, user event or temporal event. Actions are used to control the execution of the PLM Flow instance.
  Example 3 (*PLM Flow Instance Management Rule*).
  Event (ACTION, CostEstimate, *, FINISHED) |(part='engine' ∧ cost > \$2000){Suspend(ClashAnalysis(engine))}
  In this example, if the engine's CostEstimeate is finished and cost is greater than \$2000, the task of ClashAnalysis on the engine needs to be suspended. □

- *Service Coordination Rules* are used to specify data flow among the task execution.
  Expression: Event(*)|(C){SendMSG()}
  The event corresponds to task event, user event or temporal event. The result of an action is the issuance of a message from one task to another.

3   Dynamic Business Processes Composition and Execution

In this section, we first present the PLM Flow process model, and then give details on how to realize the dynamical business process composition and execution.

3.1   PLM Flow Process Model

In this subsection, we introduce the PLM Flow process model that facilities dynamic business processes composition. The following is the formal definition of PLM Flow schema.

Definition 1 (*PLM Flow Schema*). A PLM Flow Schema is a 2-tuple ⟨*Tasks, DataPool*⟩, where

1. *Tasks* is a set of *Task*. A *Task* is further defined by 3-tuple ⟨ *ServiceSchema, BCTasks, FCTasks* ⟩ where

  - *ServiceSchema* gives details of task's functionality.
  - *BCTasks* are tasks that are inferred by backward-chain rules.
  - *FCTasks* are tasks that are inferred by forward-chain rules.
2. *DataPool* is data pool for input and output data.

□

PLM Flow is a task centric process model. In this model, instead of requiring end users to predict how to achieve a certain goal by defining detailed workflow schemas, end users only need to specify the service schema of the target task (that represents the end objective of the business process) and provide necessary input data. Initially, the target task is sole task in the PLM Flow schema. Based on rule inference, the system dynamically adds tasks into the PLM Flow schema to compose the projected execution path from start to finish.

Business process composition and execution in PLM_{flow} involves four major steps (see Figure 1) : backward-chain inference, forward-chain inference, PLM Flow schema selection and PLM Flow instance execution. In the following subsection, details about each step are given.

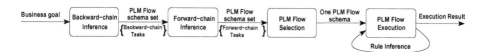

Fig. 1. Business Process Composition and Execution in PLM_{flow}

3.2 Backward-Chain Inference

In this subsection, we introduce the Backward-chain Inference algorithm. A formal description is found in [8]. This algorithm discovers task execution paths for the target task using backward-chain rules as follows:

1. It searches the backward-chain rules for the target task. Then, starting at the target task, rules are used to infer backward-chain tasks that compose an execution path. The algorithm recursively infers backward-chain tasks and the inference will not stop until there are no more new backward-chain tasks found.
2. In the case that there exists OR operations in backward-chain rules, more than one PLM Flow schema may be generated. If so, the output of the algorithm is a set of PLM Flow schemas. Prior to execution, only one of the PLM Flow schema is selected. The selection method is described later in this paper.
3. If the inferred task already exists in the execution path, the algorithm detects whether there is a cyclic graph in the path (see example in 2). Such a cyclic graph indicates there is a conflict among backward-chain rules, which causes the target task to be unreachable. In such case, the inference process terminates and the PLM Flow schema is abandoned.

An example of backward-chain inference is illustrated in Figure 3. In this example, the target task is `Create New Part`. Based on backward-chain rule r_{b1}, `Clash Analysis` and `BOM Rollup` are added into the PLM Flow schema as backward-chain tasks. Since `Clash Analysis` also has a backward-chain rule r_{b2}, `Clash Design` is added into the PLM Flow schema as the backward-chain task of `Clash Analysis`.

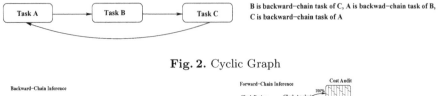

Fig. 2. Cyclic Graph

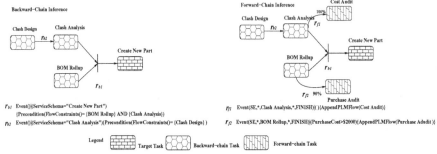

Fig. 3. Backward-chain Inference and Backward-chain Inference

3.3   Forward-Chain Inference

A PLM Flow schema that is generated by backward-chain inference is not complete, since the forward-chain rules may add new tasks to PLM Flow schema. In this subsection, we introduce a **Forward-chain Inference** algorithm to predict additional forward-chain tasks that are added into PLM Flow instance during execution time. A formal description of this algorithm is found in [8]. For each task t in PLM Flow schema, we assume t has been completed; R is the set of forward-chain rules that are triggered by the event of completing task t. For each of r in R, the condition part is regard as a *condition tree*. The formal definition of a condition tree is as follows:

Definition 2 (*Condition Tree*). CT is a Condition Tree of the condition C in rule r, if CT has two types of nodes: parent nodes and leaf nodes. Parent nodes represent the Boolean operations in condition C. Each atomic condition in C is represented by two kinds of leaf nodes that share an AND node. One type of leaf node represents state the function of data. The state function returns true when the data is available, otherwise returns uncertain. The operation on uncertain is given in table 1. Each data item in an atomic condition has one state function. Another type of leaf node represents the expression of atomic condition, for example, budget> $1000. □

Example 4 (*Condition Tree*). Figure 4 gives the condition tree of condition C, where $C = ((Role = TestEngineer) \wedge (partName = Engine)) \vee \neg ((Role = SystemEngineer) \wedge ((Budget > \$1000)))$. □

If the condition tree test result is true or false (and not uncertain), then the **Forward-chain Inference** algorithm infers forward-chain tasks. In the case that condition tree is true, a forward-chain task is added into the PLM Flow schema. If the result is false, then the algorithm checks whether there are conflicts among the rules. There are two types of conflicts: a conflict between a

Table 1. Operation Result on Uncertain

Operation	Expression	Result
AND	True ∧ Uncertain	Uncertain
	False ∧ Uncertain	Uncertain
	Uncertain ∧ Uncertain	Uncertain
OR	True ∨ Uncertain	True
	False ∨ Uncertain	Uncertain
	Uncertain ∨ Uncertain	Uncertain
NOT	¬ Uncertain	Uncertain

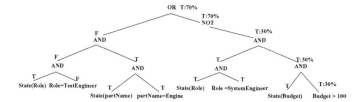

Fig. 4. Annotated Condition Tree

forward-chain rule and a backward-chain rule; or a conflict between two forward-chain rules. For example (see Figure 5 case 1), in backward-chain rule r_b, task t_i is backward-chain task of task t_j, while in forward-chain rule r_f, task t_j is forward-chain task of t_i. If the condition in r_f is false, then there is a conflict between the forward-chain rule and the backward-chain rule. In another example (see Figure 5 case 2), forward-chain rule r_{f1} enables the task t_j, while forward-chain rule r_{f2} disables the task t_j. Here there is a conflict between r_{f1} and r_{f2}. Such conflicts indicate the target task is unreachable in the PLM Flow schema. In this case, the inference procedure terminates and the PLM Flow schema is abandoned. Forward-chain Inference algorithm also detects whether there existing a cyclic graph in PLM Flow schema as previously discussed. In the case that the test result of the condition tree is uncertain, the algorithm conducts a non-deterministic inference. The basic idea in non-deterministic inference is to use past task execution results to predicate that the condition is true or false. If the probability of the enabling task is greater than a given threshold then the algorithm adds the task into PLM Flow schema, otherwise, the algorithm disables the task. Non-deterministic inference also detects the potential conflicts in PLM Flow schemas. Due to space constraints, detail description of non-deterministic inference is outside the scope of this paper.

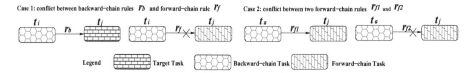

Fig. 5. Conflict between the rules

Figure 3 gives an example of forward-chain inference. In this example, there is a forward-chain rule r_{f1} for `Clash Analysis`. Since the condition part is empty, the probability of `Cost Audit` is 100%. For `BOM Rollup`, the forward-chain rule's condition is `PurchaseCost > $400`. Suppose based on past task execution result, we know the probability of `PurchaseCost > $400` is 90%, then the probability of enable the rule is 90%. So, `Purchase Audit` is added into the PLM Flow instance with probability of 90%.

In backward chain inference and forward chain inference, a set of candidate PLM Flow schemas will be generated. For each PLM Flow schema, the system uses service provider selection rules to select service providers for each the task. Based on these service provider selections, the workflow engine can estimate the quality of PLM Flow schemas. The quality criteria include total execution time, execution cost, etc. Here, we adopt the Multiple Criteria Decision Making approach to select a PLM Flow schema; we skip the details since it is similar to the procedure that is described in [7]. The PLM Flow schema that is selected to be of the highest quality is used for creating PLM Flow instance.

3.4   Executing PLM Flow Instance

When a PLM Flow schema is selected, the workflow engine starts the execution of PLM Flow instance. Assume that PLM Flow $P = \langle T, DataPool \rangle$ is selected, an executing scenario for P as follows:

1. **Creating PLM Flow instance.** A PLM Flow instance is created based on P. At the start of execution, assume T_s is set of tasks in P that does not have any precursor tasks. Each task in T_s is started after PLM Flow instance is created.

2. **Assigning executable tasks to service providers.** When the workflow engine assigns a task to a service provider, it need to consult the business rule bases and generate an event table for the service class or service composition schema, where the entry is defined as $\langle RuleID, Event \rangle$. During the execution of task, the service provider needs to send `Event Notification` to system when any events in the event table occur.

3. **Handling events.** The execution of the PLM Flow instance is driven by events. During the execution of PLM Flow instance, when the workflow engine receives an event notification from a service provider, it uses the event to re-evaluate PLM Flow instances and to dynamically modify PLM Flow instances as required. An `Event handler` algorithm (formal description is found in [8]) is used to handle the event. The algorithm takes the event as an input and initiates the forward-chain inference to determinate whether actions (e.g. add new task) are required. The execution of PLM Flow instance is completed when the target task and all the forward-chain tasks are finished.

3.5   Resolving the Conflicts during Execution

During the execution, the PLM Flow's target task becomes unreachable if there is a conflict among rules. There are two approaches to resolve conflicts: modify the rules or change PLM Flow schema. In the first approach, the system reports the conflicts and related rules to the user allowing them to modify the rules or input data. The PLM Flow instance then resumes from the conflict point. In the second approach, the system automatically tries to find another PLM Flow schema that can avoid the conflict. In this approach, the system resolves the conflict by removing the sources of the conflict; the system selects an alternative PLM Flow schema that excludes the offending task. When a new PLM Flow schema is identified the system migrates the conflicted PLM Flow instance to the new PLM Flow schema.

4   Related Works

There are many on going research efforts in the workflow management area. In this section we review some related work on aspects of business rules and dynamic workflows. Business rules are used in several research projects. In the WIDE project [1], a workflow management system is built to support distributed workflow execution. ECA rules are used to support exceptions and asynchronous behavior during the execution of workflow. In the EvE project [2], ECA rules are used to address the problem of distributed event-based workflow execution, which is a fundamental metaphor for defining and enforcing workflow logic. Both WIDE and EvE are static predefined workflow schemas using the ECA rules. However, PLM_{flow} uses business rules to dynamically infer workflow schemas. Dynamic workflow management systems [4][6] focus on the evolution of business processes by adapting to business changes based on pre-defined workflow schema. PLM_{flow} differs from these existing works in its ability to dynamically predict and modify workflow based on business rules and rule inference.

Decision Flow [3] focuses on providing a high level business process specification language with declarative semantics, which can be understood by users throughout an enterprise. It provides an algorithm for eager detection of eligible, unneeded or necessary tasks to support efficient execution of decision flow. However, the decision flow is predefined and the business rules are statically bound into the decision flow. ISEE [5] introduces events and rules into the business process, which enables runtime modifications; but again, the business processes are predefined and events and rules are static bound. Different from [3] and [5], PLM_{flow} composes the business processes dynamically at pre- execution and continues evaluation of the workflow as events occur during execution, during which time business rules are dynamically bound to the workflow.

5   Conclusion

We describe a PLM_{flow} framework that dynamically generates workflow schema to enable business process composition by rules inference. As a result, end user can focus their business goals to be achieved, instead of having to provide the detail control flows and data flows about the business processes. The execution of a PLM Flow instance is enabled by business rules, which provide flexibility to adapt to changing business environments. Currently, we have implemented a PLM Flow manager that realizes dynamic business process composition and are validating the approach using real industry scenarios. Ongoing research includes optimization of workflow and automatic business rule learning.

Acknowledgments. The authors would like to thank Dr. Boualem Benatallah for his helpful directions and comments.

References

1. Stefano Ceri, Paul W. P. J. Grefen, and Gabriel Sanchez. WIDE: A distributed architecture for workflow management. 1997.
2. Andreas Geppert and Dimitrios Tombros. Event-based distributed workflow execution with EVE. Technical report, 1998.
3. Richard Hull, Bharat Kumar, Gang Zhou, Francois Llirbat, Guozhu Dong, and Jianwen Su. Optimization techniques for data-intensive decision flows. In *Proceeding of 16th International Conference on Data Engineering*, 2000.
4. Pinar Koksal, Ibrahim Cingil, and Asuman Dogac. A component-based workflow system with dynamic modifications. In *Next Generation Information Technologies and Systems*, pages 238–255, 1999.
5. J. Meng, S. Y.W. Su, H. Lam, and A. Helal. Achieving dynamic inter-organizational workflow management by integrating business processes, events, and rules. In *Proceedings of the Thirty-Fifth Hawaii International Conference on System Sciences (HICSS-35)*, 2002.
6. Manfred Reichert and Peter Dadam. ADEPT flex -supporting dynamic changes of workflows without losing control. *Journal of Intelligent Information Systems*, 10(2):93–129, 1998.
7. Liangzhao Zeng, Boualem Benatallah, and Anne Hee Hiong Ngu. Dynamic web service integration and collaboration (submit for publication). Technical report, School of Computer Science and Engineering, University of New South Wales, 2002.
8. Liangzhao Zeng, David Flaxer, Henry Chang, and Jun-Jang Jeng. PLM_{flow} - on demand business process composition and execution by rule inference. Technical report, IBM Research Division, 2002.

Trust-Based Security Model and Enforcement Mechanism for Web Service Technology

Seokwon Yang, Herman Lam, and Stanley Y.W. Su

Database Systems Research and Development Center
University of Florida, Gainesville, FL
{seyang, hlam, su}@cise.ufl.edu

Abstract. The emerging Web service technology has enabled the development of Internet-based applications that integrate distributed and heterogeneous systems and processes which are owned by different organizations. Compared to centralized systems and client-server environments, the Web service environment is much more dynamic and security for such an environment poses unique challenges. For example, an organization (e.g., a service provider or a service broker) cannot predetermine the users of its resources and fix their access privileges. Also, service providers come and go. The users of services must have some assurances about the services and the organizations that provide the services. Thus, the enforcement of security constraints cannot be static and tightly coupled. The notion of trust agreement must be established to delegate the responsibility of certification of unknown users, services, and organizations. In this paper, we describe a Trust-based Security Model (TSM) that incorporate the traditional security concepts (e.g., roles, resources, operations) with new security concepts that are specific to the Web service environment. The security concepts of TSM are then applied to the general Web service model to include security considerations. Finally, an event-driven, rule-based approach to the enforcement of security in a Web service environment is described.

1 Introduction

The emerging Web service technology provides a systematic and standard-based approach (e.g., UDDI, SOAP, WSDL, WSFL) to enable application-to-application integration [1]. Figure 1 shows the general Web service model [2] that models the interactions among three roles: Service Provider, Service Registry, and Service Requestor. In the *publish* phase of the model, a service provider, representing an organization that provides its resources as Web services, describes its services using WSDL (Web Service Definition Language) and publishes the services to a service registry using UDDI (Universal Description, Discovery and Integration). In the *discover* phase, a service requestor, also using UDDI and WSDL, queries the registry to find the required service and to obtain the information required to contact the service provider. In the *bind* phase, the service requestor contacts a service provider to dynamically bind and invoke a Web service application by sending a SOAP (Simple Object Access Protocol) message via HTTP.

Security issues have long been investigated in centralized systems and client-server environments in which the focus is on the protection of resources of a central-

A. Buchmann et al. (Eds.): TES 2002, LNCS 2444, pp. 151–160, 2002.
© Springer-Verlag Berlin Heidelberg 2002

ized server from illegitimate accesses and malicious attacks. Intra-organizational approaches to security such as identity-based authentication and role-based access control for authorization have been shown to be effective. However, the intra-organizational approach is not adequate to support security in inter-organizational collaboration using Web services. There is an increasing interest in cross-organizational, joint security, which deals with security issues in connection with trust relationships among cooperating organizations. In the Web service environment, the development of Internet-based applications requires the integration of distributed and heterogeneous systems and processes that are owned by different organizations. Also, the Web service environment is highly dynamic. Thus, security for such an environment poses unique challenges. For example, an organization (e.g., a service provider or a service registry) cannot predetermine the users of its resources and fix their access privileges. Also, service providers come and go. The users of services must have some assurances of the quality and availability of services to be used. Service providers and requestors, who may not be known to each other beforehand, have to rely on trusted third party organization to authenticate each other. Moreover, no single organization can dictate what security, privacy, and safety policies should be enforced across organizational boundaries. Instead, responsibilities and administrative authorities for managing the network and services must be agreed, distributed, and shared.

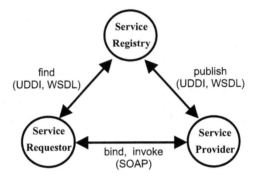

Fig. 1. The General Web service model

While trust issues cover both non-technical (e.g., license, copyright law, etc.) and technical issues (e.g., membership, certification, delegation, and global/local security constraints), this paper focuses on the technical ones. In particular, we address trust management with regard to security issues in the context of the Web service model. After we survey some related works in Section 2, we describe a Trust-based Security Model (TSM) in Section 3, which incorporates the traditional security concepts (e.g., roles, resources, and operations) with new security concepts that are specific to the Web service environment. In Section 4, the security concepts of the TSM are applied to the general Web service model to include security considerations. In Section 5, an event-driven, rule-based approach to the enforcement of security in a Web service environment is described. Finally, a summary and some concluding remarks are given in Section 6.

2   Related Works

Many of the security technologies that have been developed for Internet communication can be applied to Web Services at the transport and message layer (e.g., IPSec [3], SSL [4], SOAP security [5]). In this work, we concentrate on trust-based security in the context of Web services. The concept of trust management was first introduced in PolicyMaker as a distributed security solution [6]. The work investigated how security rules and digital credentials can be integrated for security enforcement in a distributed system, and proposed a decentralized authorization mechanism. The SDSI/SPKI project [7] studied similar issues and introduced the concept of "linked local names". It proposed a simple distributed approach to the limitation of the current PKI technology in building a global trust model. Similar works in the area of trust management are KeyNote, REFEREE, and TPL [8,9,10].

In terms of security in a wide area network, security in the context of the service discovery service (SDS) was addressed in [11]. The authors investigated on how a service provider can advertise its service safely and securely, and how a service requestor can find the trusted service it needs. From the service provider's perspective, SDS allows a service provider to advertise its private service securely so that the service is available to only those clients designated by the service provider. For clients to get a required credential, they need to contact a capability manager (CM). CM is responsible for issuing capability (or credential) certificates to each individual client after receiving a list of authorized clients from the service provider. From the client's perspective, a client trusts SDS to return the service description of a service that meets the client's interest and trust requirement. Therefore, SDS aids the client in determining the trustworthiness of services, as well as in locating services.

A digital certificate [12] is a data record or document about a subject, digitally signed by a trusted entity (e.g., a certificate authority (CA)). It is used as a digital proof of a business entity's attributes, such as distinguishable attributes (name, address, public key), demographic information (age, sex), transactional information (credit card number, credit limit, available credit), and relationship information (group membership, relationship to other groups). Trust is an issue because a certificate is accepted and honored only if there exists a trust relationship between an organization authenticating the certificate and an authority issuing the certificate. Each organization has its own definition of what the trusted entities are and has its own trust policy for determining which certificates to accept. As described later, the use of certificate authorities (CAs) and digital certificates for authenticating security attributes of business entities is an alternative to password-based authentication.

3   Trust-Based Security Model (TSM)

Although a wide range of security models has been proposed over the past years [18], we introduce a formal Trust-based Security Model (TSM) because none of the models addresses trust relationships among collaborating organizations. As illustrated in Figure 2, TSM incorporates the traditional security concepts (e.g., roles, service resources, and operations) with new security concepts that are specific to collaborative interactions using Web services (e.g., delegation, membership, and CA). It captures the semantics of distributed trust management, decentralized access control, security constraint enforcement, and certification-based authentication.

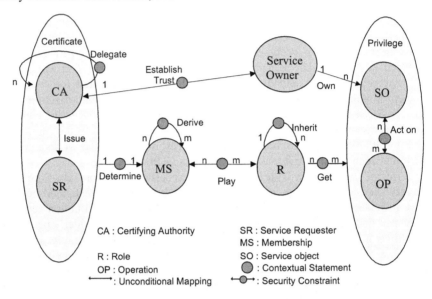

Fig. 2. Trust-based Security Model

Access control in TSM is based on the role-based access control (RBAC) model [12, 13]. As shown on the right side of Figure 2, a *service owner* (e.g., a Web service provider or the owner of a registry service) can own many *service objects* (SO) (i.e., 1-to-n cardinality). In turn, a service object can have many *operations* (OP) and an operation can be performed on many service objects (m-to-n cardinality). A set of such associations defines a *privilege*. A *role* (R) can acquire one or more privileges and a privilege can be acquired by one or more roles (m-to-n). Role entities are organized in a role hierarchy (1-to-n "inheritance") to exploit the commonality between roles. When a role inherits from a parent, it inherits all of the privileges of its parent role in the hierarchy and can acquire additional privileges.

In TSM, the RBAC model is extended by incorporating recently established concepts: *membership* [13, 15], role membership credential [16] and *certification-based authentication* [10, 12, 17]. They are added to TSM to support the distributed and dynamic nature of collaborative computing. Unlike the traditional RBAC, the identities of service requestors are not static and not *directly* assigned to roles. Instead, a requestor is assigned to a role indirectly through its membership. More specifically, a service owner defines rules that relate membership (MS) entities to roles according to an agreement between the collaborating organizations. The membership of a service requestor (SR) can be **determined** from a digital certificate that has been obtained from a trusted CA. A trusted CA is one who has established a trust relationship with the service owner or one whose authority has been delegated by another trusted CA. Furthermore, the membership of a requestor can be **derived** from other membership(s) (m-to-n). For example, a requestor may be accepted as a member of a group if it is a member of another group.

Note that responsibilities and authorities are distributed and shared in TSM. Each service owner manages trust-based access control rules, controlling membership-based role authorization and enforcing global/local security constraints. Authentication is certification-based. The responsibility of certification is entrusted to a third party CA or the CA of a collaborating organization.

Finally, TSM provides a basic mechanism for defining a variety of security constraints. In TSM, security constraints are represented by conditional mappings between entities defined in the model (shown in Figure 2 as arrows with "bubbles"). The conditions are defined in terms of contextual information that is accessible within a Web service environment.

4   Web Service Model with Trust and Security Considerations

Figure 3 illustrates how the trust and security concepts of TSM can be applied at each phase of the general Web service model. An additional role, certificate authority (CA), is included in the model. A certificate authority is responsible for certification and authentication of attributes associated with the each role player (that is, service requestor, service provider, and service registry).

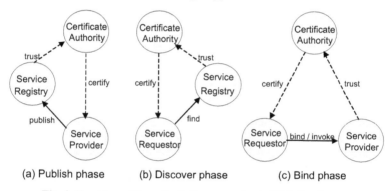

(a) Publish phase   (b) Discover phase   (c) Bind phase

Fig. 3. Trust-based Security Enforcement in the Web Service

In order to provide *trusted* registries in a collaborative e-business environment, the registry services must be restricted only to *certified* service providers. This means a service provider can publish to a registry only if it has a membership certificate that is trusted by the service registry, as shown in Figure 3 (a). A certificate is said to be trusted if a certifying organization (here, CA) is trusted by a verifying organization (e.g. service registry). Once authenticated, the membership of the service provider can be determined from the certificate and a role (and its associated privileges) can be assigned. For example, a service provider assigned to a certain role may be able to publish new services, but not to update the service descriptions of already published services of an organization.

Along with the conventional service description of Web services, a service provider may provide additional security-related information to the registry during publication. In order to increase the trustworthiness of its services and thus attract more customers, a service provider provides additional certification concerning the trust-worthiness and quality of the service provided (e.g., a certified rating of the Web service). The provider may also specify credential requirements of and restrictions on the service users. For example, the provider may not want its service descriptions, which contains metadata about its services, to be given to unauthorized parties, who may utilize the descriptions for security attacks.

Similarly, during the discover phase, the access to a service registry should be re-stricted to requestors who has a certificate that is trusted by the service registry, as shown in Figure 3(b). In addition, a service requestor can find the metadata of only those services which his membership is allowed to access. The metadata for a service that is intended for a particular group is available only to those members of the group. For example, let us assume that an insurance company decides to provide a free quote service to accredited banks and the customers of the banks. Its clients (either the banks or the customers) need to show their membership credentials in order to get information about how to invoke the service.

During the bind phase, as shown in Figure 3(c), a service requestor must present a certificate from a CA that is trusted by a service provider. Based on the contents of the certificate, the service provider determines a service requestor's membership and thereby its access privileges.

In each of the three phases, while processing a service request, the service provider can enforce its own security rules and constraints defined on the service. For exam-ple, before returning the resulting data, the service provider may trigger rules to filter out personal information so that privacy constraints are enforced. An event-driven, rule-based approach to security constraint enforcement will be described in the next section.

Note that there are trust relationships among different roles in the Web service model. A registry trusts and relies on a certificate authority (CA) to authenticate ser-vice providers and service requestors. It employs a certification-based authentication and authorization, rather than maintaining a database of end users' personal identifi-cation numbers (PIN) and roles. In the same way, service providers can authenticate and authorize service requestors based on trust in CA and its certification. In addition, a service provider trusts a service registry in the sense that the registry would deliver the metadata of its services only to trusted service requestors and protect the metadata from unauthorized access. In turn, service requestors rely on a service broker for discovering only trusted services provided by certified service providers. Requestors may review certificates for trustworthiness or QOS (quality of the service) before selecting services.

5   Event-Driven, Rule-Based Enforcement of Security Constraints

A key feature of the Trust-based Security Model (TSM) shown in Figure 2 is that complex security rules or constraints can be defined on relationships among elements of TSM. In this section, we describe an event-driven, rule-based approach to enforce these security constraints.

There are three general types of rule systems developed in academic research and the commercial world: logic rule systems, production rule systems, and event-condition-action (ECA) rule systems. The first two types do not allow the specification and processing of events in an explicit manner. ECA rules have been used in active database management systems, including our own work on an object-oriented knowledge base management system [19]. In our work, we have generalized the ECA paradigm into an Event-Trigger-Rule (ETR) paradigm [20, 21]. In the ETR paradigm, events can be all things of interest that occur in a collaborative environment (e.g., the sending or receiving of a business document, the shipping of a product, before or after the activation of an application program, a user's action through a user interface, etc.). Rules are condition-action-alternative-action rules. A trigger specification consists of three parts: a specification of trigger events, an event history (or composite event) specification, and a specification of a rule structure. If any one of the trigger events occurs, the event history specification is evaluated. If and only if the result is True, the rule structure is processed. Events can carry the data that are relevant to the occurrences of events and be processed by rules. Events, rules and triggers can be defined independently by different people/organizations.

The ETR paradigm improves the ECA paradigm in several ways. First, it readily supports event and rule specification and execution in a Web service environment. It separates the specifications of events from those of rules. By allowing this separation, the events can be defined independently of the rules and vice versa, which is essential in a Web service environment. Events can be defined at one site and rules can be defined at another site. The remote event can be associated to a local rule by a trigger specification. For example, in TSM, a revocation of a certificate or a change made in the delegation of certifying authority can be an event. Organizations can define their own rules to respond to this remote event. Second, it has the built-in consideration for performance issues. As an example, the ETR server provides a more efficient mechanism to process composite events. In most ECA rule systems, a composite event is specified by creating a single large expression, which includes all the participating events and their relationships. The processing of composite events in ECA rule systems is initiated when "any" of the participating events in the expression occurs. In many real world situations, the occurrence of any event in only a subset but not the entire set of events given in a composite event expression should trigger the processing of rules. The ETR paradigm separates the TRIGGER EVENT and EVENT HISTORY to add a finer control on the evaluation of composite events. Third, the condition part of a rule can be a guarded expression, which can contains a number of guard expressions and a final condition expression. If any of the guard expression is evaluated to False, the entire rule will be skipped (i.e., not applicable). If all the guard expressions are evaluated to True and the final condition expression is also True, then the action part of the rule will be processed. Otherwise, the alternative action will be performed. Lastly, ETR allows complex structures of rules to be triggered by events. A linear tree or graph structure of rules can be given in a trigger specification, and a rule can participate in many rule structures. This kind of rule specification is more general and powerful than a set of prioritized rules, which is used in most ECA rule systems.

The ETR technology has been incorporated into our Trusted Computing (TC) Architecture to support the dynamic and adaptive properties of the system by using an event-driven, rule-based approach to enforce security constraints. All the security constraints in the Trust-based Security Model can be translated into events, triggers, and rules to be installed in and enforced by ETR servers installed at the sites of service providers, requestors, and registry.

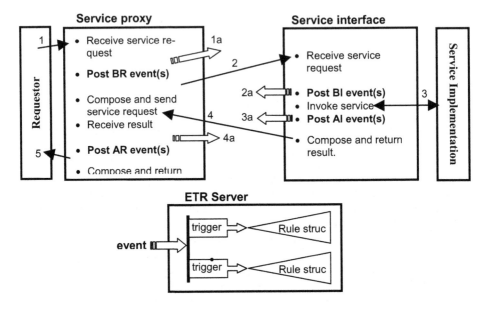

Fig. 4. Integration of ETR technology into TC component interactions.

In the Web service environment, interactions among collaborating organizations can be viewed as service requests at the requestors' sites and the activation of the requested services at the service providers' sites. The ETR technology provides "hooks" (by means of events) into the interactions to trigger rules to enforce security constraints. Shown in Figure 4 are some possible places where events can be posted. Normal course of an interaction is illustrated by the path labeled 1,2,3,4, and 5. The ETR technology is incorporated at the points labeled 1a, 2a, 3a, and 4a, where synchronous and/or asynchronous events can be posted by the service proxy and the service interface to enforce the security rules & constraints. Suppose that a requester makes a service request to a Web service using a service proxy. On the requestor side, the service proxy would post a Before Request (BR) event (label 1a) before composing and sending the corresponding request message in SOAP to the service provider (label 2). The BR event can trigger some rules managed by the ETR Server to enforce global (mutually agreed upon) and/or local constraints. If all constraints are satisfied, the process can then continue. For example, a rule may modify the service request itself (e.g., parameter values associated with a request) to comply with a service agreement.

On the service provider side, after the service request is received, a Before Invocation (BI) event can be posted to trigger rules in the ETR Server to enforce any global or local constraints (label 2a) before the actual service is invoked (label 3). Rules may invoke a retrieval operation for information (such as a credit report) from a trusted third party for validating the requestor' credential. After the execution of the service, an After Invocation (AI) event can be posted to trigger any necessary rules on the provider side (label 3a). For example, privacy rules can be enforced by performing post-processing or data filtering on the result to be returned by the provider-side application (label 4). Another example would be a rule for monitoring data access, which records the access history upon the requestor's access. Back on the service requestor side, the service proxy can post an After Request (AR) event to trigger some other rules (label 4a) before returning the result to the client component (label 5).

6 Summary and Conclusion

There is an increasing need for basic research to make large-scale Internet-based information systems trustworthy for the purposes of security, privacy, safety, and reliability. These properties are of paramount importance for Internet users and organizations to securely share their data, applications, software systems, and hardware facilities, and to promote and enable collaborative efforts in solving complex problems. In this paper, we have described a Trust-based Security Model (TSM) to address this need. TSM incorporates the traditional security concepts (e.g., roles, resources, operations) with new security concepts (e.g., membership, delegation, certificate-based authentication) that are specific to the Web service environment. It captures the semantics of distributed trust management, decentralized access control, security constraint enforcement, and certification-based authentication. These security concepts of TSM are applied to the general Web service model to include security considerations.

TSM also provides a basic mechanism for defining a variety of security constraints in the form of conditional mappings between entities defined in the model. An event-driven, rule-based (ETR) approach was described to enforce the security constraints in a Web service environment. By using events to trigger rules managed by ETR Servers distributed throughout the Web service environment, the ETR technology provides a very dynamic and flexible mechanism to enforce security constraints. These constraints include global security constraints resulting from mutually agreed upon trust agreements and local constraints needed to preserve local autonomy. Control and logic specified by rules are not hard-coded in application programs or enforcement components. Rules can be more easily changed and understood.

Based on TSM, our on-going effort is to develop a Trusted Computing Architecture and implement a trust-based security server to provide distributed trust management and security services. We plan to continue our investigation on trust monitoring using the event-driven, rule-based approach, and on a model-driven approach to automatically deploy trust agreements and security requirements.

References

1. Curbera, Francisco, et al., "Unraveling the Web Services Web: An Introduction to SOAP, WSDL, and UDDI," IEEE Internet Computing , March/April, 2002.
2. Vaughan-Nichols, Steven, "Web Services: Beyond the Hype," IEEE Computer, February 2002, Vol. 35, No. 2, pp. 18-21.
3. http://www.ietf.org/html.charters/ipsec-charter.html

4. http://www.netscape.com/eng/ssl3/
5. http://www.w3.org/TR/SOAP-dsig/
6. Blaze, Matt, Feigenbaum,Joan, and Lacy, Jack, "Decentralized Trust Management," Proceedings 1996 IEEE Symposium on Security and Privacy, May 1996.
7. http://theory.lcs.mit.edu/~cis/sdsi.html
8. Blaze, Matt, Feigenbaum, Joan, and Lacy, Jack, "Trust management for public-key infrastructures," Cambridge 1998 Security Protocols International Workshop, England, 1998.
9. Chu, Y., Feigenbaum, J., LaMacchia, B., Resnick, B, and Strauss, M., "REFEREE: Trust management for Web applications," The World Wide Web Journal, 1997.
10. Herzberg, A., Mass, Y. and Mihaeli, J., "Access Control Meets Public Key Infrastructure," IEEE Symposium on Security and Privacy 2000.
11. Czerwinski, Steven E., Zhao, Ben Y., Hodes, Todd, Joseph, Anthony D., and Katz, Randy, "An Architecture for a Secure Service Discovery Service," Fifth Annual International Conference on Mobile Computing and Networks (MobiCOM '99) , Seattle, WA, August 1999.
12. Johnston, W., Mudumbai, S., and Thompson, M., "Authorization and attribute certificates for widely distributed access control," IEEE 7th International Workshop on Enabling Technologies: Infrastructure for Collaborative Enterprises - WETICE, 1998, pp. 340-345.
13. Nyanchama, M., and Osborn, S., "The Role Graph Model and Conflict of Interest," ACM Transactions on Information and System Security, 2 (1), February 1999, pp. 3-33.
14. Ferraiolo, D., Sandhu, R., Gavrila, S., Kuhn, D. and Chandramouli R.. "Proposed NIST Standard for Role-Based Access Control," ACM TISSEC, Volume 4, No. 3, August 2001.
15. Hildmann, T. and Barholdt, J., "Managing trust between collaborating companies using outsourced role based access control," Proc. of 4th. ACM Workshop on Role-based Access Control, Oct. 28-29, 1999, Fairfax, VA, USA, pp. 105-111.
16. Hayton, R. J., Bacon, J. M., and Moody, K., "Access control in an open distributed environment," IEEE Symposium on Security and Privacy, May 1998, pp. 3-14.
17. Winslett, M., Ching, N., Jones, N. and Slepchin, I., "Assuring security and privacy for digital library transactions on the web: client and server security policies," Proceedings of ADL '97, Washington, DC, May 1997.
18. Bertino, Elisa, and Ferrari, E., "Data Security," Proc. of 22nd IEEE Annual International Computer Software & Application Conference (COMPSAC), Vienna (Austria), August 19-21, 1998, IEEE Computer Society Press.
19. Su, S.Y.W., Lam, H., Arroyo, J., Yu, T. F., and Yang, Z., "An Extensible Knowledge Base Management System for Supporting Rule-based Interoperability among Heterogeneous Systems," Proc. of the Conf. on Information and Knowledge Management, Baltimore, MD, Nov. 28-Dec. 2, 1995, pp. 1-10.
20. Su, S.Y.W., Lam, H., Lee, M., Bai, S., and Shen, Z., "An Information Infrastructure and E-services for Supporting Internet-based Scalable E-business Enterprises," Proceedings of the 5th International Enterprise Distributed Object Conference (EDOC 2001), Seattle, WA, Sept. 4-7, 2001, pp. 2-13.
21. Lee, M.S., Su, S.Y.W., and Lam, H., "A Web-based Knowledge Network for Supporting Emerging Internet Applications," WWW Journal, Vol. 4, No. 1/2, 2001, pp. 121-140.

Fair Exchange under Limited Trust

Chihiro Ito, Mizuho Iwaihara, and Yahiko Kambayashi

Department of Social Informatics, Kyoto University,
Yoshida Sakyo Kyoto, 606–8501 Japan
{chihiro, iwaihara, yahiko}@db.soc.i.kyoto-u.ac.jp
http://www.db.soc.i.kyoto-u.ac.jp/

Abstract. The Internet technology encourages electronic commerce between people and/or organizations that are physically distributed in different locations, which makes it difficult to trust each other. The existing work of electronic trades have proposed protocols and mechanisms with mediation by Trusted Third Parties (TTP), on the assumption that the third parties could be trusted without reservation by each party on a trade. Such an assumption, however, is sometimes not applicable to businesses via the Internet where various parties are trading each other, and it is not practical to give infinite trust to the parties regardless of the scale or period of trades. This paper proposes the degree of trust which limits the amount of money or goods that can be sent at one time according to the risk of the parties on trades. Each of risk limits is assumed to be determined through information from credit facilities or by the decision of each party. Then we discuss the feasibility of transactions within given credit limits and propose algorithms to judge the feasibility.

1   Introduction

The Internet technology encourages electronic trades between people and/or organizations that are physically distributed in different locations. The improvement of the performance of personal computers and network technologies enables people to exchange data from a personal computer to another not by way of servers but directly, and such technologies are called *"peer-to-peer."* In such a peer-to-peer environment, it may be mistrustful between different parties without appropriate user authentication on servers.

The existing studies on electronic trades have proposed protocols and mechanisms to enforce fair exchange through mediation by Trusted Third Parties (TTPs) [4][8][5][2]. An example of simple trade through a TTP is shown in Figure 1. A vendor commits items to a TTP and a consumer sends the TTP payment for the items. After receiving both the TTP sends the items to the consumer and sends the payment to the vendor respectively, and the trade completes. This protocol is based on the assumption that TTPs are always honest and trouble-free. Such an assumption, however, is sometimes not applicable to businesses via the Internet where various parties are involved, and it is not practical to give infinite trust to other parties regardless of the scale or period of transactions.

A. Buchmann et al. (Eds.): TES 2002, LNCS 2444, pp. 161–169, 2002.
© Springer-Verlag Berlin Heidelberg 2002

Fig. 1. The exchange through a TTP.

Thus we propose the notion of credit limits not only to the consumer and the vendor on a trade but also to the TTPs. The credit limits define the maximum amount of money or item that can be sent at one time to improve diversification of risk. We assume that the target items for trades are digital data or services deliverable in installments and that each of divided articles retains commercial value. The way of dividing an item varies for the types of the item. Video images in a series of volumes, for example, may be separately delivered in number order for each payment. Electronic service such as e-learning can be charged by per use or par period basis. Software licenses can also be divided by per use or par period basis by delivering keys for divided licenses from a vendor. Another way of dividing software product is to deliver licenses for minimum functionalities at the beginning, and gradually removing restrictions according to payment.

In delivering items it is suitable for the vendor to send encrypted data to consumers and encryption key to their mediators [8] to reduce the load of mediators and networks. As for payment, we assume a bank transfer to the account of the mediator through Web banking. Mediators shall be selected dynamically with the information on their costs and risks, such as their charge and credibility.

The remainder of the paper is organized as follows. In Section 2, the terms *"fairness"* and *"risk"* in electronic commerce are addressed. The notation used in this paper is defined in Section 3. We propose protocols by installment payment and delivery for risk diversification, and we discuss feasibility of trades within given credit limits in various settings in Section 4. Related work are referred in Section 5, and Section 6 concludes this paper.

2   Fairness and Risk in Exchanging Items and Payments

"Fair exchange" is an essential keyword for electronic commerce. Franklin and Reiter defined fair exchange as *"a protocol by which two parties swap secrets without allowing either party to gain an advantage by quitting prematurely or otherwise misbehaving*[2].*"*

Gärtner, Pagnia and Vogt defined the notion of fairness in a formal way and they classified the fairness condition into two flavors: *"strong fairness"* and *"week fairness*[3].*"* The former ensures that nobody can make fraud in any case. The latter means that if a party has suffered a disadvantage, it should be possible to start a dispute outside of the system, and if it can prove its disadvantage strong fairness can be re-established. They however pointed out that guaranteeing strong fairness has much difficulty since mediators are supposed to be completely fair, and thereby they showed more detailed classification of fairness including the notions of following up a dispute, revocability of items and compensation [10]. The protocols we propose achieve the weak fairness mentioned above. However, suffered disadvantages are kept within the predefined limit of credit.

On an electronic trade it is difficult in general to exchange goods and the payment for them simultaneously. Hence a party involved in a trade suffers disadvantages through illegal abort of the trade at some point of time, and the amount of the disadvantage is called "*risk.*"

In a direct trade between a vendor and a consumer, possible risks are such that a consumer does not pay for the item he/she has received, and that a vendor does not send items even though it has received their payment. Disadvantages may also be brought if a consumer receives the items different from the one in the contract after payment, and if items are not delivered or payment is not accomplished within a previously agreed period of time.

The risks may derive either from the intention of a party or from disorder of networks or servers. On trades through mediators, they may become unable to continue their tasks while items or payments are entrusted to them. Some mediators may coalescence with one party so that the party gains items or value without sending anything.

Thus in practical electronic trades involving multiple parties have inherently inerasable risks, so that it is necessary to have a mechanism to limit loses.

3 Notations

In general the acceptable risk in trades depends on the trustworthiness of parties involved in the trades, and the trustworthiness from a party A to another party B does not always correspond to the one from B to A. We hence represent risk limit by a directed graph, where directed edges represent directions of trust.

Definition 1. (*Risk limit graph*) Let M be a set of mediators, let S be a set of suppliers and let C be a set of consumers. A *risk limit graph* $G = (V, E)$ is a directed graph such that each edge $(u, v) \in E$ has a nonnegative *risk limit* $L(u, v) \geq 0$, where $V = M \cup S \cup C$ and $E \subseteq V \times V$. A risk limit $L(u, v)$ means maximum acceptable risk to u against v.

In case of $L(u, v) = 0$, u has no trust to v, and direct exchanges between them are infeasible. Each of risk limits is asuumed to be determined through information from credit facilities or by the decision of each party.

Definition 2. (*Division*) A *division* is a function D that maps an item g into a sequence of m subitems such that $D(g) = \langle g_1, g_2, ..., g_m \rangle$, where each g_i is a subitem which can be delivered separately and cannot be decomposed further.

Some types of items may require to be sent in the order of the sequence, such as movies, for example. We denote the price of an item g by $P(g)$. For simplicity, we assume that the sum of each price of $D(g)$ is equal to $P(g)$, not taking into account of split commission.

Definition 3. (*Action*) A trade is a sequence of *actions* by participating parties, denoted as follows:

$$u \rightarrow v : g \qquad \text{Party } u \text{ sends item } g \text{ to party } v$$
$$u \rightarrow v : P(g) \qquad \text{Party } u \text{ pays for } g \text{ to party } v$$

Definition 4. (*State variables*) A *risk* $r_t(u, v)$ is the possible amount of disadvantage just after time t when party u sends items or money to v, and $d_t(u, v)$ is u's *debt* to v at time t.

Let p_t be the value sent by u to v, then the variables have the following properties:

$$r_{t_i}(u, v) = r_{t_{i-1}}(u, v) + p_{t_i}, \quad r_{t_i}(v, u) = r_{t_{i-1}}(v, u) - p_{t_i},$$
$$d_{t_i}(u, v) = d_{t_{i-1}}(u, v) - p_{t_i}, \quad d_{t_i}(v, u) = d_{t_{i-1}}(v, u). \tag{1}$$

Definition 5. (*Available amount*) The *available amount* $a_t(u, v)$ is the maximum amount of the value or the price of an item that can be sent from u to v after the action at time t, defined as follows:

$$a_{t_i}(u, v) = L(u, v) - r_{t_i}(u, v). \tag{2}$$

We denote the state of each party by the three variables throughout the paper. The risk of a party may be negative at a point of time, which implies that the party has possible advantage if the trade aborts irregularly at that time.

At time t_0 when a trade begins, the risk of each party is 0 and the debt is equal to the price of items to be sent, and at time t_e when the trade ends, both the risk and the debt of each party shall be equal to 0. A trade is *feasible* if there exists a sequence of actions that leads the state variables from $r_{t_0}(u, v) = 0$, $d_{t_0}(u, v) = P(g)$ to $r_{t_e}(u, v) = 0$, $d_{t_e}(u, v) = 0$, where the trade starts at t_0 and ends at t_e, and the price item or payment of each action is not greater than the available amount of the action.

4   Exchange Protocols and Feasibility

4.1   Direct Exchange

At first we discuss feasibility of a trade without mediators. Assume that consumer C purchases an item g from vendor S. The item g can be divided into m subitems as $\langle g_1, g_2, ..., g_m \rangle$. An example of an installment exchange is shown in Figure 2. In general, it is beneficial for a trade to begin with the payment of C to S, since the available amount $a_1(S, C)$ is greater in this case than that of pay later, and S will be able to send more items to C at one time.

Thereby at first C sends payment of $a_1(C, S) = L(C, S)$ to S. Then S is able to send the subitem g_1 to C if and only if $P(g_1)$ is no greater than S's available amount $a_2(S, C)$. Every time C sends payment to S, $a(S, C)$ becomes $L(C, S) + L(S, C)$. Thus an installment exchange without mediators is feasible if and only if for every subitem g_i, $P(g_i) \leq L(C, S) + L(S, C)$ ($i = 1, 2, \cdots, m$).

If a trade is found to be infeasible, we assume that negotiations for expanding the risk limits or request for smaller divisions are carried out to realize the trade.

4.2   Exchange through a Single Mediator

Now we discuss the exchange through mediators. Well-known and trustworthy parties may be chosen as mediators, hence the risk limit of them can be set higher in general. Upon accidents, mediators are supposed to compensate for the damage of entrusted values. The risk and debt of a mediator are set to both against the consumer and against the vendor.

For sending items there are two ways: (1)sending the next item only after the settlements of previously sent items are accomplished, (2)sending the next item without confirming the settlements of previously sent items. In case 2, a vendor's available amount of item to be sent becomes smaller than case 1 because the risk and debt are increased by unsettled items. We hence consider the feasibility of trades only under case 1.

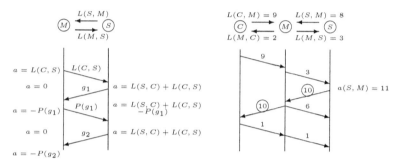

Fig. 2. Direct trading.   **Fig. 3.** Trading with a mediator.

At first we discuss installment with a single mediator. Suppose that consumer C purchases an item g of ten dollars in lump sum from vendor S. Let $L(C, S)$ be $1 and $L(S, C)$ be $3. In this case S cannot send the item to C because the sum of risk limits $L(C, S) + L(S, C) = \$4$. We thus employ a mediator M, whose risk limits are as shown in Figure 3. With the mediator S becomes able to send the item after receiving the payment because $a(S, M) = min(L(C, M), L(M, S)) + L(S, M) = \$11$, which is greater than the price of the item. M can send the item to C likewise because $a(M, C)$ is $L(C, M) + L(M, C) = \$11$.

Consequently, the installment trade of g is feasible through a mediator M if and only if every sum of $L(M, S) + L(S, M)$, $L(C, M) + L(S, M)$ and $L(C, M) + L(M, C)$ is no smaller than $P(g_i)$, where $i = 1, 2, \cdots, m$.

4.3   Exchange through Multiple Mediators

Employing multiple mediators is necessary when the vendor and customer have no common trusting mediators. It is also effective to find a path of multiple mediators having high credit limit. We first consider the case where the risk limit graph is a bidirectional list as shown in Figure 4.

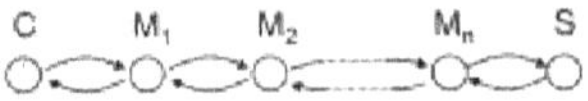

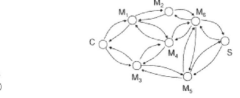

Fig. 4. Risk limit graph in list structure

Fig. 5. Risk limit graph in general form

C shall purchase from S an item g which can be divided into m pieces $\langle g_1, \cdots, g_m \rangle$. As with a single mediator, an exchange begins after the completion of the previous exchange. Suppose that there are n mediators $M_1, M_2, \cdots, M_n$ between C and S. We denote $\min(\ L(M_{j-1}, M_j)\ )\ |\ j = 1, 2, \cdots, i)$ as $L^{min}(C, M_i)$. The exchange of g_1 is carried out as follows:

1. The first action is $C \rightarrow M_1 : L(C, M_1)$ at time t_1. The amount of money S receives from M_n is $L^{min}(C, S)$ at t_{n+1}.
2. At t_{n+2}, S sends subitem g_1 to M_n whose value is not greater than $a_{t_{n+2}}(S, M_n) = L^{min}(C, S) + L(S, M_n)$. Similarly, M_n sends the items to M_{n-1} if its value is not greater than $a_{t_{n+3}}(M_n, M_{n-1}) = L^{min}(C, M_n) + L(S, M_n)$.
3. C receives the items at t_{2n+1}, and at t_{2n+2} C pays $a_{t_{2n+2}}(C, M_1) = P(g_1)$ to M_1.

The subitem g_1 can be sent from S through M_n, and received by M_i if $P(g_1) \leq L^{min}(C, M_i) + L(M_i, M_{i-1})$. Then a trade for g is feasible if and only if

$$P(g_{\max}) \leq L^{min}(C, M_i) + L(M_i, M_{i-1})\ (i = 1, 2, \cdots, n+1), \qquad (3)$$

where $P(g_{\max})$ is the maximum value of all subitem of g.

An algorithm to judge the feasibility is as follows:

Algorithm Find Trade 1 *Let M_0 be C and M_{n+1} be S.*

1. *Set $L^{min}(C, M_0)$ to be infinite.*
2. *Repeat the following 3-4 for $i = 1$ to $n + 1$.*
3. *Compare $L^{min}(C, M_{i-1})$ with $L(M_{i-1}, M_i)$, and set the smaller one to $L^{min}(C, M_i)$.*
4. *If $L^{min}(C, M_i) + L(M_i, M_{i-1}) \geq P(g)$, then*
   - *if $i = n$, then the trade is feasible.*
   - *if $i \neq n$, then add 1 to i and go to 2.*
   If $L^{min}(C, M_i) + L(M_i, M_{i-1}) < P(g)$, then the trade is infeasible.

The algorithm runs in $O(n)$ time, which is practical because n is the number of mediators in the trade.

At last we consider the risk limit graph has a general form as in Figure 5. In general, the payment and delivery of items are not always done via the same mediators. We consider the case where one exchange is done on the same path of mediators. Then the feasibility problem is to find a bidirectional list between C and S satisfying the formula (3).

We describ an algorithm to find maximum price $P_G^{\max}$ of items that can be sent under the condition of a risk limit graph G.

Algorithm Find Trade 2

1. For a risk limit graph $G = (V, E)$, let V^a be the set $\{C\}$. Assign infinity to both $L^{\min}(C, C)$ and $P^{\max}(C)$.
2. Select a node v which is not in V^a. Note that S is the last node to be selected. For every node $V^a (i = 0, 1, \cdots, m)$,

$$L^{\min}(C, v) = \max(\min(L^{\min}(C, v_i^a), L(v_i^a, v)))$$
$$P^{\max}(v) = \min(P^{\max}(v_i^a), L^{\min}(C, v) + L(v, v_i^a))$$

3. If $P_v^{\max} > 0$, then add v into V^a.
4. If $v \neq S$, then go to 2.
5. If $v = S$, then $P_G^{\max} = P_S^{\max}$.

A trade on G is feasible if $P_G^{\max}$ is greater than the price of items or subitems. This algorithm uses a greedy method and its time complexity is $O(n^2)$, where n is the number of mediators in G.

5   Related Work

Various fair exchange protocols mediated by TTPs have been proposed in the literature. Ketchpel and Garcia-Molina noticed the trust problem in electronic trades[4]. Su and Manchala remarked the problems which occur if the size of information goods is very large and showed the solution using cryptographic techniques [8]. They both have assumption that TTPs are honest and trouble-free.

Pagnia, Vogt, Gärtner and Wilhelm proposed protocols to enforce fair exchange between two mobile agents, which autonomously gather information about items on World Wide Web and can perform purchase on behalf of the user [6]. The basis for ensuring the security properties of fair exchange is a tamper-proof hardware device, such as the trusted processing environment (TPE) [12]. Another solution using hardware devices is that implementing a kind of protocols [1] into smart cards to perform fair exchange, which does not require an external TTP in the faultless case [11]. It is true that smart cards are structurally tamper-proof, however, participants have to face the risk of defects in the algorithms or their implementations. which discourages large trades via smart cards.

These protocols, giving infinite trust onto TTPs or some hardware device, may bring enormous disadvantages on accidents, whereas our approach, limiting the amount of trust, is able to suppress losses for some extent.

Franklin and Reiter proposed protocols for data exchange through third parties whom are not always trusted[2]. In their protocols if one party acts dishonestly in a transaction, the transaction may fail but no one suffers disadvantage. When two of the parties collude, however, the other party may incur loss.

The idea of suppressing losses on trades with *gradual exchange* protocols was presented by Sandholm and Lesser[7]. The protocols assume a direct trade between a vendor and a consumer, who may not give much trust to each other. Their protocols do not have the concept of credit limit which vary among parties and also do not utilize mediators, resulting in reduced possibilities of establishing deals. Choosing mediators having large credit limits can reduce network transaction costs. We proposed employing mediators, whom are more credible than consumers and vendors in general, to deal with the problems that came from shredding of items. Through the mediators, the number of deliveries is reduced and more items are available without division.

To enable flexible trades on the Internet, we require dynamic routing of exchange through multiple mediators since it is difficult in general to find one mediator to be trusted by both a consumer and a vendor. Manchala [5] also discussed about the dynamic network of trusted agents but he did not addressed risk aversion between agents. We consider that installment payment and delivery enables not only risk diversification but also privacy preservation of vendors or consumers through multiple intermediaries.

6   Conclusion

In this paper we introduced the notion of credit limits and installment into electronic trades through mediators. We proposed risk limit graphs to judge the feasibility of a trade protocol with installments. Employing mediators increases credit limits and trade chances with various parties. More detailed protocol design is future work. The protocol of setting risk limits, which are assumed to be based on the information from credit facilities or the decision of each party, are to be defined with probability variables of failure of each party. Protocols for recovery from accidents also need to be addressed in the exchange protocols.

Acknowledgments. The authors thank the members of Kambayashi Laboratory for helpful suggestions and useful discussions.

References

1. N. Asokan, M. Schunter, and M. Waidner, "Optimistic Protocols for Fair Exchange", *Proc. 4th ACM Conf. on Computer and Communications Security*, pp. 6–17, Zürich, Switzerland, April 1997.

2. M. K. Franklin, M. K. Reiter, "Fair Exchange with a Semi-Trusted Third Party", *Proc. 4th ACM Conf. on Computer and Communication Security*, April 1997.

3. F. C. Gärtner, H. Pagnia, and H. Vogt, "Approaching a Formal Definition of Fairness in Electronic Commerce", *Proc. International Workshop on Electronic Commerce (WELCOM'99)*, pp. 354–359, Lausanne, Switzerland, Oct, 1999.

4. S. P. Ketchpel, H. Garcia-Monia, "Making Trust Explicit in Distributed Commerce Transactions", *Proc. 16th ICDCS*, pp. 270–281, Hong Kong, May 1996.

5. D. W Manchala, "Trust Metrics, Models and Protocols for Electronic Commerce Transactions" *Proc. 18th ICDCS*, pp. 312–321, Amsterdam, May 1998.

6. H. Pagnia, H. Vogt, F. C. Gärtner, and U. G. Wilhelm, "Solving Fair Exchange with Mobile Agents", *Proc. 2nd ASA/MA*, pp. 57–72, 2000.

7. T. W. Sandholm and V. R. Lesser, "Equilibrium analysis of the possibilities of unenforced exchange in multiagent systems", *Proc. 14th International Joint Conf. on Artificial Intelligence*, pp. 694–703, San Mateo, August 1995.

8. J. Su, D. Manchala, "Building Trust for Distributed Commerce Transactions", *Proc. 17th ICDCS*, pp. 322–329, Baltimore, May 1997.

9. J. Su, D. Manchala, "Trust Vs. Threats: Recovery and Survival in Electronic Commerce", *Proc. 19th ICDCS*, pp. 126–133, 1999.

10. H. Vogt, H. Pagnia, and F. C. Gärtner "Modular Fair Exchange Protocols for Electronic Commerce", *Proc. 15th Annual Computer Security Applications Conf.*, pp. 3–11, Phoenix, December 1999.

11. H. Vogt, H. Pagnia, and F. C. Gärtner, "Using Smart Cards for Fair Exchange", *Proc. International Workshop on Electronic Commerce (WELCOM 2001)*, pp. 101–113, Heidelberg, Germany, November 2001.

12. U. G. Wilhelm, L. Buttyán, and S. Staamann, "On the Problem of Trust in Mobile Agent Systems", *Symp. on Network and Distributed System Security*, pp. 114–124, March 1998.

Author Index

Abrahams, Alan S.   97
Aiello, M.   76
Akhounov, Alexei   29
Alonso, Gustavo   118

Bacon, Jean M.   97
Bussler, Christoph   19

Carman, M.   76
Chang, Henry   107, 141
Cingil, Ibrahim   9

Dogac, Asuman   9

Eyers, David M.   97

Flaxer, David   141

Helal, Abdelsalam   65

Ito, Chihiro   161
Iwaihara, Mizuho   161

Jain, Rajiv   48
Jeng, Jun-Jang   107, 141
Joosery, Vinay P.   6

Kabak, Yildiray   9
Kambayashi, Yahiko   161

Laleci, Gokce   9
Lam, Herman   151
Li, Haifei   107

Li, Jing   131
Lu, Jingting   65

Mecella, Massimo   38
Mohan, C.   1

Nori, Anil K.   48

Ordille, Joann J.   86

Papazoglou, Mike P.   54, 76
Parisi Presicce, Francesco   38
Pernici, Barbara   38
Petsche, Thomas   86
Pistore, M.   76
Popovici, Andrei   118

Ronström, Mikael   6

Schmidt, Andreas   29
Serafini, L.   76
Su, Stanley Y.W.   151

Tian, Zhong   131
Traverso, P.   76

Valikov, Alexey   29

Yang, Jian   54, 76
Yang, Seokwon   151

Zeng, Liangzhao   141
Zhang, Xin   131

Lecture Notes in Computer Science

For information about Vols. 1–2341
please contact your bookseller or Springer-Verlag

Vol. 2342: I. Horrocks, J. Hendler (Eds.), The Semantic Web – ISCW 2002. Proceedings, 2002. XVI, 476 pages. 2002.

Vol. 2345: E. Gregori, M. Conti, A.T. Campbell, G. Omidyar, M. Zukerman (Eds.), NETWORKING 2002. Proceedings, 2002. XXVI, 1256 pages. 2002.

Vol. 2346: H. Unger, T. Böhme, A. Mikler (Eds.), Innovative Internet Computing Systems. Proceedings, 2002. VIII, 251 pages. 2002.

Vol. 2347: P. De Bra, P. Brusilovsky, R. Conejo (Eds.), Adaptive Hypermedia and Adaptive Web-Based Systems. Proceedings, 2002. XV, 615 pages. 2002.

Vol. 2348: A. Banks Pidduck, J. Mylopoulos, C.C. Woo, M. Tamer Ozsu (Eds.), Advanced Information Systems Engineering. Proceedings, 2002. XIV, 799 pages. 2002.

Vol. 2349: J. Kontio, R. Conradi (Eds.), Software Quality – ECSQ 2002. Proceedings, 2002. XIV, 363 pages. 2002.

Vol. 2350: A. Heyden, G. Sparr, M. Nielsen, P. Johansen (Eds.), Computer Vision – ECCV 2002. Proceedings, Part I. XXVIII, 817 pages. 2002.

Vol. 2351: A. Heyden, G. Sparr, M. Nielsen, P. Johansen (Eds.), Computer Vision – ECCV 2002. Proceedings, Part II. XXVIII, 903 pages. 2002.

Vol. 2352: A. Heyden, G. Sparr, M. Nielsen, P. Johansen (Eds.), Computer Vision – ECCV 2002. Proceedings, Part III. XXVIII, 919 pages. 2002.

Vol. 2353: A. Heyden, G. Sparr, M. Nielsen, P. Johansen (Eds.), Computer Vision – ECCV 2002. Proceedings, Part IV. XXVIII, 841 pages. 2002.

Vol. 2355: M. Matsui (Ed.), Fast Software Encryption. Proceedings, 2001. VIII, 169 pages. 2001.

Vol. 2356: R. Kohavi, B.M. Masand, M. Spiliopoulou, J. Srivastava (Eds.), WEBKDD 2002 – Mining Log Data Across All Customers Touch Points. Proceedings, 2001. XI, 167 pages. 2002. (Subseries LNAI).

Vol. 2358: T. Hendtlass, M. Ali (Eds.), Developments in Applied Artificial Intelligence. Proceedings, 2002 XIII, 833 pages. 2002. (Subseries LNAI).

Vol. 2359: M. Tistarelli, J. Bigun, A.K. Jain (Eds.), Biometric Authentication. Proceedings, 2002. X, 197 pages. 2002.

Vol. 2360: J. Esparza, C. Lakos (Eds.), Application and Theory of Petri Nets 2002. Proceedings, 2002. X, 445 pages. 2002.

Vol. 2361: J. Blieberger, A. Strohmeier (Eds.), Reliable Software Technologies – Ada-Europe 2002. Proceedings, 2002 XIII, 367 pages. 2002.

Vol. 2362: M. Tanabe, P. van den Besselaar, T. Ishida (Eds.), Digital Cities II. Proceedings, 2001. XI, 399 pages. 2002.

Vol. 2363: S.A. Cerri, G. Gouardères, F. Paraguaçu (Eds.), Intelligent Tutoring Systems. Proceedings, 2002. XXVIII, 1016 pages. 2002.

Vol. 2364: F. Roli, J. Kittler (Eds.), Multiple Classifier Systems. Proceedings, 2002. XI, 337 pages. 2002.

Vol. 2365: J. Daemen, V. Rijmen (Eds.), Fast Software Encryption. Proceedings, 2002. XI, 277 pages. 2002.

Vol. 2366: M.-S. Hacid, Z.W. Raś, D.A. Zighed, Y. Kodratoff (Eds.), Foundations of Intelligent Systems. Proceedings, 2002. XII, 614 pages. 2002. (Subseries LNAI).

Vol. 2367: J. Fagerholm, J. Haataja, J. Järvinen, M. Lyly. P. Råback, V. Savolainen (Eds.), Applied Parallel Computing. Proceedings, 2002. XIV, 612 pages. 2002.

Vol. 2368: M. Penttonen, E. Meineche Schmidt (Eds.), Algorithm Theory – SWAT 2002. Proceedings, 2002. XIV, 450 pages. 2002.

Vol. 2369: C. Fieker, D.R. Kohel (Eds.), Algorithmic Number Theory. Proceedings, 2002. IX, 517 pages. 2002.

Vol. 2370: J. Bishop (Ed.), Component Deployment. Proceedings, 2002. XII, 269 pages. 2002.

Vol. 2371: S. Koenig, R.C. Holte (Eds.), Abstraction, Reformulation, and Approximation. Proceedings, 2002. XI, 349 pages. 2002. (Subseries LNAI).

Vol. 2372: A. Pettorossi (Ed.), Logic Based Program Synthesis and Transformation. Proceedings, 2001. VIII, 267 pages. 2002.

Vol. 2373: A. Apostolico, M. Takeda (Eds.), Combinatorial Pattern Matching. Proceedings, 2002. VIII, 289 pages. 2002.

Vol. 2374: B. Magnusson (Ed.), ECOOP 2002 – Object-Oriented Programming. XI, 637 pages. 2002.

Vol. 2375: J. Kivinen, R.H. Sloan (Eds.), Computational Learning Theory. Proceedings, 2002. XI, 397 pages. 2002. (Subseries LNAI).

Vol. 2377: A. Birk, S. Coradeschi, T. Satoshi (Eds.), RoboCup 2001: Robot Soccer World Cup V. XIX, 763 pages. 2002. (Subseries LNAI).

Vol. 2378: S. Tison (Ed.), Rewriting Techniques and Applications. Proceedings, 2002. XI, 387 pages. 2002.

Vol. 2379: G.J. Chastek (Ed.), Software Product Lines. Proceedings, 2002. X, 399 pages. 2002.

Vol. 2380: P. Widmayer, F. Triguero, R. Morales, M. Hennessy, S. Eidenbenz, R. Conejo (Eds.), Automata, Languages and Programming. Proceedings, 2002. XXI, 1069 pages. 2002.

Vol. 2381: U. Egly, C.G. Fermüller (Eds.), Automated Reasoning with Analytic Tableaux and Related Methods. Proceedings, 2002. X, 341 pages. 2002 .(Subseries LNAI).

Vol. 2382: A. Halevy, A. Gal (Eds.), Next Generation Information Technologies and Systems. Proceedings, 2002. VIII, 169 pages. 2002.

Vol. 2383: M.S. Lew, N. Sebe, J.P. Eakins (Eds.), Image and Video Retrieval. Proceedings, 2002. XII, 388 pages. 2002.

Vol. 2384: L. Batten, J. Seberry (Eds.), Information Security and Privacy. Proceedings, 2002. XII, 514 pages. 2002.

Vol. 2385: J. Calmet, B. Benhamou, O. Caprotti, L. Henocque, V. Sorge (Eds.), Artificial Intelligence, Automated Reasoning, and Symbolic Computation. Proceedings, 2002. XI, 343 pages. 2002. (Subseries LNAI).

Vol. 2386: E.A. Boiten, B. Möller (Eds.), Mathematics of Program Construction. Proceedings, 2002. X, 263 pages. 2002.

Vol. 2387: O.H. Ibarra, L. Zhang (Eds.), Computing and Combinatorics. Proceedings, 2002. XIII, 606 pages. 2002.

Vol. 2388: S.-W. Lee, A. Verri (Eds.), Pattern Recognition with Support Vector Machines. Proceedings, 2002. XI, 420 pages. 2002.

Vol. 2389: E. Ranchhod, N.J. Mamede (Eds.), Advances in Natural Language Processing. Proceedings, 2002. XII, 275 pages. 2002. (Subseries LNAI).

Vol. 2391: L.-H. Eriksson, P.A. Lindsay (Eds.), FME 2002: Formal Methods – Getting IT Right. Proceedings, 2002. XI, 625 pages. 2002.

Vol. 2392: A. Voronkov (Ed.), Automated Deduction – CADE-18. Proceedings, 2002. XII, 534 pages. 2002. (Subseries LNAI).

Vol. 2393: U. Priss, D. Corbett, G. Angelova (Eds.), Conceptual Structures: Integration and Interfaces. Proceedings, 2002. XI, 397 pages. 2002. (Subseries LNAI).

Vol. 2395: G. Barthe, P. Dybjer, L. Pinto, J. Saraiva (Eds.), Applied Semantics. IX, 537 pages. 2002.

Vol. 2396: T. Caelli, A. Amin, R.P.W. Duin, M. Kamel, D. de Ridder (Eds.), Structural, Syntactic, and Statistical Pattern Recognition. Proceedings, 2002. XVI, 863 pages. 2002.

Vol. 2398: K. Miesenberger, J. Klaus, W. Zagler (Eds.), Computers Helping People with Special Needs. Proceedings, 2002. XXII, 794 pages. 2002.

Vol. 2399: H. Hermanns, R. Segala (Eds.), Process Algebra and Probabilistic Methods. Proceedings, 2002. X, 215 pages. 2002.

Vol. 2401: P.J. Stuckey (Ed.), Logic Programming. Proceedings, 2002. XI, 486 pages. 2002.

Vol. 2402: W. Chang (Ed.), Advanced Internet Services and Applications. Proceedings, 2002. XI, 307 pages. 2002.

Vol. 2403: Mark d'Inverno, M. Luck, M. Fisher, C. Preist (Eds.), Foundations and Applications of Multi-Agent Systems. Proceedings, 1996-2000. X, 261 pages. 2002. (Subseries LNAI).

Vol. 2404: E. Brinksma, K.G. Larsen (Eds.), Computer Aided Verification. Proceedings, 2002. XIII, 626 pages. 2002.

Vol. 2405: B. Eaglestone, S. North, A. Poulovassilis (Eds.), Advances in Databases. Proceedings, 2002. XII, 199 pages. 2002.

Vol. 2406: C. Peters, M. Braschler, J. Gonzalo, M. Kluck (Eds.), Evaluation of Cross-Language Information Retrieval Systems. Proceedings, 2001. X, 601 pages. 2002.

Vol. 2407: A.C. Kakas, F. Sadri (Eds.), Computational Logic: Logic Programming and Beyond. Part I. XII, 678 pages. 2002. (Subseries LNAI).

Vol. 2408: A.C. Kakas, F. Sadri (Eds.), Computational Logic: Logic Programming and Beyond. Part II. XII, 628 pages. 2002. (Subseries LNAI).

Vol. 2409: D.M. Mount, C. Stein (Eds.), Algorithm Engineering and Experiments. Proceedings, 2002. VIII, 207 pages. 2002.

Vol. 2410: V.A. Carreño, C.A. Muñoz, S. Tahar (Eds.), Theorem Proving in Higher Order Logics. Proceedings, 2002. X, 349 pages. 2002.

Vol. 2412: H. Yin, N. Allinson, R. Freeman, J. Keane, S. Hubbard (Eds.), Intelligent Data Engineering and Automated Learning – IDEAL 2002. Proceedings, 2002. XV, 597 pages. 2002.

Vol. 2413: K. Kuwabara, J. Lee (Eds.), Intelligent Agents and Multi-Agent Systems. Proceedings, 2002. X, 221 pages. 2002. (Subseries LNAI).

Vol. 2414: F. Mattern, M. Naghshineh (Eds.), Pervasive Computing. Proceedings, 2002. XI, 298 pages. 2002.

Vol. 2415: J. Dorronsoro (Ed.), Artificial Neural Networks – ICANN 2002. Proceedings, 2002. XXVIII, 1382 pages. 2002.

Vol. 2417: M. Ishizuka, A. Sattar (Eds.), PRICAI 2002: Trends in Artificial Intelligence. Proceedings, 2002. XX, 623 pages. 2002. (Subseries LNAI).

Vol. 2418: D. Wells, L. Williams (Eds.), Extreme Programming and Agile Methods – XP/Agile Universe 2002. Proceedings, 2002. XII, 292 pages. 2002.

Vol. 2419: X. Meng, J. Su, Y. Wang (Eds.), Advances in Web-Age Information Management. Proceedings, 2002. XV, 446 pages. 2002.

Vol. 2420: K. Diks, W. Rytter (Eds.), Mathematical Foundations of Computer Science 2002. Proceedings, 2002. XII, 652 pages. 2002.

Vol. 2421: L. Brim, P. Jančar, M. Křetínský, A. Kučera (Eds.), CONCUR 2002 – Concurrency Theory. Proceedings, 2002. XII, 611 pages. 2002.

Vol. 2423: D. Lopresti, J. Hu, R. Kashi (Eds.), Document Analysis Systems V. Proceedings, 2002. XIII, 570 pages. 2002.

Vol. 2430: T. Elomaa, H. Mannila, H. Toivonen (Eds.), Machine Learning: ECML 2002. Proceedings, 2002. XIII, 532 pages. 2002. (Subseries LNAI).

Vol. 2431: T. Elomaa, H. Mannila, H. Toivonen (Eds.), Principles of Data Mining and Knowledge Discovery. Proceedings, 2002. XIV, 514 pages. 2002. (Subseries LNAI).

Vol. 2436: J. Fong, R.C.T. Cheung, H.V. Leong, Q. Li (Eds.), Advances in Web-Based Learning. Proceedings, 2002. XIII, 434 pages. 2002.

Vol. 2440: J.M. Haake, J.A. Pino (Eds.), Groupware – CRIWG 2002. Proceedings, 2002. XII, 285 pages. 2002.

Vol. 2442: M. Yung (Ed.), Advances in Cryptology – CRYPTO 2002. Proceedings, 2002. XIV, 627 pages. 2002.

Vol. 2444: A. Buchmann, F. Casati, L. Fiege, M.-C. Hsu, M.-C. Shan (Eds.), Technologies for E-Services. Proceedings, 2002. X, 171 pages. 2002.